Our Changing World

Book 4: The Responsibility Renaissance

Business as a Catalyst for Environmental and Social Ethics

James Fountain

Acknowledgments And Dedication

Before we venture into the heart of this series, let's take a moment to acknowledge the hands and hearts that have been instrumental in bringing this work to life. It is with deep gratitude that I recognize the individuals and communities whose unwavering support and boundless inspiration have laid the cornerstone for these pages. Their contributions have not only enriched this journey but have also been pivotal in shaping the narratives that unfold within.

To start, this series stands as a testament to the guardians of wisdom through the ages—Indigenous peoples, whose very essence is woven into the Earth's rhythms, educators and seekers of knowledge who illuminate our understanding, and you, the valiant souls navigating the sustainability frontier. Your endeavors, though often stretched thin by the magnitude of your obligations and the ceaseless demands for your expertise, are the cornerstone upon which we dare to envision a future brimming with hope and harmony. In these pages lies a shared reservoir of insights, a lighthouse for those teetering on the edge of this crucial movement, aiming to cast light on the path ahead with lessons from my journey, igniting a spark within yours.

The dedication you exhibit, even when overwhelmed and overcommitted, underscores a collective resolve that transcends personal accolades. It's driven by a deep-seated desire for impact, a shared obsession with catalyzing meaningful change in the realms of sustainability, climate action, and human rights. Your commitment speaks to a profound yearning for a deeper connection with the world around us, a connection that is less about individual recognition and more about the collective soul of our planet. In an era shadowed by division, your tireless efforts weave a narrative of unity and hope, showcasing the monumental impact we can achieve through values-driven action and the pursuit of real, tangible solutions. This series seeks not only to honor your undertaking but to amplify it, offering it as a clarion call to all who dream of a tomorrow where our planet is revered, and our collective well-being is cherished.

In this vast journey, Mona, your steadfast support has been my compass, guiding me through the tumultuous and the tranquil alike. Your sacrifices, quietly monumental, from the solitary evenings while I was ensconced in thought or sequestered at the local bar, to the boundless reservoir of patience and encouragement you offered amid my sea of doubts. Our countless brainstorming sessions—naming series, books, and chapters—have been pivotal. This endeavor, imbued with your love and belief, mirrors not just my efforts but the essence of your spirit. The laughter we shared, our nocturnal dialogues, and even the moments of companionable silence have woven a rich tapestry into this work. You have been my muse, my confidante, and my untiring partner through every zenith and nadir. Your love, steadfast and grounding; your incredible life story, a wellspring of inspiration; this milestone bears witness to the enduring strength of our shared journey.

As we stand on the cusp of new adventures, I am buoyed by the knowledge that with you by my side, there are no bounds to the stories we can tell, the worlds we can explore, and the impacts we can make. Here's to the chapters yet unwritten, the tales yet untold, and the journey that continues to unfold with you, Mona, as my guiding star.

And finally, to Liam, my cherished companion whose absence has left a silence too profound for words. I miss you, buddy. In my heart, I envision you in a realm where the forest trails stretch into eternity, where mountain meadows sprawl under the open sky, where tennis balls are abundant, and marrow-filled bovine bones are yours for the taking.

Liam, you exemplified the essence of an ideal Earth citizen—your love, dedication, empathy, and compassion were lessons in themselves, showing me the heights to which we can aspire. Your soul, luminous and guiding, illuminated the path of what life should embody. Through your eyes, I learned to see the world not just as it is but as it could be, filled with love and boundless joy. This book and the series that contains it, while a dedication to the guardians of our planet and the stewards of knowledge, is also a tribute to you, Liam. Your spirit, a guiding star in the vast cosmos of our journey, continues to lead me toward love, empathy, and the profound connections that weave the fabric of life. Thank you for teaching me, for being my compass in exploring what it truly means to live fully and love unconditionally. Your legacy is etched not just in these pages but in my ambition of the being I hope to become.

-JF

Table of Contents

Preface

The transformative potential of business in shaping a sustainable future is immense and undeniable. Our era stands as a pivotal crossroads, where the actions and decisions of today's enterprises will echo into the lives of future generations. This book delves into the heart of environmental and social responsibility within the commercial world, seeking to illuminate the pathways for businesses to embody a role far beyond profit maximization—becoming stewards of our planet and champions for equitable societies.

At a time when ecological crises and social disparities demand urgent attention, this work does not merely present theoretical musings but aims to spark a practical and inspirational movement. As businesses contend with the complexity of integrating ecological dynamics and social ethics, this volume provides a comprehensive exploration of how such integrations are not only feasible but indeed necessary.

Metamorphosis in the business landscape is already underway—driven by visionaries and innovators who recognize environmental and social well-being are inseparably linked to long-term corporate success. This book is a conversation with those visionaries, an exchange of ideas for skeptics, and a guiding light for changemakers. Their shared insights and stories weave through the pages, bearing witness to the unprecedented opportunity lying before us: to be architects of a future that is resilient, just, and vibrant.

Drawn from the confluence of environmental ethics, cultural studies, and sustainability practices, the content here does not shy away from challenging the status quo. It dares to question deep-seated corporate paradigms and offers a new compass by which to navigate the evolving landscape of global business. Innovation, as revealed in these chapters, is not tethered solely to technology and markets; it is equally about revolutionizing mindsets, values, and purposes.

From the ethics of AI to the intricacies of the circular economy, and from the nuances of cultural perspectives on sustainability to the bold assertions of conscious capitalism, the diverse topics addressed establish a multilayered narrative that acknowledges the complexity of business in *Our Changing World*.

To academics, sustainability professionals, policymakers, environmental activists, human rights champions, and anyone with an investment in our collective future, this book speaks to you. It serves as a repository of knowledge, a source of motivation, and a catalyst for action.

This preface, therefore, is an invitation—an opening note warming the readers to the richness of discussions that follow. It is not an exhaustive revelation of what lies within, for each chapter burgeons with its own depth and breadth of insight. Instead, consider this preface a prologue to a journey of transformation—one that each reader will chart through their engagement with the material and ensuing actions.

The author's own journey, summarized in a personal recounting, is testament to the power of inspiration and fortitude in manifesting this work. In every anecdote and reflection, the intricate tapestry of experiences unravels to show passion combined with purpose can indeed foster change.

In an era that craves authenticity and a genuine commitment to the greater good, businesses have a unique opportunity to redefine their legacy. This text illustrates operating within a framework of ethical rigor does not preclude success; rather, it marks the dawning of a new kind of prosperity—one that accounts for the well-being of all stakeholders and the planet itself.

Amidst a backdrop of rapidly shifting societal expectations, technology advancements, and climate imperatives, these pages hold conversations of realities and possibilities. They offer not only academic discourses, but also practical steps toward enacting meaningful corporate transformations.

Now, more than ever, we have access to an arsenal of tools, knowledge, and collaborative potential to forge ahead with confidence and clarity. *Our Changing World* is not just a series title but a declaration that the status quo is in flux—and this flux is ripe with opportunities for those prepared to lead the vanguard of an ethical renaissance.

Though challenges loom large, the evidence presented here demonstrates solutions are within our grasp. The commitments articulated, the frameworks proposed, and the innovation showcased provide a hope that's grounded in reality, a hope that pragmatic and conscientious business practice can, and will, elicit positive global impact.

This preface sets the stage for what is to be a formative exploration into the essence of ethical business and a vocation for all who take up this reading to embark on a transformative exchange that transcends the pages, influencing the fabric of the world we are collectively shaping.

In the following chapters, the convergence of multiple disciplines will weave a rich discourse on how business excellence can be redefined to harmoniously align with sustaining life on Earth. May this preface serve as the opening melody to a powerful symphony of change, resonating with scholars and practitioners alike and heralding a new epoch in which enterprise becomes synonymous with ecological and social guardianship.

To conclude, the essence of this book is not captured merely by its written content but by its potential to inspire change. Let's ensure the legacy we leave behind is one of courage, sustainability, and great respect for the interconnectedness of all life. The task ahead is monumental, but together, we can redefine the very foundations upon which business and society stand. Let the chronicles of *Our Changing World* continue.

Introduction and a Note from the Author

As we embark on the elaborative journey that is this book, it's imperative to acknowledge the urgency and gravity of the narrative ahead. The world is at an ecological and sociocultural crossroads; the decisions we make and the paths we take are determinative of our collective future—a future in which sustainability isn't an option but a necessity. This book seeks to serve as both a call to action and a source of hope for those standing at the vanguard of change: academics, sustainable professionals, policymakers, activists, and humanitarians alike.

The shifting paradigms within the spheres of business and environmental ethics that this book addresses are more than mere academic considerations. The impacts of these discussions reach the core of our existence and the continued prosperity of our planet. To all who engage with the ideas enclosed within these pages, you are partaking in a movement that shuns complacency in favor of a transformative shift toward environmental and social responsibility. It's a cause demanding our utmost dedication and innovative capacity.

This book does not only aspire to inform, but also to inspire. The integration of ecological and social ethics into the operational DNA of businesses can indeed become a pivotal driver in the global sustainability movement. Furthermore, the mission extends to fostering a robust paradigm wherein businesses act not merely as commercial entities but as engaged stewards of a more sustainable and equitable future.

My goal, as the author, is not to preach to the converted. Rather, it's to present a framework that is scientifically robust, ethically sound, and grounded in real-world applicability—one that persuades skeptics, motivates the ambivalent, and fuels the passion of advocates. This book is an amalgamation of perspectives, blending philosophies and practices to illumine a path forward for all sectors and stakeholders within our global patchwork.

In crafting the narrative that lies ahead, I have drawn upon interdisciplinary research to substantiate the dialogues and debates that permeate the text. The scientific rigor is intentional, designed to underpin the arguments and recommendations with evidence and expertise. This rigorous approach provides a foundation upon which we can confidently build our understanding and strategies for sustainable business models.

As we address the intricate relationship between business operations and environmental stewardship, the ethical considerations at play are manifold. No aspect of commerce is exempt from scrutiny; from the boardroom to the supply chain, every decision is a thread in the fabric of our societal impact. These considerations frame the discussions to follow, ensuring ethical rigor is maintained in conjunction with strategic innovation.

I urge you, the reader, to approach each chapter with an open mind and a willingness to engage with new and sometimes challenging ideas. The content is structured to provoke thought, incite discussion, and, ultimately, catalyze action. Indeed, the intent is not merely to expound upon theoretical constructs but to offer tangible, actionable insights that can be implemented in the realms of policy, practice, and personal conduct.

The role of diversity in shaping our interpretations and approaches to sustainability is central to the conversation. This book embraces a multiplicity of cultural perspectives, recognizing the paramount importance of inclusivity and equity within sustainable business practices. The amalgamation of these perspectives is key to understanding the nuanced and multifaceted challenges we face.

It is my conviction that businesses, when guided by a strong ethical compass, can be profound agents of change. Whether you are an entrepreneur, an executive, or an employee, there lies within you the potential to be a harbinger of the future we aspire to create. The visionary leadership needed to propel us forward is not confined to a select few; it is a mantle that each of us can, and must, assume as part of the collective effort.

The local and global spheres of operation may appear diametrically opposed, but within this book's discourse, you'll find they are complementary facets of the same initiative. Balancing engagement with local communities against the backdrop of global standards is not only possible but intensely beneficial in harnessing the full spectrum of sustainable innovation.

Through this introduction and the chapters to come, we shall explore the symbiosis of human rights, supply chain ethics, technological innovation, and the diverse facets of corporate responsibility. Each topic is addressed not in isolation but as integral parts of a cohesive strategy toward business sustainability.

To you, the readers, I extend an invitation to immerse yourselves in the forthcoming narrative and to reflect deeply on your role within this systemic transformation. This book is the culmination of extensive research, contemplation, and the fervent belief in our shared capacity for good. It is my deepest hope that what follows will not only inform your understanding, but also ignite your commitment to fostering a better world through the principles and practices of sustainable business.

Let us now delve into this endeavor with open hearts and minds, recognizing the journey ahead is both our responsibility and our greatest opportunity.

Embracing Curiosity: A Conversation with Skeptics

In the journey towards understanding and implementing sustainable practices, skepticism is inevitable. This section isn't just about confronting skepticism but rather engaging with it. It's about embracing the inherent curiosity that drives skeptics to question what they're told about environmental issues, the green economy, and sustainability in general. Skeptical interrogation, after all, can be a forceful ally in refining our ideas and strategies to foster a more resilient world.

Environmental skepticism can manifest in many forms – from those who doubt the severity of environmental problems to those who question the efficacy of proposed solutions. Often, skeptics demand evidence, rigor in research, and compelling arguments to be convinced of the need for change. This can inspire thorough investigation and innovation within the scientific community and technology sectors engaged in environmental studies and applications. Engaging skeptically provides a platform to confront the very myths that hamper progress and erode trust in scientific consensus.

To forge a productive dialogue with skeptics, we must first understand their perspective. Is their skepticism rooted in a lack of information, conflicting information, or perhaps a deep-seated ideology? Rather than dismissing their concerns outright or bombarding them with data, it's vital to listen, show empathy, and attempt to understand what drives their skepticism. Science matters, but so do the concerns of individuals and communities, and these need to be contextualized within a broader social discourse.

Conversations with skeptics must remain open and involve effective communication strategies. We need to frame our arguments in ways that resonate with the values of our audience, whether they are policymakers who prioritize economic growth or communities concerned about their ancestral lands. It's not just about proving a point; it's about creating an inclusive narrative that acknowledges the diverse interests and values of all stakeholders involved.

The engagement with skeptics is not a battle to be won but an opportunity to broaden the support base for sustainability initiatives. It's by recognizing the strength of diverse opinions and fostering a culture of continuous learning and improvement that we can truly move forward. While not all skepticism can be quelled, each conversation held in good faith is a step closer to creating a collaborative environment essential for the kind of wide-scale change we aspire to achieve.

As we move forward in this book, exploring the nuances of our changing world and the imperatives of sustainability, let us remember that the dialogue with skeptics is integral to our collective progress. It provides a critical mirror to our assertions and helps us approach the grand challenge of sustainability with humility, rigor, and determination.

Series Overview: Exploring *Our Changing World* and its Central Ideas

Culminating the journey of *the Our Changing World* series, *The Responsibility Renaissance: Business as a Catalyst for Environmental and Social Ethics* represents a critical convergence of the insights and challenges explored in the preceding volumes. From the cultural tapestry of sustainability in *Threads of Green*, through the societal transformations in *A Sustainable Civilization*, and the socio-cultural landscapes navigated in *A Planet in Balance*, this final installment turns our attention to the pivotal role of business in steering our collective future toward sustainability and ethical integrity. Here, the series reaches its zenith, offering a profound exploration of how the corporate world can and must align with the principles of environmental stewardship and social responsibility to catalyze meaningful change.

This volume serves as a testament to the power of business as a force for good, challenging conventional narratives around capitalism and corporate practices. By drawing on the foundations laid by the previous books, *The Responsibility Renaissance* advocates for a new paradigm wherein business operations are intrinsically linked to sustainability goals and ethical considerations. It presents a vision of the future where companies are key players in the pursuit of a balanced, just, and sustainable world, emphasizing that the path forward requires a radical rethinking of business models, corporate governance, and consumer engagement. In doing so, the series not only concludes its comprehensive exploration of our changing world but also sets forth a blueprint for the critical transformations needed within the business sector to ensure a thriving planet for future generations. From here, the Series will take the following exploration:

Threads of Green: Weaving Sustainability into the Cultural Fabric

Threads of Green presents a detailed examination of how cultural diversity and unity are essential to achieving sustainability. This book positions itself at the intersection of cultural studies and environmental science, arguing that a truly sustainable future cannot be realized without a deep understanding of the varied cultural perspectives that shape our interactions with the environment.

By tracing the evolution of cultural landscapes over time, the book showcases how traditions, beliefs, and practices from around the world offer unique insights and solutions to contemporary ecological challenges. It stresses the importance of integrating traditional wisdom with modern technological and scientific advancements to address these issues effectively. This fusion not only enriches our approach to sustainability but also ensures that solutions are culturally sensitive and widely applicable.

The narrative underscores the critical role of cultural diversity in enriching the global sustainability discourse. It illustrates how embracing the interconnectedness of global and local efforts is vital for the stewardship of our planet. Through stories of resilience, innovation, and collective action, *Threads of Green* highlights how cultural insights and practices contribute to building a sustainable world.

In essence, the book serves as a call to action for individuals, communities, and policymakers to recognize and harness the power of cultural diversity and integrated system thinking in crafting a sustainable future. It's an essential guide for anyone looking to understand the complex relationship between culture and sustainability, offering a rich perspective on how to weave these threads into the fabric of our everyday lives.

A Sustainable Civilization: Unraveling the Threads of Change

A Sustainable Civilization embarks on a comprehensive exploration of the sustainability movement, tracing its roots from the past, navigating through the present, and extending into the future. This journey highlights the essential contributions of diverse cultures, integrating ancient wisdom with contemporary principles to tackle the multifaceted challenges of industrialization, population expansion, and rapid technological innovations. The book lays bare the pressing environmental issues that threaten our planet, emphasizing a pivotal shift from initial conservation efforts to a deeper understanding of ecological interconnectedness.

Central to the narrative are the influential figures and landmark events that have significantly molded the sustainability discourse, offering readers an inspirational glimpse into the evolving ethical landscape that seeks to redefine humanity's bond with nature. *A Sustainable Civilization* delves into the critical battles against climate change and biodiversity loss, underscoring the indispensable role of Indigenous knowledge in weaving a resilient and sustainable future.

By presenting a vision of a world where humanity and nature exist in harmonious coexistence, the book aspires to inspire a collective movement toward sustainable living. It portrays a future where the lessons of the past and the innovations of the present converge to create a sustainable civilization, underlining the importance of unity, innovation, and respect for the natural world in shaping the future we aspire to leave for generations to come.

A Planet in Balance: Exploring the Socio-Cultural Landscape of Sustainability

A Planet in Balance provides a thorough examination of the intricate relationships between sustainability, ethics, and multicultural perspectives. The book investigates the ethical bases that support the pillars of environmental, social, and economic sustainability, presenting a nuanced discussion on how these ethical considerations are essential for understanding and advancing sustainability goals. It explores how individual values, cultural backgrounds, and societal frameworks critically shape our perceptions and engagements with sustainability.

Central to the book's discourse is the vital role that education, art, and storytelling play in enhancing sustainability awareness and motivating societal action. These elements are portrayed as powerful tools for bridging the gap between knowledge and action, effectively engaging diverse audiences and fostering a deeper connection to sustainability issues.

The narrative further extends into the realm of global governance and international cooperation, scrutinizing the mechanisms of policy development and the execution of international environmental agreements. This examination reveals the complexities and challenges of global collaboration, while also highlighting successful strategies that have led to meaningful progress in sustainability efforts.

By providing an in-depth analysis of how ethics, culture, and governance intersect with sustainability, *A Planet in Balance* offers a comprehensive perspective on the socio-cultural dimensions of sustainability. The book encourages readers to reflect on their roles within this global framework and inspires collective efforts toward achieving a sustainable and balanced planet.

The Backstory of the *Our Changing World* Series

What compels a person to delve into the deep river of sustainability, cultural geography, and executive leadership and to emerge with a story to tell? It is the richness of the world's cultural tapestry and the pressing urgency of our environmental crises that fuels the *Our Changing World* series, a narrative canvas I have woven with countless threads of knowledge and experience acquired over twenty years.

My voyage began over two decades ago on the familiar shores of academic rigor, within the bastions of public accounting and professional services firms. Here, the grasp of corporate sustainability strategy was not merely a trade; it was a craft honed through persistence akin to a blacksmith shaping iron. My tenure at prominent Big Four firms was merely the prologue to a much grander tale.

Academia and boardrooms could only teach me so much. It was outside, in the expanse of the living, breathing world, where I would uncover the most poignant lessons. I traversed the globe, journeying through Indigenous territories, sitting with elders, listening to stories of lived experiences from the people living in these remote villages, and understanding the vital pulse of sustainability beat strongest within the communities that have revered the Earth long before the term "sustainability" was even coined.

Amidst these encounters, the inkling that Western ideologies and Indigenous knowledge could converge grew into a bold conviction. As a cultural geographer, I sought to explore not just the physicality of places, but the ethereal sense of "place" embedded in the narratives and rituals that define human-environment interactions.

This exploration transformed me, carving into my consciousness the necessity of a holistic outlook. I saw not only the fragility of nature but the resilience of cultures. Witnessing firsthand the intricate symbioses between communities and their lands, I was heartened by the demonstrated potential for both conservation and sustainable development.

The more communities I visited, the more apparent it became that sustainability is as much about maintaining cultural identity as it is about promoting green technologies. This symphony of sustainability resonates on multiple frequencies—environmental, social, cultural, and spiritual. Each note is crucial for the harmony of the whole.

As I journeyed on, camera in hand and heart open, the diversity of our world unraveled before me in exquisite complexity. Through the lens, each photograph captured a story, a piece of wisdom, a moment where the dance of culture and nature was in perfect step.

My storytelling, thus, is not a mere recapitulation of facts and figures but an endeavor to touch the soul of the reader. The aromas, colors, and textures of distant lands must leap off the pages and draw one into a gentle embrace with the world's myriad societies and ecosystems.

The Responsibility

The *Our Changing World* series is inspired by this wealth of discovery. It is a guided expedition that introduces renowned leaders, humble farmers, wise elders, and enterprising youths, all of whom share a common thread—they are the vanguards of sustainability, each in their own right.

In the crafting of this narrative, my objective has never been to merely educate. It has been to awaken a sense of wonderment and responsibility, to ignite the flame of activism within each reader, and to rally a community of kindred spirits that will champion the cause for a sustainable planet.

This is a tale of unity in which science and story coalesce. The scientific underpinnings are undeniably crucial—they provide the framework upon which our understanding of sustainability rests. But the story is the heart, beating life into the framework and inspiring action.

The *Our Changing World* series, therefore, is not a single chorus but a tapestry of voices—a multidisciplinary narrative that seeks to connect the pragmatic solutions of scientific inquiry with the emotional impetus that only a compelling story can provide.

My aim is to capture and translate the soul of sustainability as I have experienced it: in the boardroom and in the wild, in policy and in practice. It is to lay bare the intrinsic connections that interweave humanity with the broader ecology of the Earth.

Thus, each chapter in this series serves as a waypoint on a quest, beckoning readers to journey through the nexus of environment, culture, and leadership. It is an invitation to envision a new paradigm in which humanity thrives not apart from, but as a part of the natural world.

It's a narrative that asserts we are at our best when we recognize the interconnectedness of our world, champion diversity, and walk hand in hand toward sustainability. The *Our Changing World* series is my ode to our planet—a call to all who will listen to join in the dance of change and become stewards of a world that endlessly gives and asks only that we respect its delicate balance.

Chapter 1:
Navigating the Paradigm Shift in Business and Sustainability

I n an age in which environmental catastrophes headline the daily news and social inequalities deepen, businesses must fundamentally reconsider their role in an evolving global ecosystem. We're witnessing a critical juncture where ignoring the shift toward sustainability spells obsolescence while adapting promises revitalization and relevance.

Swift action has become imperative. Industries across sectors have begun to recognize not only the inherent responsibilities nested within their operations, but also the expansive opportunities sustainability offers—signaling a remarkable paradigm shift from the traditional profit-centric models. A new era beckons—one where ecological integrity and social equity become core to corporate strategy, establishing a symbiotic relationship between enterprise success and planetary well-being.

This initial chapter embarks on unfolding how businesses can align with environmental and societal imperatives, thereby turning into potent allies in the quest for a sustainable future that embraces the interdependence of economic growth, environmental stewardship, and social justice.

Welcoming a New Era

As the curtain falls on traditional business practices that privileged profit over people and planet, a new stage where sustainability and corporate responsibility take the spotlight is set. This crucial transition isn't merely an optional adjustment; it is an imperative pivot to ensure the survival of ecosystems, economies, and communities around the globe. Recognizing this shift is the first step in embracing it.

The transformation we are experiencing is profound, echoing the calls of countless stakeholders who demand transformative action. Sustainability, once seen as a nice-to-have or a regulatory burden, has now been recognized as the linchpin of long-term success, resilience, and ethical leadership in business. Companies that have already begun weaving sustainability into their core strategies are setting themselves apart as frontrunners in a world reshaped by ecological awareness.

This new era, however, poses monumental challenges. To navigate this uncharted territory, businesses must rapidly adapt and embed sustainability into every aspect of their operation. Leaders and decision-makers face the Herculean task of striking a balance between generating profit and preserving the planet for future generations.

The pressure to change comes from multiple directions; consumers growing more conscious, governments implementing stricter regulations, and investors increasingly favoring sustainable practices. In this context, businesses that can't— or won't—adapt risk obsolescence, as failing to pivot to sustainability is a failure to recognize the interconnectedness of all life and commerce.

The call to action is clear, and the avenues for transformation are manifold. Innovation in product design, supply chain management, and energy efficiency are not merely good practices but essential elements of a new competitive advantage. The very conception of value creation is being redefined as businesses direct their ingenuity toward positive environmental and social impact.

As with any significant shift, there is a learning curve. We're seeing a rapidly developing landscape where savvy businesses aren't just engaging with sustainability as a compliance issue but as a strategic imperative and a source of opportunity. This approach is about identifying how sustainable practices can lead to new markets, enhance brand reputation, and drive innovation. It's a move toward authentic integration rather than superficial adoption.

Moreover, the focus is widening from environmental concerns to encompass social justice, human rights, and inclusive growth. The triple bottom line—people, planet, profit—becomes not just a tagline but a framework for measuring business success. Corporate actions are now scrutinized by how they affect all stakeholders and wider communities, making ethical considerations central to day-to-day operations and long-term strategies.

The shift toward a sustainable business paradigm isn't just a passive journey; it's a proactive endeavor requiring leadership, creativity, and persistent commitment. Beyond adopting existing practices, it calls for pioneering new approaches that will serve as blueprints for the businesses of tomorrow.

Leaders at the helm of this transformative wave are themselves undergoing a metamorphosis. The competencies needed to succeed in the past are different from those imperative now and in the future. Adaptability, a deep understanding of ecological systems, empathy toward a diverse workforce and consumer base, and uncompromising ethical standards are elements of the new ethos of leadership.

This is a journey of both disruption and discovery, where tradition may be challenged, but potential is unleashed. The businesses that flourish will be those that have physical and moral courage and that are relentless in their pursuit of sustainability because they recognize their fate is inseparable from the health of the world at large.

Embracing this new era is also a call to academia and practitioners to join forces in generating and disseminating knowledge that can guide and empower businesses. Collaborations across disciplines and sectors are needed to create an ecosystem supportive of sustainable advances. The fostering of forums for dialogue, research initiatives, and platforms for sharing best practices are all integral in aligning efforts toward common goals.

The new era of business and sustainability is not just on the horizon; it is already upon us. It's a period defined by the understanding that business does not exist in a vacuum and that the long-term prosperity of companies and the health of the planet are inextricably linked.

In welcoming this new era, businesses must learn to thrive not just economically but ethically and ecologically. We are tallying the true costs and gains of our business practices, not only on balance sheets, but in the lives of people and the vitality of our environment. Herein lies our greatest challenge and our most significant opportunity.

The narrative of our times unfolds, emphasizing economic growth and sustainability do not have to be in opposition. Instead, they can progress hand in hand if we harness our collective talent and will. This is more than an invitation; it is a necessity, a call to action for a conscientious and determined march toward a sustainable future—a future we can all welcome with open arms.

Embracing Change for Sustainability and Corporate Responsibility

The unyielding march of progress has brought humanity to the precipice of a momentous juncture. In the realm of business, this juncture demands an unprecedented shift toward sustainability and corporate responsibility. As we delve deeper into this chapter, we shall explore the dimensions of this transformation, acknowledging the shift to sustainable business may be the grandest Organizational Change Management (OCM) endeavor in modern business history.

Untangling the complex web of traditional business practices requires a bold reassessment of corporate values and operations. Companies that used to prize financial performance as the sole barometer of success must now account for a much more intricate set of metrics that gauge environmental impact, social responsibility, and overall sustainability.

The concept of sustainability has matured beyond a mere buzzword to become a cornerstone of corporate strategy. It is no longer enough for companies to simply "do no harm." They must actively do good, instilling positive change within their organizations and the broader communities they serve. With this change comes a demand for transparency and accountability that can no longer be sidestepped.

A key driver in this significant shift is the understanding business systems do not operate in isolation. They are deeply embedded in the environmental and social fabric of our world. Hence, corporate strategies must align with ecological imperatives, becoming a reflection of higher ethical standards in business conduct.

To this end, executives and boards are recognizing the power of their influence. They are starting to augment their governance structures, incorporating sustainability into their core ethos and decision-making processes. The process of incorporating these ideals is intricate and challenges deeply ingrained habits and expectations, both internally and externally.

Change management, in this context, isn't merely about enacting policies—it's about cultivating a corporate culture that breathes sustainability. Motivating employees and stakeholders to embrace this new paradigm requires a hands-on approach to leadership and a commitment to ongoing education and engagement.

Centered on the pillars of change management, companies are now actively redefining their missions and business models. The traditional profit-centered model is becoming outdated, making room for models that prioritize social and ecological outcomes alongside financial returns.

Collaborations across industries and sectors are becoming more common as organizations recognize tackling sustainability challenges often requires joint effort. Public-private partnerships reflect the synergistic possibilities and the shared responsibility to act with foresight and conscience.

The sustainability narrative in business has evolved to not only address environmental concerns, but also to grapple with societal issues such as inequality and human rights. Corporate responsibility now extends to ensuring fair labor practices, ethical sourcing, and supporting the communities where businesses operate.

Innovation, too, has taken on a new hue. Sustainable innovation isn't just about creating products and services that sell, but also about designing solutions that contribute positively to the planet and society. Many companies are turning to biomimicry and circular economy principles to revolutionize their product life cycles and reduce waste.

As businesses adopt these new practices, they face the daunting task of communicating their shifts in a genuine manner. The market's skepticism toward greenwashing demands authentic, substantiated claims about sustainable practices and results. This, in turn, necessitates rigorous standards for measuring and reporting sustainability performance.

Financial institutions and investors are catching up to the paradigm shift, with sustainable investing rapidly expanding. Investment decisions are increasingly made based on Environmental, Social, and Governance (ESG) factors, which are seen as indicative of long-term profitability and risk management.

Education plays a crucial role in this transformative process. Continuous learning and skill building for sustainability are not only valuable but essential for company personnel at all levels. Fostering a culture of curiosity and learning ensures the company and its staff will be adaptable and innovative in the face of sustainability challenges.

Ultimately, the commitment to sustainability and corporate responsibility is a commitment to future generations. It requires a long-term vision that transcends the immediate quarterly earnings report. Businesses that embrace this mindset position themselves as leaders and pioneers, playing a pivotal role in shaping a more sustainable and equitable future.

The narrative of embracing change for sustainability and corporate responsibility is far more than a tale of compliance and adaptation. It is a story of foresight, innovation, and, most importantly, of moral imperative. Companies that understand and embody this ethos are not only navigating the paradigm shift, but also steering it, becoming the vanguards in a world thirsting for sustainable leadership.

The Interconnection of Sustainability, Corporate Responsibility, and Ecological Economics

The discourse of sustainability often orbits around a core of ecological responsibility. As we've seen previously, it's no longer a marginal aspect of corporate ethics but a central pivot in the nexus where business intersects with society and the environment. Understanding this intersection is crucial as it pushes further into the realms of an evolving economic paradigm—ecological economics.

The fulcrum of ecological economics rests on the principle that the economy is a subsystem of the Earth's larger ecosystem, which is finite, nongrowing, and materially closed. This viewpoint challenges traditional economic paradigms that hinge on the assumption of infinite growth and resource availability. It posits a crucial question: How can corporations operate sustainably within a system with clear physical boundaries?

Corporate responsibility has transcended beyond mere compliance with legal standards and into the realm of proactive environmental stewardship and societal well-being. This concept encompasses a holistic view of how businesses can be agents of positive change rather than mere adherents to statutory obligations. Corporations have an innate potential to foster innovation that can lead humanity into a more sustainable future.

Businesses encounter a multitude of challenges and opportunities in addressing sustainability. Traditional business models and strategies are being upended by the pressure to adapt to the ecological limits posed by our planet. This adaptation involves not just technological innovation but a transformation in the value propositions businesses offer. Firms are encouraged to consider the full life cycle impact of their products and services, and to become stewards of resources rather than mere consumers.

One could argue the convergence of sustainability, corporate responsibility, and ecological economics signifies a potent blend of ethics, strategy, and practical necessity. This triad suggests businesses must evaluate their operations, products, and services through the lens of environmental impact, resource use efficiency, and social welfare contribution. It's about extending the time horizon from quarterly profits to long-term sustainability goals.

In acknowledging this interconnectedness, corporations must grapple with new metrics of success. Whereas financial benchmarks have long stood as the primary measure of corporate performance, parameters such as carbon footprint reduction, social impact, and resource efficiency become equally significant. This shift necessitates a fundamental reevaluation of what constitutes corporate achievement.

Engaging with stakeholders is another integral part of this interconnection. As transparency becomes a non-negotiable demand from consumers and investors alike, companies must open the channels of communication regarding their environmental and social initiatives. Sustainability reporting and consumer education, thus, become pivotal in solidifying the corporate responsibility mandate.

This synthesis of sustainability, corporate responsibility, and ecological economics also influences supply chain management. Ethical sourcing and procurement policies, coupled with sustainable logistics operations, endorse the interconnection while addressing the critical concerns of resource depletion and environmental degradation.

When addressing the pressing needs of today's world, companies are increasingly expected to apply circular economic principles, integrating waste reduction, reuse, and recycling into their business operations. This approach underpins both ecological economics and the broader sustainability agenda by disrupting the traditional "take-make-waste" industrial model.

Moreover, the rise of conscious capitalism highlights the idea that businesses can build a flourishing and just economic system for all within ecological limits. It's a model that urges businesses to be conscious about the purpose and the impacts of their actions on all stakeholders, including the environment.

Financial practices, too, must align with the principles of sustainable and ethical management. The blooming field of sustainable finance is a testament to this integration, drawing attention to investments that deliver long-term sustainable returns while positively impacting society and the environment.

The integration of ecological economics principles into corporate strategy represents more than a mere operational shift; it is an entire philosophical realignment. It imbues every aspect of business with the ethos of sustainability and responsibility, thus, recalibrating the meaning of business success.

This paradigm shift is not without its challenges. It demands innovative thinking, long-term planning, unwavering commitment, and, often, a readiness to confront short-term financial trade-offs for long-term societal gains. But the evidence is mounting that integrating sustainability deeply into business practices is not only ethically sound but strategically smart and financially beneficial in the long run.

Companies that have embraced this interconnected approach find themselves as leaders of a new vanguard, one positioned to harness collective corporate influence for the well-being of society and the health of the planet. This evolution in thinking and acting lights our way to a sustainable future marked by a rekindled hope for the integration of human economies with nature's economies.

Chapter 2:
Innovating for the Environment: Business Strategies for the Twenty-First Century

Building on the understanding that our planet's resources are not infinite, this chapter turns to the crux of innovation, where businesses are not just participants but pioneering architects of a sustainable future. In "Innovating for the Environment: Business Strategies for the Twenty-First Century," we delve into the reshaping of corporate landscapes through the lens of ecological stewardship and social responsibility. Here, the transformation is not just technological but deeply entrenched in every facet of business ethos.

This chapter illuminates the emerging paradigms where enterprises thrive by harnessing creativity with an Earth-first approach, boldly transitioning from traditional profit-centric models. We explore how innovative practices encompassing product design, material sourcing, and green technologies interweave to scribe the blueprint of eco-friendly and socially conscious business methodologies. It's a meticulous orchestration, akin to a symphony, where diverse instruments—start-ups, small and medium-sized enterprises (SMEs), and large conglomerates alike—play harmoniously to drive the narrative of sustainable change. They collectively champion the cause, embedding the sustainability narrative into the very DNA of business models, thereby changing the conventions of industry and influencing a global culture of resilience and regeneration. The commitment to a greener future is not only a strategic imperative but a moral compass directing corporate journeys toward a more equitable, conscientious, and flourishing world.

Rethinking Innovation: Eco-friendly and Socially Conscious Approaches

In the quest for a sustainable future, businesses are increasingly compelled to reimagine what innovation means in the context of environmental and social well-being. In this essential shift, economic success is no longer solely harnessed by profit margins but aligned with the planet's finite resources and the equitable treatment of its inhabitants.

Eco-friendly and socially conscious approaches to innovation necessitate a transformation within industries. These changes imply the design and production of goods and services that minimize environmental harm and prioritize long-term ecological balance. Innovators are now tasked with the vital challenge of creating solutions that do not simply reduce harm but actively contribute to the health of the environment and communities.

One emerging perspective sees waste as a valuable input rather than an output. The circular economy model revolutionizes the traditional "take-make-dispose" industry structure, offering a system in which resources are reused, repaired, and recycled, creating a closed-loop system that minimizes environmental impact.

Companies are now exploring how to use less to produce more, encouraging resource efficiency and a departure from the linear economy. These efforts are not simply about reducing consumption but redefining success—where quality supplants quantity, and innovation is tied to sustainability.

Moreover, innovation today demands a recognition of the deeply intertwined nature of ecological and social issues. The fair and equitable treatment of labor within supply chains, for instance, is not separable from environmental considerations. Ethical business practices must acknowledge the human aspect of sustainability by ensuring fair wages and safe working conditions as well as rigorously opposing labor exploitation.

Embracing diversity becomes a cornerstone of these innovative strides, enabling the incorporation of a broader range of perspectives and solutions to sustainability challenges. Businesses must lean not only on technological advances, but also on the rich variety of human experiences and knowledge systems that exist around the world.

This journey toward eco-friendly and socially conscious innovation is not without challenges. It requires a systemic change in the way we understand business and its relationship to society and the environment. Long-standing business practices are deeply entrenched, making the pivot to sustainability both a strategic and a cultural challenge.

However, these challenges are accompanied by a myriad of opportunities. Research indicates eco-friendly and socially conscious approaches can lead to new market opportunities, enhance brand reputation, and create economic advantages through increased operational efficiencies.

Strategies for sustainable innovation may include product life extension; servitization, which offers a service rather than a product; and product-as-a-service models, which focus on providing the functionality of a product without the need to own it. These models disrupt traditional market dynamics and reflect a growing consciousness among consumers who prefer access over ownership.

Integrating the perspectives of various stakeholders—from customers to non-governmental organizations (NGO) partners—informs businesses about material concerns that may not have been identified from a purely internal viewpoint. This broader lens uncovers risks and opportunities earlier, allowing companies to be proactive rather than reactive in their innovation strategies.

This proactive stance is increasingly recognized as essential for long-term viability. Businesses that predict and prepare for societal shifts toward sustainability are likely to lead their industries. By embedding these approaches into their core strategies, companies do not just navigate the shifting landscape; they help to shape it.

In rethinking innovation, it's clear the essence of creativity must evolve alongside our understanding of what it means to inhabit a more equitable and sustainable world. The surge of social entrepreneurship exemplifies this evolution, showcasing how businesses can solve societal problems through innovative, scalable models that prioritize public benefit over profit.

Despite the significant progress in eco-innovation, challenges remain in measuring and communicating its impact clearly and transparently to stakeholders. Robust frameworks for assessing the social and environmental footprint of innovations are critical in demonstrating their legitimacy and operationalizing continuous improvement.

As we continue to witness the unfolding consequences of unsustainable practices on our planet and communities, it is incumbent upon businesses to adopt a forward-thinking approach where social and environmental priorities are not just an afterthought but are deeply integrated into the very notion of innovation. In this way, businesses can become champions of a sustainable future, inspiring industries and consumers alike to redefine the boundaries of what is possible and desirable in a world where the health of the planet, and all its inhabitants, is the ultimate measure of success.

Driving Sustainable Change Through Business Models

As we forge ahead within the pages of innovation, we arrive at a critical juncture where the architecture of business models must be scrutinized under the magnifying glass of sustainability. Business models are not just the gears of commerce; they are foundational blueprints that dictate the ways firms create, deliver, and capture value. The pursuit of a sustainable future directs us to reimagine these blueprints with the intent to harmonize economic success with ecological stewardship and social equity.

Traditional business models operate on linear principles of "take-make-waste," which perennially harvest resources and generate waste with little regard for environmental constraints or social welfare. A sustainable business model, however, is engineered to operate within the planetary boundaries and foster social well-being. This reconceptualization is not just an option; it is an imperative for preserving our biosphere and ensuring the longevity and relevance of enterprises in a world that increasingly values the principles of sustainability.

To be agents of sustainable change, businesses must pivot toward models that thrive on circularity. Herein, instead of a linear flow, resources move through cycles of use, reuse, and regeneration. The circular economy is not a mere buzzword—it's a revolution in redefining growth and reframing consumption patterns. In this ecosystem, businesses model resilience by designing products for longevity, repurposing materials, and strategically aligning with waste-to-resource narratives.

Moreover, the service-dominant logic presents another pathway for sustainable transformation. This perspective shifts focus from product-centric models to service-based ones, where the value is co-created through the continuous engagement between firms and customers. Here, businesses are not merely vendors of commodities but facilitators of experiences and solutions that support sustainable lifestyles.

Adopting a sustainable business model often demands a bold overhaul in operational practice, requiring deep integration of sustainability goals across the organization. Yet, it's a transformation that begins with the simple step of articulating a clear vision for sustainability within the company's mission. Aligning the core business strategy with ecological priorities and social imperatives ensures every decision made propels the business toward sustainability.

Collaborative consumption is another facet of sustainable business models that is gaining traction. The paradigm of sharing, leasing, or renting products rather than owning them outright presents an opportunity to optimize asset utilization, reduce waste, and cater to the modern consumer's desire for flexibility and variety. By embedding themselves in the narrative of shared economies, businesses can demonstrate the practicalities of sustainable living.

Yet, the path to sustainable change isn't solely about internal recalibrations within business operations; it's equally about external partnerships and systemic engagement. Collaborative networks that bind together corporations, governments, non-profits, and academia are vital. These networks craft a mutual language of sustainability, push forward collective efforts, and expand the reach and impact of sustainable practices.

Performance metrics are the compass that guides the ship of sustainable business. Without robust and transparent performance measurement, it's challenging to gauge the impact of sustainable business models. Firms need to adopt and report on qualitative and quantitative metrics that reflect their environmental and social performance. These metrics not only serve as internal checkpoints, but also help build trust with stakeholders by demonstrating accountability and progress.

Evolving consumer expectations act as a forceful wind in the sails of businesses sailing toward sustainability. As awareness and demand for ecological and ethical products and services escalate, businesses that align their models with these expectations distinguish themselves within the market. It's imperative that firms listen intently to their customers and embed their insights into the core of their sustainable business strategies.

This transformative journey entails risks. The redesign of conventional business models to fit into the procrustean bed of sustainability is littered with financial, practical, and cultural challenges. However, if navigated judiciously, these challenges can be converted into innovative opportunities. By facing these risks head-on, businesses demonstrate fortitude and leadership that can redefine entire industries.

Leadership commitment is the spearhead of driving sustainable change through business models. It requires executives and managers to not only endorse sustainable principles but to embody them in their leadership styles and business philosophies. When leadership echoes sustainability in its decisions and actions, it permeates throughout the organizational culture and galvanizes collective momentum for change.

In the grand theater of sustainability, technology plays a starring role. Businesses must leverage technology to enhance operational efficiency, reduce environmental impact, and innovate for sustainability. From data analytics that optimize resource use to blockchain systems that ensure supply chain transparency, technology is a potent enabler of sustainable business models.

Education and training are indispensable for actualizing sustainable business models. They equip employees with the knowledge and skills necessary to implement and advocate for sustainability. As such, organizations must invest in continuous learning programs that provide their workforce with tools to innovate and drive the sustainable agenda from within.

The pursuit of sustainable change through business models is an ongoing narrative. It is a story of evolution, replete with moments of insightful breakthroughs and resilient strides against formidable barriers. Firms must be agile, continually learning and adapting their models as new challenges emerge and new solutions arise. The journey is complex, but the destination—a sustainable and equitable world—is unquestionably worthwhile.

The Role of Start-Ups and SMEs in Sustainable Innovation

Start-ups and small to medium enterprises (SMEs) have positioned themselves as the crucibles for sustainable innovation as they carve out their unique roles in the modern business ecosystem. Their agility and inherent culture of innovation allow them to act as catalysts for change, challenging established norms with eco-friendly and ethical business models.

The very fabric of these smaller entities often reflects a flexible and responsive framework. Unlike their larger counterparts, start-ups and

SMEs can pivot and adapt rapidly, integrating sustainability into their core without the entrenched resistance seen in legacy corporate structures. This nimbleness lends itself to the kind of transformative innovation that the twenty-first century demands.

SMEs and start-ups, often borne of a passion for addressing specific societal or environmental issues, treat sustainability not as an add-on but as an essential component of their proposition. Such a perspective aligns seamlessly with today's conscious consumerism, where customers increasingly seek out brands with a purpose beyond profit.

The ability of these smaller businesses to contribute meaningfully to sustainable innovation can be seen in various sectors. From clean technology to sustainable fashion and from waste management to green architecture, their breakthroughs are driven by a dedication to the environment that is, at times, part and parcel of their mission statements. These enterprises don't just adapt to change; they aspire to be the authors of it.

In providing sustainable solutions, start-ups often leverage the latest technologies, formed by leaders who are digital natives and inherently understand the power of tech-driven change. SMEs become testbeds for sustainability, where blockchain, artificial intelligence, and other cutting-edge tools are applied to solve age-old problems in resource management, supply chain transparency, and energy efficiency.

Their financial structures also enable a focus on long-term value creation rather than short-term profit maximization. This is essential for fostering sustainable practices, which may require upfront investment and patience to realize returns—a luxury start-ups and SMEs can afford if supported by the right investors.

Furthermore, these smaller entities are often deeply embedded within their communities, which allows them to craft solutions that are humane, contextually relevant, and culturally sensitive. By operating close to the ground, they can foster a deep connection with local stakeholders and directly witness the impacts of their sustainable practices.

Additionally, partnerships among SMEs, start-ups, and larger corporations can be a powerful force for wider sustainable innovation. The agility of smaller firms, combined with the scale and resources of established entities, can accelerate the development and adoption of groundbreaking sustainability solutions.

Yet, the pathway for start-ups and SMEs is not without its hurdles. Access to capital, regulatory challenges, and the capacity to scale without compromising sustainability principles are lingering concerns. These hurdles must be addressed through collaborative efforts among governments, investors, and the broader business community.

Capital investment targeted at green and social ventures is growing, acknowledging the pivotal role start-ups and SMEs play in sustainable development. This trend toward impact investment is a clear indicator of confidence in the potential of these smaller entities to lead the way in crafting a sustainable future.

Recognition and support from regulatory frameworks that understand the unique position and potential of SMEs and start-ups are also essential. Policies that ease their burdens, offer incentives, and promote sustainable practices can create a fertile environment for these businesses to thrive and innovate for the greater good.

However, the journey toward sustainability is a shared endeavor. Start-ups and SMEs, with their inherent ability to innovate and disrupt, must be integrated into broader platforms that address sustainability issues. Peer networks, incubators, and consortia dedicated to sustainability can serve as collective powerhouses driving systemic change, with start-ups and SMEs at their heart.

Ultimately, start-ups and SMEs embody hope; a promise that business can be a force for good. Through their pursuit of sustainable innovation, they demonstrate how enterprises can operate responsibly while still pursuing success. In their resilience and creativity rest the seeds for a regenerative and equitable future that benefits business, society, and the planet alike.

The Responsibility

As the global business landscape continues its shift toward a more sustainable and ethically responsible future, the central role played by start-ups and SMEs in this transformation cannot be overstated. They are not just participants but pioneers, leading us toward a horizon where innovation and integrity walk hand in hand. Their stories and strategies underscore the narrative that the future of business is one in which success is measured not just by profit but by positive impact on the world.

Chapter 3:
Navigating the Ethical Quandary: Moral Philosophies in Business

In the quest to redefine the essence of business in the age of sustainability, we've come to the vital crossroads where ethical considerations are not simply niceties but necessities for corporate longevity. As we delve into this chapter, the narrative shifts toward the intricacies of moral compasses guiding business decisions. It's here that the convergence of environmental ethics and corporate behavior charts a course for enterprises to act as stewards of both profits and the planet.

An in-depth exploration of moral philosophies provides companies with the philosophical frameworks that can reconcile profit goals with the greater good. From the Kantian imperative of duty to the utilitarian pursuit of the greatest happiness, businesses must steer through these philosophies to inform their strategies—ensuring each decision aligns with a commitment to ecological preservation and social justice. By instilling a culture that prizes ethical reflection, corporations can lead the charge in the sustainability movement, transforming the marketplace into a force for positive change.

Such moral underpinnings invite leaders and teams to ask not only what can be done to succeed, but also what should be done to honor our collective responsibilities. In this pivotal chapter, businesses are equipped to navigate the ethical quandary, emerging as architects of a future in which integrity and innovation are inextricably linked.

The Intersection of Environmental Ethics and Business Decisions

As we delve into the myriad challenges businesses face in today's complex socio-environmental landscape, it's clear that environmental ethics cannot be an afterthought in business decisions. Balancing profitability with ecological care is a tightrope walk, demanding a nuanced understanding of moral philosophies. Businesses that embrace environmental ethics do not just contribute to the greater good—they also position themselves as leaders in the innovation-driven economy that characterizes the twenty-first century.

To comprehend the intersection of environmental ethics and business decisions, we must first acknowledge that corporations are pivotal actors on the environmental stage. Not only do they have the power to inflict considerable damage, but they also possess the creativity and resources to forge new paths toward sustainability. It is now widely recognized that long-term business success is tethered to the health of our planet.

Integrating environmental ethics into business requires a foundational shift in perspective. A business operating solely on profit-maximizing principles is akin to an organism ignoring the health of its own ecosystem. The reality is businesses do not exist in a vacuum; they are interwoven with the natural world, and every decision resonates across ecosystems and communities. Therefore, environmental ethics must be tightly woven into every business strategy and decision-making process.

The philosophical principles guiding environmental ethics in business often draw from the deep well of sustainability, stewardship, and intergenerational justice. Companies that acknowledge their dependency on the environment, envisioning themselves as stewards rather than exploiters, find sustainable practices are not just ethical—they're indispensable for resilience and relevance in a rapidly changing global marketplace.

One of the essential tenets in this intersection is the concept of the triple bottom line, wherein success is measured through the lenses of profit, people, and the planet. It advocates for a form of capitalism that does not solely pursue financial gains, but also seeks to ensure social equity and environmental conservation. Each decision point, then, becomes an intersection where ethical considerations must balance with business imperatives.

Embracing environmental ethics in business implicates the entire supply chain—from raw material sourcing to end user. Ethical sourcing, for instance, isn't just about minimizing environmental impact, it's also about fostering resilience in local economies and communities both now and for future generations. It's no longer a question of whether businesses should adopt sustainable practices, but how they will do so in order to remain competitive and relevant.

There are numerous examples where environmental ethics have steered companies toward innovation and competitive advantage. The adoption of renewable energy sources, reduction in waste, and water conservation efforts not only reduce ecological footprints, but also result in operational cost savings. Furthermore, transparency in reporting environmental initiatives has become a driver for building consumer trust and brand loyalty.

The finance sector, too, can't be overlooked in these ethical considerations. Sustainable investing is on the rise, showing profitability can be aligned with ethical goals. Investors increasingly use Environmental, Social, and Governance (ESG) criteria to screen potential investments, leading businesses to prioritize sustainability goals in their decision-making processes.

However, the path of integrating environmental ethics into business operations is fraught with challenges. Traditional economic models and short-term financial pressures often conflict with the long-term perspectives required by sustainability. Overcoming such institutional inertia demands courage, leadership, and a deep commitment to ethical values that resound beyond the boardroom.

Moreover, in embracing environmental ethics, businesses must also contend with the complexities of global operations. What is considered environmentally ethical can vary between cultures and economies, raising intricate questions about global standards versus localized practices. This demands a nuanced, culturally sensitive approach to implementation.

In light of the urgency of environmental crises, businesses must adopt a proactive stance. Reactive stances that only address environmental concerns when they reach a critical point are no longer adequate—nor are they ethical. Proactivity in this realm entails not only complying with existing regulations but innovating beyond them, setting new standards for industry and society alike.

The role of leadership in this ethical journey is also paramount. Leaders who embody environmental values and articulate a clear vision for sustainability can drive a culture shift throughout their organization. Their ability to inspire and mobilize teams toward a shared vision of environmental stewardship is critical for effecting transformative change.

Environmental ethics and business decisions intersect at a point that defines the future not only for a company but for the planet. As the world faces increasingly pressing environmental challenges, it is incumbent upon businesses to evolve and reconceive their roles not as conquerors of nature but as collaborators with it. Such a transformative shift is not just morally imperative—it's essential to the survival and prosperity of businesses in the long term.

Conclusively, the entwinement of environmental ethics and business decisions signals a paradigm shift. It ushers in an era in which the two aren't competing ideals but are complementary forces driving innovation, profitability, and, fundamentally, the responsible stewardship of our planet. Thus, companies that take this intersection seriously will not only thrive but will lead the charge in fostering a more sustainable and equitable future.

The Ethical Obligations of Corporations

In modern commerce, corporations wield unprecedented influence over the social and environmental fabrics of our global community. Recognizing this influence, there is an inescapable ethical imperative for businesses to engage proactively with the problems facing our ecosystem and society. This paradigm shift is not merely altruistic; it responds to the clarion call of our times, demanding a blend of integrity and innovation to support a world where all life thrives.

The ethical obligations of corporations extend beyond mere compliance with laws or the pursuit of profit. They encompass a broader commitment to sustainable development and the well-being of all stakeholders, including employees, customers, communities, and the environment. The very ethos of a company must pivot toward a realization that safeguarding our common home transcends balance sheets and quarterly reports.

Companies today must navigate complex moral terrain where every decision can have far-reaching impacts. This requires a commitment to ethical decision-making processes that consider not only the financial, but also the social and environmental ramifications of the outcomes. The emergence of these ethical considerations reflects an understanding that the long-term success of a company is deeply interwoven with the health of the planet and its inhabitants.

Ranging from climate change to social inequalities, the challenges are both vast and varied. Corporations must adopt a holistic approach to ethics that integrates ecological sensitivity and social justice—a commitment to do no harm, and indeed, to do good. This stance aligns with an emerging consciousness that sees the well-being of the individual and the collective as fundamentally connected.

The pursuit of sustainability has become an undeniable trend among leading corporations, driven both by ethical reflection and strategic foresight. The integration of sustainable practices is seen not as a cost but as an investment—an investment in a more stable, prosperous future for both businesses and society.

An ethical corporation looks beyond short-term gains and embraces its role in fostering long-term resilience—be this through the responsible sourcing of materials, minimizing waste, reducing carbon footprints, or ensuring fair labor practices across the supply chain. Such measures are not solely environmental or social concerns; they are strategic business imperatives that preserve the very ecosystems and social structures upon which commerce itself depends.

Transparency and accountability stand as pillars in the ethical corporation's endeavor. Stakeholders—bolstered by digital connectivity and a burgeoning awareness—demand greater insight into corporate practices and their consequences. In response, businesses are increasingly held to their commitments, scrutinized not only for their policies but for their actions and their impact.

The ethical obligations of corporations also involve active engagement and leadership within their spheres of influence. Companies can be powerful advocates for change, fostering innovation that promotes sustainability and lobbying for policies that support responsible business practices.

Education and dialogue form the cornerstone of an ethical corporate culture. Companies have a responsibility to educate their workforce, partners, and customers about the importance of sustainability, empowering them to make informed decisions and to act with ethical purpose.

To navigate this evolving ethical landscape, corporations require leaders who possess not only business acumen, but also a deep moral compass—creating a leadership that fosters a culture where ethical considerations are woven into the very fabric of the organization's operational strategy.

Harnessing the power of innovation to meet environmental challenges head-on is another area where businesses have a key role to play. Developing new products, services, and processes that mitigate environmental harm and contribute positively to ecosystems illustrates the ongoing, dynamic nature of ethical corporate responsibility.

Partnerships and collaboration across sectors amplify a corporation's ability to affect positive change. By aligning efforts with governments, nongovernmental organizations (NGOs), and civil society, corporations can engage in initiatives that address pressing environmental and social issues more effectively than they may alone.

Ethical corporations also recognize the importance of their consumers in shaping a sustainable future. By offering products and services that reflect ethical values and engaging in honest marketing practices, companies can inspire consumers to make choices that support environmental and social sustainability.

The notion of corporate social responsibility (CSR) is evolving. No longer confined to peripheral "add-on" initiatives, CSR must become embedded within the core strategy and operations of corporations to meet the moral imperatives of our era.

In conclusion, the ethical obligations of corporations in the modern age are multifaceted and pervasive. Meeting these obligations is about more than compliance or philanthropy; it's about embracing a more insightful, purpose-driven approach to business. By upholding these ethical standards, corporations not only ensure their own longevity but contribute to the well-being of society and the preservation of the planet.

Fostering an Ethical Corporate Culture

In the pursuit of an ethical corporate culture, we find that business isn't just about the bottom line—it's about the values we imbue within our enterprises and how these values manifest in the global community. Forging an ethical corporate culture is paramount in guiding businesses toward a more sustainable, equitable future, where ecological and social considerations are harmoniously integrated into the fabric of corporate decision-making.

The essence of an ethical corporate culture begins with clear moral guidance. This ethical framework should be built not only on the prohibitions of malpractice, but also on promoting a spectrum of pro-social behaviors. As such, companies ought to cultivate environments where integrity flourishes and every employee, from the C-suite to interns, internalizes the company's commitment to doing good as much as doing well.

Leadership plays a pivotal role in fostering an ethical culture. Leaders must exemplify the values they espouse, demonstrating a commitment to ethical principles consistently and visibly. It is not enough to draft policies; leaders must actively support initiatives that advance sustainability, social responsibility, and fair dealings at every level of their organization.

Transparency is another cornerstone of an ethical corporate culture. Openness in operations and decision-making processes helps build trust among stakeholders and ensures accountability. In this light, encouraging candid communication throughout the organization is critical. Employees should feel confident that their voices are heard and that their concerns, especially regarding ethical quandaries, are taken seriously and addressed appropriately.

Empowerment of employees is vital. A truly ethical corporate culture doesn't just discourage wrongdoing—it encourages individual agency in stewarding the company's values. Staff at all levels should feel that they have the power and responsibility to make choices that align with the company's ethical stance, bolstering a collective sense of purpose and moral direction.

Implementation of ethical training programs can also enhance the fiber of corporate culture. Such programs should not only convey the expected ethical standards, but also provide practical tools and scenario-based training to help individuals navigate complex situations where decisions may not be clear-cut.

Reward systems that incentivize ethical behavior reinforce a culture where doing the right thing is recognized and valued. Aligning evaluations, promotions, and incentives with ethical performance ensures individuals at every level are motived to uphold and advance the company's ethical framework.

Espousing a stakeholder perspective is crucial. Ethical culture is enriched when companies recognize and respond to the needs of all stakeholders, including employees, customers, local communities, and the environment. Engaging in open dialogue with stakeholders to understand their concerns and integrating their feedback into business practices fortifies the ethical grounding of a company.

Continuous evaluation of company practices against ethical standards allows for growth and improvement. This process should be rigorous and carried out with the same seriousness as financial audits. Regular ethical audits can help identify areas for improvement and create a roadmap for ongoing development of the corporate culture.

Collaboration with external bodies, such as NGOs, can give depth to an ethical corporate culture. These partnerships can help ensure companies maintain a focus on the wider societal and environmental impacts of the business and can elevate standards across industries.

Integrating considerations of global sustainability trends into corporate strategies is essential. As the planet faces unprecedented environmental and social challenges, companies that incorporate long-term sustainability goals into their core operations will not only foster ethical cultures, but also secure their relevance in a rapidly evolving marketplace.

Businesses must understand that fostering an ethical culture is not a one-time achievement but a dynamic process that adapts to changing moral insights and societal expectations. Just as businesses evolve to stay competitive, they must also evolve to stay ethically aligned with the world's transforming values.

Finally, recognizing that an ethical corporate culture is an investment, not an expense, is fundamental. The payoff of this investment isn't merely in risk mitigation or compliance—the true return comes in the form of trust, innovation, and the long-term loyalty of stakeholders. Companies that thrive ethically contribute to a regenerative economy that benefits all.

In sum, as we venture to make businesses conduits of global sustainability, the cultivation of ethical corporate cultures stands out not as an optional addendum but as a pillar in constructing a more sustainable, just, and prosperous world. And while the path forward may be complex, the drive to mold corporate ethics into a force for worldwide betterment is both a moral imperative and a strategic necessity.

Chapter 4:
The Power of Diversity:
Cultural Perspectives on Sustainability

Building on ethical quandaries and the foundation of environmental ethics explored in previous chapters, this chapter delves into the rich blending of global cultures and the multifaceted perspectives on sustainability they offer. In the kaleidoscope of human experience, diversity is not just a strength but an essential component of innovation and resilience. When businesses embrace the myriad of cultural lenses through which sustainability may be viewed, they tap into a wellspring of knowledge and practice that can drive the transformative shift toward environmental and social responsibility.

The integration of cultural diversity into sustainable business practices yields a multitude of strategies that reflect the deep-seated values and traditions of various communities, demonstrating inclusivity goes beyond mere representation; it's about genuinely understanding and valuing different ways of seeing the world.

Organizations that cultivate a global mindset are positioned to set the pace in the sustainability movement, pioneering pathways that respect the planet's needs while fostering a more equitable future. By learning from the intricate blend of cultural norms, values, and Indigenous wisdom, businesses can craft an approach to sustainability that's as adaptive and dynamic as the world's myriad of cultures, anchoring ecological and social stewardship in the heart of corporate practice and ethos.

Inclusion and Equity in Sustainable Business Practices

In the quest for sustainability, a crucial component often overlooked is the need for an inclusive and equitable approach in business practices. Businesses, large and small, have a unique opportunity—and some would argue an imperative—to build frameworks that go beyond environmental conservation to include social equality and community empowerment. This section explores the intricate relationships between diversity, inclusion, and sustainable business operations, demonstrating how equity can be both a goal and a strategic advantage.

Inclusion embodies more than just the notion of "having a seat at the table." It pertains to having one's voice heard and integrated within the operational and decision-making processes of businesses. When perspectives from varied cultural, gender, racial, and socioeconomic backgrounds are not only recognized, but also valued, businesses can foster creativity and innovation that is essential for sustainability.

An equitable business environment, on the other hand, ensures policies and practices are fair, transparent, and promote justice within the organization and its community. Equity aims to understand and give people what they need in order to enjoy full, healthy lives. In practice, this means ensuring equitable access to opportunities and resources—a concept often summarized in the "Triple Bottom Line" accounting framework, which emphasizes people, planet, and profit.

Historically, corporate social responsibility (CSR) initiatives have focused predominantly on environmental sustainability. However, there is a growing recognition that true sustainability cannot be achieved without addressing the systemic inequalities that exist within and around business ecosystems. This involves critically examining supply chains, labor practices, community engagement activities, and overall corporate governance.

Practically, inclusive business models may involve collaboration with local communities in decision-making processes or investing in community development projects that address needs identified by those living in the communities. It also entails promoting diversity in leadership roles within organizations and offering fair and equal compensation across the company.

Employee resource groups (ERGs) and diversity councils have become popular tools for supporting inclusion and equity in the workplace. They provide platforms for minority groups to share insights, raise concerns, and shape corporate policies. These groups are not just support networks, they can offer vital perspectives that challenge the status quo and spark more sustainable business innovations.

Inclusion is not only morally imperative, but also economically beneficial. Research has shown that diverse companies are more likely to achieve better financial performance and are more innovative. In terms of sustainability, this could translate to more holistic and impactful environmental strategies that take into account various stakeholder perspectives.

As businesses move toward more inclusive models, they also enhance their accountability in terms of social equity. This includes reducing the gender pay gap, promoting equal opportunity employment, and creating more accessible work environments for individuals with disabilities. Equity-focused policies contribute to a healthier society and, by extension, a more stable and receptive market for business growth.

However, integration of inclusion and equity doesn't come without its challenges. Resistance to change, unconscious biases, and a lack of understanding of different cultural norms can create barriers. Addressing these obstacles with sensitivity and determination is crucial for the successful implementation of inclusive practices within an organization.

Training and development programs are fundamental in equipping employees with skills to understand and manage diversity. Through these programs, employees can become more aware of their biases and learn how to work collaboratively with people from different backgrounds.

Transparency is another key factor in fostering inclusion and equity. When businesses are transparent about their sustainability efforts, including their successes and failures, they build trust with consumers and stakeholders. Transparency can also lead to more rigorous and honest assessments of where equity needs to be improved within the business.

Thinking globally but acting locally can help businesses to achieve equity in sustainability. While global standards provide a benchmark, they must be adapted to fit the cultural and social contexts of each locale. Engaging local stakeholders in the conversation around sustainable practices ensures these practices are both effective and respectful of the local norms and values.

Looking outward, businesses can influence their suppliers and partners to adopt similar inclusion and equity practices. This push can create a ripple effect, transforming industries and markets toward more sustainable and just operations. Collective action, driven by a network of businesses with aligned values, holds immense power in promoting global change.

In closing, businesses play a pivotal role in shaping the future of our planet. Creating business practices that prioritize inclusion and equity is not just beneficial; it is a necessity for those seeking to lead in sustainable development. While there are challenges to such a transformative shift, businesses that seize this opportunity can expect to see not only increased innovation and profitability, but also become key drivers in the global sustainability movement.

In the following sections, we will delve into the role of a global mindset, explore case studies where cultural diversity is driving sustainability, and investigate how businesses balance local and global imperatives. But first, let us carry forward the understanding that sustainable practices integrated with inclusion and equity are not just additions to a business's strategy—they are the foundations upon which lasting success is built.

Global Mindset: Embracing Cultural Differences in Ethics

In the journey to foster a more sustainable and equitable future, recognizing the strength that lies in our global diversity is paramount. Cultural differences often give rise to distinct ethical viewpoints, which can greatly enrich the dialogue and development of sustainability practices. By fostering a global mindset, businesses and societies can embrace these differences, leading to more innovative and inclusive approaches to sustainability.

With the power of cultural diversity comes the acknowledgment that ethics are not universal. What one society may consider ethical, another could view as problematic. Consequently, businesses operating on a global scale must navigate this complex ethical terrain with sensitivity and intelligence. To do that, they must understand the underlying cultural values that inform ethical perspectives in various regions of the world.

Interdisciplinary approaches to sustainability must, therefore, seek to bridge the gap between these divergent ethical frameworks. Such bridging helps ensure sustainability initiatives are not only environmentally sound, but also culturally respectful and inclusive. Failure to do so can lead to initiatives that are, at best, ineffective and, at worst, damaging to the sociocultural fabric of local communities.

As businesses expand their reach, they increasingly recognize ethics cannot be siloed within cultural boundaries. Instead, they need to adopt a pluralistic stance, actively engaging with different cultural insights and values. This inclusion aids in building more holistic and adaptive ethical frameworks that are capable of accommodating various cultural perspectives and enhancing the social acceptability of sustainability initiatives.

When businesses embark on sustainability projects in unfamiliar cultural territories, it's critical they learn to listen first. The expertise and knowledge present in local ethical perspectives can provide invaluable guidance when developing and implementing sustainability strategies that are both effective and culturally congruent. Importantly, this process is not about co-opting local wisdom but rather integrating it as a key element of ethical decision-making.

Take, as an example, the principle of "Ubuntu," a South African term that translates roughly to "I am because we are." This philosophy emphasizes collective well-being and has important implications for sustainability. It suggests a shift away from purely individualistic approaches toward ethical frameworks that recognize the interconnectedness of people and ecosystems. By integrating such philosophies into their operations, businesses can resonate more deeply with local communities and foster a sense of shared responsibility.

Another important aspect of embracing a global mindset is the acknowledgment that language and communication play significant roles in the understanding and practice of ethics. In many cultures, the concepts of honor, respect, and harmony are deeply embedded in the language used to discuss ethical issues. Businesses should be aware of these nuances and ensure their communication strategies are adapted accordingly.

International businesses must be not only fluent in the language of cross-cultural ethics, but also adept at negotiating varying legal environments. Ethics and law are intimately intertwined, and what is considered ethical within the business practices in one country may be governed by law in another. A global mindset requires a keen awareness of these legal distinctions and a commitment to uphold the highest standards of ethics, regardless of regional regulations.

To support these cross-cultural ethical considerations, education plays an essential role. Ensuring employees at all levels of an organization understand the cultural dimensions of ethics can strengthen their ability to engage respectfully and effectively with diverse stakeholders. Continuous, culturally sensitive training must be a cornerstone of any business dedicated to ethical sustainability.

This cultural sensitivity extends to the realm of technology and data. In an age in which data can be shared globally in an instant, ethical considerations surrounding privacy and consent can vary greatly between cultures. Integrating technological strategies that respect these cultural views on data ethics is another layer in building a sustainable global business model.

Part of embracing a global mindset also involves recognizing and countering ethnocentric attitudes. This commitment to cultural humility means understanding no single culture has all the answers for sustainable and ethical practices. This ethos encourages collaboration and shared learning, drawing from the full spectrum of global cultures to craft sustainability strategies that are both innovative and inclusive.

Moreover, incorporating a variety of cultural ethics into sustainability efforts can lead to a more comprehensive understanding of issues such as climate change, resource management, and social equity. Diverse perspectives can highlight different aspects of a problem and suggest unique solutions that may not emerge from a monocultural viewpoint.

It's crucial to remember, however, that embracing cultural differences in ethics is not without challenges. Tensions can arise when universal sustainability goals, such as those outlined in the Sustainable Development Goals, intersect with local cultural norms and practices. Businesses and policymakers must navigate these situations with finesse, aiming for solutions that honor both global sustainability objectives and the cultural sovereignty of local communities.

With the emergence of new ethical challenges, the role of Indigenous knowledge and traditions in sustainability efforts has become increasingly recognized. This appreciation for traditional ecological knowledge reflects a broader understanding that long-standing cultural practices often embody sustainable living principles honed over generations. Integrating this knowledge with contemporary sustainability science can lead to robust, culturally informed ethical practices.

In conclusion, developing a global mindset requires an ongoing commitment to learning and adapting. As the world continues to shrink due to technological advancements and increased connectivity, the importance of embracing cultural differences in ethics becomes more pronounced. Through a thoughtful blend of respect, collaboration, and innovation, businesses can lead the charge toward a more sustainable and ethically diverse future, allowing a multitude of voices to contribute to the shared goal of preserving our planet and its people.

Case Studies: Cultural Diversity Driving Sustainability

In the previous sections, we explored how cultural diversity enhances sustainability through inclusion, equity, and a global mindset. Now, let's delve into concrete examples where cultural diversity has been a pivotal element in driving sustainable practices and business ethics forward.

Considering the weaving collective of Oaxaca, Mexico, as a pioneering case, one observes how traditionally marginalized Indigenous communities have infused ancient customs into modern business models. By preserving biodiverse farming for dye-producing plants and employing age-old weaving techniques, these cooperatives have maintained a sustainable economy that benefits people and the planet. These efforts have been recognized globally, resulting in partnerships that bolster local economies.

Crossing continents, we find a distinct example in the Maasai people of Kenya and Tanzania, renowned for their symbiotic relationship with their environment. Their nomadic lifestyle and livestock grazing practices have been studied to promote sustainable land management and conservation efforts. Companies have partnered with Maasai leaders to integrate their environmental ethics into eco-tourism, simultaneously preserving culture and boosting local economies.

In Scandinavia, the concept of "janteloven," a cultural mindset emphasizing communal success over individual accolades, has shaped corporate governance. Firms here are heralded for their sustainable business models and a cultural disposition that favors long-term environmental considerations over short-term profits, reaffirming the cultural roots of sustainability.

The "Guna People" in Panama serve as custodians of one of the most-diverse ecosystems in the world—the Guna Yala archipelago. Through community-led conservation and sustainable tourism, they showcase an exemplary balance between cultural preservation and environmental sustainability. Their traditional practices have been integrated into environmental policy, demonstrating the mutual reinforcement of cultural diversity and sustainable development.

Japan presents another compelling case with its "Satoyama" and "Satoumi" concepts, portraying traditional agricultural and coastal management that conserves biodiversity. Contemporary business strategies have embraced these practices to create sustainable supply chains, recognizing traditional knowledge can coalesce profit and ecology in harmony.

Recognizing the strength in Africa's diverse cultures, businesses have embraced models that incorporate traditional knowledge into modern agricultural practices. In this context, agroforestry systems that mirror Indigenous techniques have demonstrated both increased yields and biodiversity protection. International markets are now keen on sourcing from suppliers that align with such culturally cognizant practices.

Moving toward the fashion industry, cultural diversity is threading success in sustainability through various artisan communities around the globe. For instance, the revival of traditional Indian textile crafts, such as handloom weaving and natural dyeing, is being merged with ethical fashion movements. This not only revives fading art forms, but also enables sustainable livelihoods, all while reducing the fashion industry's notorious carbon footprint.

In Brazil, the use of Amazonian native plants in cosmetics has grown exponentially. The market favors businesses that collaborate with local communities, ensuring biodiversity is respected and residents receive fair shares of profits. Such businesses illuminate the path for utilitarian and ethical use of natural resources while honoring cultural heritage.

The Responsibility

The Indigenous concept of "Ubuntu," translating to "I am because we are," has also framed corporate social responsibility in various African businesses. This notion of interconnectedness has proven vital in crafting sustainable community-based models in industries ranging from technology to mining.

Then, there is the environmentally conscious ethos of Bhutan—where the Gross National Happiness index prioritizes sustainability and cultural values over pure economic growth. Here, businesses are intrinsically tied to these principles, creating a unique blueprint for global companies to consider happiness and sustainability as mutually inclusive metrics.

In the Pacific, the "Vale ni Vanua" framework from Fiji illustrates how traditional land stewardship can be adapted into modern environmental policy. This framework not only guides local businesses, but also informs national strategies aligning with sustainable development goals.

Furthermore, in the vibrant Andean regions, "Sumak Kawsay," a term encapsulating living in harmony with the community and nature, has been pivotal for Ecuador and Bolivia. Companies within these countries have weaved this philosophy into their operations to foster sustainable development in alignment with local worldviews.

In conclusion, these diverse case studies validate that cultural diversity isn't just an ethereal concept but a practical business asset. Taking cues from various cultures' intimate bond with nature can inspire and direct sustainable business practices that attend both to the ecological realities of our world and the longevity of human societies.

Businesses that recognize and integrate the wisdom embedded in cultural traditions will not only contribute to preserving our planet, but also exemplify the spirit of innovation grounded in humanity's rich heritage.

As we turn the pages of these case studies, they remind us sustainability isn't solely technocratic or scientific—it is deeply human and intrinsically cultural. It's this abundance of diverse wisdom that can lead us to forge a future that is as resilient as it is reflective of our global mosaic of cultures.

Chapter 5:
The Local vs. Global Paradigm in Ethical Business

This chapter engages in a crucial conversation on the conundrum businesses encounter while balancing local commitments with global responsibilities. As agents of change, businesses are increasingly discovering that local values and cultural nuances play a pivotal role in the realization of ethical operations. Yet, they operate in a globalized marketplace where standardization and efficiency drive competitive advantage. In this intricate dance, ethical businesses are tasked with respecting the unique attributes of local communities, including their economic structures, environmental concerns, and social norms, while simultaneously contributing to broader global sustainability goals.

It's here that proactive companies can serve as custodians of culture—using their influence to preserve and promote local traditions and ecological knowledge. All the while, these same entities must translate such respect into a language of universal ethical business practices. And so, we discover visionary businesses weaving a version of sustainability that honors the place-based wisdom of local economies and contributes robust threads to the global fabric of ethical commerce. The ascendancy of such a model is both an art and a science, requiring a nuanced understanding of socio-ecological systems in all their splendid diversity—as well as a heartfelt commitment to the well-being of communities, both human and more-than-human.

Supporting Local Economies While Operating Globally

The tension between global expansion and its impact on local economies represents a dichotomy at the heart of today's ethical business conversations. As we delve into the complexities of this issue, we uncover a rich set of challenges and opportunities for companies striving to support local economies within the broader scope of their global operations. This section explores the ways corporations can bolster local markets while thriving internationally, propelling both economic growth and sustainable practices.

Corporations hold immense power to transform local economies, but this transformation must be sensitively navigated to ensure empowerment rather than exploitation. When multinationals enter local markets, they bring with them a tide of capital that's potent enough to stir the local economic landscape. However, this inflow needs to be managed with care, ensuring the economic benefits are not just transient but form the bedrock for sustained growth.

One approach that's gained traction is the inclusive business model that integrates low-income communities into corporate value chains as suppliers, distributors, or customers. By doing so, companies do not just offer charity, they create profitable ventures that elevate the local economic standards.

An ethical business must look beyond the profit horizon and focus on developing symbiotic relationships with local entities. Investment in local workforce training, for instance, not only equips individuals with marketable skills, but also feeds the company's future talent pool. Partnerships with local educational institutions can catalyze this process, creating a synergy where both sides thrive. H&M's collaboration with textile factories in Bangladesh to provide better safety training is a noteworthy example.

Businesses also have the opportunity to support local economies through local sourcing. By prioritizing local suppliers and producers, companies can reduce their carbon footprint while fostering economic development in the regions where they operate. This modality of local reinforcement, when paired with commitments to fair trade practices and ethical sourcing, not only upholds the respect for human rights, but also signifies a company's dedication to nurturing local industries.

However, the path of supporting local economies isn't without its imperfections. The complexities of balancing global operational strategies with local needs can yield unintended consequences. Global business strategies may sometimes clash with local cultural practices and small economies. Therefore, it's critical for businesses to engage in active dialogue with community leaders and stakeholders, thus, ensuring local customs and economies are not only acknowledged but respected and integrated into their operational strategies.

In the face of globalization, safeguarding local industries from becoming submerged by the competitive pressures of multinational corporations is of paramount importance. Protective measures such as capacity building and advocating for equitable trade policies can insulate these local industries while allowing them to benefit from the global business network.

Another essential element in supporting local economies is innovation that addresses unique local challenges. Whether it's developing technologies that cater to local environmental issues or providing services tailored to communal customs, companies can engender goodwill and long-term loyalty by showcasing genuine commitment to resolving local problems.

Philanthropy, too, plays a role in strengthening local economies. Charitable projects can fill gaps in local infrastructure and services. The goal, however, should be to go beyond philanthropy and create long-term strategies for self-sufficiency rather than dependency. This requires a partnership mentality, where communities are equal stakeholders in projects.

The implementation of corporate social responsibility (CSR) initiatives that have local impact cannot be understated. By embedding

CSR into their core business strategy, companies can address local concerns while achieving their global objectives. Programs focused on local environmental restoration and preservation, for instance, can illustrate a company's dedication to the localities in which they operate.

Sustainable financial investments in local businesses can spearhead economic stimulation. Microfinance, for instance, has shown significant success in bolstering local entrepreneurs who, in turn, contribute to the local economy's vibrance. Collaborative investments between large corporations and local enterprises can forge strong local supply chains that benefit both entities.

It is also integral for businesses to consider the local socioeconomic landscape when determining prices and wages to avoid disrupting the local economy. A balance must be struck. Prices need reflect the true cost of sustainable practices while remaining accessible to local consumers, and the wages provided must be able to feasibly ripple benefits throughout the community.

Cross-cultural competency is essential for global corporations operating in diverse local contexts. Understanding subtleties in communication, leadership styles, and negotiation processes can preclude misunderstandings and foster inclusive, respectful business relationships that bolster local economies.

Environmental protection is inexorably linked to local economic prosperity. Companies focusing on green technologies and sustainable practices in local industries not only safeguard the environment, but also set standards for the local market, encouraging a green economy trend. The long-term economic benefits of such practices can be monumental, aiding in the resilience of local economies against ecological adversities.

In summary, operating globally with an ethos that cherishes and supports local economies is intrinsically a complex endeavor. The kaleidoscopic nature of this interaction requires a vigilant, well-informed approach that prioritizes ethical engagement and environmental stewardship. When corporations harness their resources and influence to uplift local economies, they become catalysts for genuine progress—an effort that not only redefines success in business terms but underscores an allegiance to the essence of humanity and our shared home, Earth.

Let us consider this paradigm not as an obstacle but as a canvas of potential, where the broad strokes of global operation meet the intricate details of local livelihoods to create a masterpiece of sustainable and ethical business practice.

Balancing Global Standards with Local Traditions and Values

As businesses expand their horizons beyond borders, the friction between global standards and local traditions becomes a crucible for ethical decision-making. In attempting to calibrate this balance, corporations face the perplexity of harmonizing universally accepted protocols with region-specific norms. This section distills the essence of that intricate dance—synchronizing global expectations with the rich global fabric of local values and traditions that define diverse cultures around the world.

The emergence of global sustainability standards has created a framework for businesses to benchmark their practices against universally recognized guidelines. These standards aim to ensure a level playing field while addressing universal concerns such as climate change, labor rights, and biodiversity conservation. However, these global parameters may not always align perfectly with local contexts, creating a moral quagmire for business operations.

For example, the push for gender equality in the workplace is a global movement that faces diverse cultural interpretations. The application of such standards within communities that have traditional gender roles requires sensitivity and adaptability. Businesses must work alongside local stakeholders to encourage empowerment without undermining cultural identity. Negotiating these subtleties requires more than just box-ticking; it demands an understanding and respect for the labyrinth of human diversity.

Environmental stewardship is another area where the integration of global sustainability standards and local practices can be challenging. For instance, adhering to stringent emissions controls may hamper traditional industries in developing countries that rely on older technologies. A thoughtful transition plan that supports local economies while advancing toward cleaner methods is crucial. By investing in technology transfer and capacity building, businesses can create pathways for sustainable practices that honor local contexts.

Corporations operating internationally must also grapple with the complexity of supply chains that traverse diverse cultural landscapes. The ethical sourcing of raw materials compels businesses to verify their standards for child labor, fair wages, and safe working conditions are met globally. However, this investigative process must be conducted with cultural acumen, ensuring local customs and practices are acknowledged and respected.

When engaging with Indigenous populations, for instance, businesses must adopt an approach that respects traditional ways of life and land use rights. Here, a one-size-fits-all approach to environmental management can result in severe repercussions for Indigenous communities whose subsistence and cultural heritage may be at stake. Collaborative strategies that incorporate native knowledge systems can lead to more sustainable and equitable outcomes.

Furthermore, the evolution of ethical consumerism has tightened the grip of scrutiny around how products are made and who makes them. Customers often demand transparency and want assurance that their values align with those of their preferred brands. This convergence of ethics and consumer choice highlights the importance of businesses embracing local traditions while upholding global principles.

The decentralization and localization of business activities can also offer a solution to the dichotomy between global and local responsibilities. Such a strategy allows for greater sensitivity to the nuances of local environments, leading to business practices that can be both globally responsible and locally relevant. Typifying this approach, the cooperation of transnational entities with local enterprises engenders a hybrid vigor wherein the sum is greater than its parts.

Digital technology further complicates the dynamic between the global and the local. The widespread reach of the internet has facilitated a permeation of cultural barriers, bringing to light an array of ethical implications. Businesses must be vigilant to not only what they sell, but also how they convey their message across differing geographies and cultures to maintain a principled online presence.

Education and dialogue form the backbone of effective integration between worldwide standards and local mores. Businesses must foster an ongoing conversation with local communities, practitioners, and authorities to cultivate mutual understanding and develop tailored strategies. Constructive engagement helps in identifying shared objectives and laying the groundwork for corporate policies that resonate with local belief systems.

One often-overlooked dimension is the transformational impact of respecting local traditions within global business models. When corporations acknowledge and interweave local customs into their practices, they can spark innovation that benefits all stakeholders. Respecting local heritage can become a catalyst for developing unique products and services that boast global appeal while preserving the authenticity and spirit of the communities from which they originate.

Ultimately, the harmonization of global sustainability efforts with local practices is not only an ethical imperative, but also a strategic one. Companies that succeed in this endeavor often gain a competitive advantage by building robust, culturally attuned brands. Enduring trust is forged when consumers discern a brand's authentic commitment to honoring both planetary boundaries and cultural legacies.

Yet, businesses must be aware that this is a dynamic process; it is not about finding a static balance but rather about being agile and responsive in order to evolve as expectations and norms shift over time. The transformative power of businesses in crafting sustainable practices is substantially amplified when alignment between global standards and local values is achieved.

In summary, the pursuit of ethical business within the realm of globalization is a journey of accommodation and innovation—a quest that businesses must undertake with an ear to the ground and an eye on the horizon. It's an endeavor that holds the promise of a more interconnected and sustainable world, where local traditions enrich global movements and vice versa. The mandate for businesses is clear: to be custodians of a future in which global standards do not overshadow but complement and uplift local traditions and values.

Case Studies: Impact of Local Initiatives on Global Sustainability

In contemplating the intricate dance between local initiatives and global sustainability, one can't help but recognize the burgeoning influence of grassroots movements on the broader tableau of international consciousness. The interlacing of sustainability efforts from neighborhood zealots to multinational conglomerates presents a vivid illustration of the adage "think globally, act locally." Through such local practices, the collective aspirations for a sustainable future come to life, resonating in a global harmonization of environmental ethics and corporate responsibility.

Take, for example, the case of a small town that reinvigorated its local economy by embracing sustainable agricultural practices. Not only did this bolster the town's resilience, it also played an educative role in the realm of global sustainability. By returning to crop rotation and organic farming, the town reduced its ecological footprint, which, when duplicated by others inspired by their success, cumulatively impacted ecological balance on a planetary scale.

Similarly, the rise of eco-tourism opportunities in remote areas showcases how local communities can significantly contribute to conservation efforts while fostering an appreciation for untouched landscapes on a global level. For instance, the cooperation between local tourism operators in Costa Rica and international conservation groups led to renewed efforts to save endangered species, thereby enhancing biodiversity worldwide. This initiative showcases the potential for local businesses to fuel not only economic, but also ecological viability— amplifying the entwined nature of local economies and global ecosystems.

Subsequently, urban centers are increasingly adopting the green building movement, emphasizing sustainable construction and energy efficiency. These local practices, initially adopted by pioneering cities, have reverberated globally, as international standards for green construction draw heavily from these early adopters. As a result, such standards influence construction policies and practices worldwide, demonstrating how local innovation can set the pace for global change.

A poignant study in contrast is that of a community-based waste management program in a developing country that turned waste into a resource, providing income for locals while reducing environmental pollution. This model, as it gains international attention, informs waste management strategies around the globe and serves as a testament to the potency of local ingenuity in addressing global sustainability challenges.

Furthermore, the emergence of renewable energy initiatives at a community level has paved the way for comprehensive shifts toward cleaner energy sources on a global scale. For example, a small town's transition to 100% renewable energy, through community-funded wind turbines and solar panels, illustrates local endeavors can scale and have a substantial impact on global energy policies.

Correspondingly, the commitment of local food cooperatives to sourcing locally has mitigated the impacts of food transportation, showcasing how local choices in consumption can contribute to a reduction in the global carbon footprint. By prioritizing regional agricultural products, these co-ops serve as examples of how localized behaviors can ripple outward, encouraging broader adoption of sustainable practices.

In examining sustainable water management, the initiatives by local municipalities to invest in innovative water conservation technologies provide valuable lessons for water-stressed regions around the world. The systematic application of these technologies could potentially reshape global water management strategies by providing a model for sustainable growth in the face of depleting resources.

Furthermore, when local artisans and producers adopt fair trade practices, they set ethical precedents that influence global trade dynamics. These practices protect natural resources, ensure equitable treatment of workers, and foster ethical consumption patterns that hold multinational companies to higher standards.

Additionally, the burgeoning movement of urban gardens in inner cities postulates not simply a patch of green, but a significant stride toward self-sufficient communities. These gardens can drastically reduce the urban heat island effect, a phenomenon experienced globally, thereby impacting climate regulation at a macro-environmental level.

One must also note the role of local educational institutions that incorporate sustainability into their curricula, enlightening future generations on ecological stewardship. By cultivating knowledgeable individuals, these institutions are, in essence, sowing seeds globally for a future workforce that elevates sustainability as an uncompromising pillar in all organizational undertakings.

The mosaic of local initiatives, thus, forms a global tapestry that exemplifies our interconnectedness and the scope of our shared responsibility in the endeavor for sustainability. As local efforts continue to inspire, guide, and redefine global standards, there lies an undeniable transformative potential for businesses at all scales to act as pivotal instruments in the quest for a sustainable tomorrow.

Chapter 6:
The Human Rights Dimension
of Sustainable Business

Within the verdant mosaic of sustainable business practices, the infusion of human rights principles represents not merely an adjunct but the very heartbeat of an ethical corporate identity. Far beyond the narrow scope of profits and losses, businesses that cultivate a reverence for the intrinsic worth of individuals carve out a revered place in global sustainability. They understand that their operations are enmeshed in the lives of people—employees, suppliers, and communities—and with this awareness, they become bulwarks against the specters of exploitation and inequality.

Whether it's ensuring fair wages, advocating for safe working conditions, or vehemently opposing forced labor, these enterprises become torchbearers for dignity and equality. Their journey toward sustainability becomes a testament to the ideal that we can't truly protect our planet without also uplifting every person who calls it home. The businesses that thrive in tomorrow's economy will be those who today grasp the immutable truth that the well-being of humanity is inseparable from the health of our world—the flourishing of one sustains the vitality of the other.

Integrating Human Rights into Business Ethics

As companies continue to affirm their role in shaping a sustainable future, the integration of human rights into business ethics emerges as a chief concern—a cornerstone in cultivating an environment that honors the dignity of all stakeholders. The corporate community is recognizing the kinship between profitability and principled operations, realizing the value of respecting humanity is of inestimable worth to their legacy and longevity.

The imperatives of corporate social responsibility and sustainable business are intertwined with the respect for human rights. This emerging consciousness isn't merely a trend; it's a transformative shift in how business relates to the world. There's an awakening to the idea that human rights provide a universal language of accountability that crosses cultural and geographical borders, knitting together the global community in a shared standard of ethical practice.

Businesses must start by recognizing human rights are not optional add-ons but fundamental requirements. Whether considering labor conditions, equitable treatment in the workplace, or the impacts of environmental degradation on communities, the integration of human rights into business operations must be meticulously planned and executed. This is not a superficial nod toward compliance but an authentic engagement in the welfare of humanity at every level.

Operationalizing human rights in business begins with understanding the United Nations Guiding Principles (UNGPs) on Business and Human Rights, which outline state duty to protect human rights, the corporate responsibility to respect human rights, and the need for both to remedy violations. Insight into the UNGPs offers companies a blueprint on which to base their ethics programs and stakeholder engagement strategies.

Due diligence processes are critical in this integration. An ethical business must continuously assess its impact on human rights, examining its supply chains, its operational footprint, and its product life cycles with rigor. Meticulous assessments identify risks not only to minimize legal repercussions but, more importantly, to prevent harm to people and communities, establishing a framework for accountability that extends along the value chain.

The Responsibility

Engaging with stakeholders—be they customers, workers, local communities, or shareholders—isn't just good practice; it's an ethical imperative. These interactions provide invaluable insights into the real-life implications of business operations, identifying areas where rights may be imperiled and opportunities for impactful change. Leveraging this feedback within ethical decision-making processes fortifies the nexus between human rights and corporate governance.

Education and training at all organizational levels are indispensable for integrating human rights into business ethics. When individuals across a business, from executives to floor workers, understand the importance of human rights, a culture of responsibility pervades the organization, reflecting in every action and decision.

In the landscape of international business, companies are expected to lead with a sensitivity to the variety of human rights concerns particular to different regions. This requires nuanced strategies that are both globally consistent and locally relevant. For instance, corporations operating in areas with a history of human rights abuses must exercise heightened due diligence and engage more deeply with local communities and experts to ensure their operations do not perpetuate existing disparities or injustices.

Corporate policies on human rights must be transparent, offering clear, accessible information on commitments, strategies, and progress. Transparency reinforces trust and signals a company's sincerity in its ethical undertakings. In doing so, it elevates a company's standing among consumers, investors, and partners who increasingly prioritize ethical considerations in their decision-making.

Furthermore, creating robust mechanisms for grievance and remediation is essential. These systems allow for the legitimate concerns of affected individuals or communities to be heard and addressed. They are vital in ensuring that, beyond risk mitigation, there is a commitment to redress and an acknowledgment that respecting human rights is an ongoing, responsive process.

Collaboration can magnify the impact of integrating human rights into business ethics. Companies can no longer operate in silos of self-interest; they must engage in collective industry action, join multi-stakeholder initiatives, and partner with non-governmental organizations to advance human rights agendas. Unity in ethical undertakings fosters a reinforcing network that amplifies positive impact on human rights globally.

Moreover, measurement and accountability are critical. Developing comprehensive metrics and key performance indicators for human rights aspects in businesses ensures these are not mere rhetorical commitments but are embedded in operational and strategic objectives. Regular reporting against these measures not only demonstrates progress, but also holds businesses accountable to their stakeholders for ongoing improvement.

Finally, businesses must stay abreast of emerging human rights issues, as the landscape of rights and the context in which businesses operate are in constant flux. Foresight in recognizing and deflecting potential violations is as vital as rectifying existing issues. This proactivity is a hallmark of ethical leadership in business—a commitment to the holistic well-being of society that anticipates and counters the specters of injustice before they cast long shadows.

In conclusion, integrating human rights into business ethics is less about navigating a labyrinth of external obligations and more about embracing the intrinsic value that human dignity brings to every facet of business. When companies anchor their ethics in human rights principles, they build a resilient foundation for sustainable success—one that withstands the ebbs and flows of economic trends and earns an enduring respect amongst a conscientious global citizenry.

Tackling Modern Slavery and Inequality in the Supply Chain

In the pursuit of a sustainable future, we must confront the blight modern slavery casts upon supply chains worldwide. Despite the advances made in many areas of business ethics, labor exploitation remains an open sore—a contradiction within a system striving for environmental and social justice. The presence of modern slavery, in varied forms across diverse industries, challenges us: Can businesses foster a culture of respect and fairness while operating profitably?

The manifestations of modern slavery—ranging from child and forced labor to human trafficking—are not just criminal violations, but also moral failures that no ethical business can afford to overlook. Companies have a fundamental responsibility to uphold the dignity of their workforce, transcending national borders and cultural divides. Every entity along the supply chain, be they raw material extractors, manufacturers, or service providers, must be vigilant in order to ensure their operations uphold human rights standards.

Consider the context: global business operations have created a network so complex that illegal and unethical practices can easily be obscured. The sheer breadth of today's supply chains often leads to a lack of oversight, providing a fertile ground for inequality and abuse. Yet, distance and complexity can't be excuses for inaction. Indeed, these challenges demand a more comprehensive, unwavering commitment to due diligence.

Companies can start by implementing robust mechanisms designed to identify risks and prevent labor abuses. This involves conducting audits, engaging with local NGOs, and establishing whistleblower protections. Businesses must not merely tick boxes for compliance but strive to understand and rectify the socioeconomic conditions that give rise to exploitation within the supply chain.

This is not entirely uncharted territory. A number of organizations have courageously stepped forward, integrating innovative measures to combat these issues. They perform spot checks on their suppliers, promote fair wage programs, and foster transparent relationships—even at the cost of more intensive management and additional resources.

In the fight against inequality and modern slavery, collaborations are essential. Partnerships between corporations and non-government organizations offer a powerful combination of resources and expertise. Together, they can address systemic issues at their root rather than simply treating the symptoms.

Transparency is another powerful tool. With consumers becoming increasingly conscientious, they demand to know that the products they purchase aren't tainted by exploitation. By providing consumers with detailed information about the origins and handling of their products, companies can not only fulfill this demand, but also build brand loyalty and trust.

Moreover, the narrative extends to the shareholders and investors who increasingly evaluate companies on the basis of their ethical practices. The integration of socially responsible investment criteria has transformed conscientious business practice from a moral choice into an economic imperative.

Advocacy plays a vital role as well. Businesses possess a unique position of influence and can leverage this to advocate for stronger regulations and enforcement against labor abuses. Aligning their influence with their values, companies can become champions for human rights on a legislative level.

Yet, the battle against modern slavery and inequality in the supply chains isn't won solely by businesses acting individually. It calls for a paradigm shift in how we reward corporate performance, measure success, and craft legislation. The global community must support a business culture that equally values profits and people.

Education of all actors in the supply chain is crucial. By fostering an understanding of the basic principles of human rights among their employees, suppliers, and partners, businesses can create a more informed and observant network that actively works against exploitation.

Even as we advocate for the eradication of modern slavery, we must also work proactively to remedy the inequality that breeds it. This means investing in communities, offering fair and equitable pay, and creating opportunities for advancement and education. Businesses can lead the charge in creating a global workforce that is valued and supported, breaking the cycle of poverty and exploitation.

As we close this section, let us consider that every effort made to embed human rights within corporate strategies symbolizes progress. It's an acknowledgment that business benefits transcend financial gain and can reverberate positively within the social fabric of communities. It challenges others to step up and illuminates the path toward a more equitable and sustainable future for all.

Businesses as Advocates for Social Justice

The integration of social justice advocacy into the corporate ethos is not just a moral imperative, but also a compass for navigating the evolving landscape of sustainable business. As pillars of the economy, businesses have a unique platform to influence societal norms, practices, and policies. This section delves into the multifaceted roles that companies can play as advocates for social justice, drawing a vital link between corporate responsibility and human rights.

At the forefront of this advocacy is the recognition of human rights as fundamental to sustainable operations. Progressive businesses understand respecting these rights goes beyond compliance; it's about leadership and commitment to creating a fair world. This extends beyond their immediate operations to their influence on partners, suppliers, and even within the communities where they operate. The power of business advocacy lies in their ability to spearhead initiatives for social change, set industry standards, and foster an environment where human rights are non-negotiable.

Corporations can serve as voices for the voiceless by highlighting issues that affect marginalized communities. Whether it's fair labor practices, gender equality, or access to essential services such as healthcare and education, businesses have the resources and networks to bring attention to these critical areas. They can champion policies that aim to dismantle systemic barriers and create inclusive opportunities for all.

Moreover, businesses have the potential to amplify their impact by collaborating with non-profits, civil society, and governments. Through strategic alliances, they can confront prevalent issues such as racial injustice, economic disparities, and environmental degradation, aligning their operations with a broader societal cause. This is not merely altruism but a strategic paradigm that recognizes the interdependence of a healthy society and a robust economy.

Transparency is also a critical component of corporate advocacy. By being open about their practices, businesses not only build trust with consumers and stakeholders, but also encourage industry-wide transparency. This can lead to a domino effect, compelling other businesses to follow suit and creating a culture of accountability.

Education and awareness-raising are vital tools at the disposal of corporate entities. By leveraging their consumer reach, companies can educate the public on social justice issues, thereby shifting perceptions and encouraging responsible consumer behavior. This not only furthers the cause of social justice, but also reinforces the business's image as a responsible corporate citizen.

Leading by example, businesses can also implement inclusive employment practices within their own organizations. This ranges from diverse hiring and promotion policies to providing a living wage, offering mentorship programs for underrepresented groups, and accommodating different cultural practices. Doing so not only creates a more fair and equitable workplace, but also sets a precedent for other organizations to emulate.

The role of businesses as advocates for social justice extends into influencing policy and legislative frameworks. Companies can use their lobbying power to promote laws and regulations that advance human rights and equality, rather than preserving the status quo of privilege. Corporate activism can help to shift the focus from mere profit maximization to a balance between profit and purpose, signifying a mature understanding of the real costs and benefits of business activities.

The sphere of influence businesses possess is further augmented when they take a stand on current issues. This can involve public endorsements of social movements, offering support for initiatives that address inequality, or even internally reformulating products and services to be more socially just. For instance, committing to fair trade or environmentally friendly materials not only benefits affected communities, but also supports sustainable development.

In the digital age, this advocacy is particularly potent. Social media and online platforms have given businesses unprecedented access to engage with both local and global audiences. They can use these tools to push for change, support social justice campaigns, or provide platforms for activist voices to be heard.

Internally, fostering an ethical corporate culture encourages employees to be mindful of the societal impacts of their work. This culture is the bedrock on which advocacy efforts are built, ensuring the commitment to social justice permeates every level of the organization.

Financial investment in social justice projects reflects a tangible commitment to societal betterment. Instead of mere token gestures, substantive financial backing for education, housing, and poverty alleviation affirms a business's dedication to effecting real change. Their investment can make a significant difference in the capability and reach of projects aiming to rectify social disparities.

In the quest for social justice, there's a necessity for accountability measures. Setting internal benchmarks for social performance and regularly evaluating them ensures a company's advocacy is not only vocal, but also effective. The same rigor applied to financial performance should be applied to social impact assessments.

Corporate social justice advocacy is not without its challenges. It requires a long-term commitment and, often, substantial resources. However, the return on this investment isn't just a more equitable society—it's also the development of consumer trust and loyalty. In an era in which consumers are increasingly aligning their spending with their values, having a genuine commitment to social justice can be a competitive advantage.

To conclude, businesses, as societal powerhouses, have both the opportunity and responsibility to advocate for social justice. Their leadership can drive systemic change and create a legacy that transcends traditional business achievements. In wielding their influence thoughtfully, businesses can nurture a world where sustainable success is measured not only in profitability, but also in the upliftment of society.

Chapter 7:
The Sustainable Supply Chain:
From Raw Materials to End Users

From the extraction of raw materials to the moment a product reaches the end user, every step in a supply chain holds power to shape our planet's future. A sustainable supply chain isn't simply an option but a necessary commitment in our journey toward a resilient and equitable world. In this convergence of raw materials, production, and consumption, leaders are learning that efficiency paired with environmental stewardship can drive performance as well as purpose.

Within these global networks, each decision ripples across communities and ecosystems, urging entities to adopt practices that honor both people and the planet. Ethical sourcing becomes a meticulous dance of balancing cost, quality, and social impact, leading to the evolution of procurement strategies that consider the long-term well-being of suppliers and their environs. At the logistics frontier, innovations aim to minimize the footprint through smarter planning and cleaner technologies, with companies aspiring to near-mythical efficiency without compromising ethical accountability. And as the veil lifts on supply chain operations, transparency and traceability become not just buzzwords but benchmarks for consumer trust and loyalty.

If businesses harness the transformative potential of new technologies such as blockchain and artificial intelligence, they can achieve a remarkable feat—orchestrating supply chains that not only meet economic goals, but also become steadfast allies in our global sustainability movement, serving as a testament to human ingenuity in harmonizing with nature's intricate web.

Challenges of Implementing Sustainable Supply Chain Management

The journey toward a sustainable supply chain is fraught with complexities and obstacles, with each step from raw materials to end users presenting its own unique set of challenges. While the aspiration to integrate ecological and social ethics into supply chain operations has gained considerable momentum, the reality is that achieving a fully sustainable supply chain is an endeavor that requires not just intention, but also deep systemic change. Let us explore the multifaceted hurdles organizations face and propose pathways for addressing these pervasive challenges.

Firstly, there is the issue of visibility. Supply chains, often global in nature, can be labyrinthine and opaque, with many tiers of suppliers and sub-suppliers. Achieving full transparency is daunting as businesses frequently lack direct control over their entire supply chain, making it difficult to ensure every actor complies with sustainability standards. This lack of visibility not only complicates monitoring, but also obscures the true environmental and social impact of the supply chain activities.

Secondly, sustainable practices often come at a cost—a cost not all businesses are willing or able to bear. Investments in greener technologies, ethical sourcing, and fair labor practices can result in higher upfront costs. In a market driven by profit maximization, organizations may fear sustainable practices will undermine their competitiveness. Companies, thus, grapple with balancing ethical imperatives with financial realities.

Another challenge is the lack of standardization in sustainability metrics and reporting. Organizations face a corridor of diverse certifications, each with its own criteria and benchmarks. This inconsistency makes it harder for businesses to measure their performance and for consumers to understand and trust sustainability claims.

Supply chain sustainability also intersects unavoidably with complex regulatory environments that vary across countries and regions. Companies must navigate a maze of international laws, trade agreements, and local regulations, which can sometimes be contradictory or underdeveloped in certain aspects of sustainability.

Furthermore, technological limitations hinder the transformation to a sustainable supply chain. Although new technologies such as blockchain and AI promise greater traceability and efficiency, integrating these technologies poses major challenges in terms of cost, scalability, and technical expertise.

When attempting to foster sustainable practices, companies may encounter resistance from within. Changing supplier relationships and internal processes can be met with organizational inertia. Shifting the entrenched ways of doing business requires not only new processes, but also an evolution in corporate culture.

Another stumbling block is consumer demand. While many consumers express a preference for sustainable products, their purchasing decisions often reflect a disparity between stated values and actual behavior, sometimes due to the price premium associated with sustainable products.

In addition, the drive toward sustainability requires extensive collaboration among stakeholders, including suppliers, customers, NGOs, and governments. However, the alignment of interests and the creation of effective partnerships is a challenging task. Each stakeholder group has its own set of priorities and expectations, making consensus-building a slow and complex process.

The procurement of sustainable raw materials is an additional hurdle. The availability and steady supply of certified sustainable materials can be limited, and there's also the challenge of ensuring the integrity of these materials throughout the supply chain.

Moreover, risk management becomes more complex in a sustainable supply chain. Companies must address not only traditional operational and financial risks, but also reputational risks associated with environmental and social issues.

Adapting to new sustainability regulations can be a double-edged sword. Regulatory changes can drive improvement in supply chain practices but they can also pose adaptation challenges for businesses, especially small and medium-sized enterprises that may lack the resources to quickly comply with new regulations.

Geopolitical instability and economic uncertainty can disrupt supply chains and derail sustainability initiatives. Political unrest, economic sanctions, or natural disasters in one part of the world can have a ripple effect throughout the global supply chain.

Lastly, while there may be a consensus on the urgency of implementing sustainable supply chains, a shared vision on how to achieve this is less common. Different industries and sectors may have conflicting ideas about the best path forward, and without a unified direction, efforts can become fragmented.

Despite these numerous challenges, the transition to sustainable supply chains remains imperative. It's a transformation that organizations must navigate with determination and creativity, understanding each hurdle overcome is a step toward a more resilient, just, and ecologically sound future. Indeed, as daunting as these challenges may be, they are not insurmountable. With steadfast commitment, collaborative innovation, and a dedication to ethical principles, businesses can be powerful agents of sustainable transformation—nurturing the planet and its inhabitants while building stronger, future-proof enterprises.

In conclusion, the path to sustainable supply chain management is certainly challenging, but it is one that is filled with opportunities for innovation, leadership, and positive impact. As businesses press forward, adjusting strategies and practices, they contribute to a broader momentum—a swell of transformative change that can redefine industry standards and spur a global sustainability movement.

Strategies for Sustainable Supply Chain Management

In navigating the shift toward sustainability, effective strategies for sustainable supply chain management are pivotal. With increasing environmental concerns and social scrutiny, businesses must prioritize sustainability not only to mitigate risks and comply with regulations, but also to seize opportunities for innovation and competitive advantage.

One indispensable strategy involves the integration of sustainability goals with traditional supply chain objectives. The alignment of environmental and social benchmarks with efficiency and cost targets requires a thorough reevaluation of supply chain design and practices.

To establish responsible procurement, firms must adopt ethical sourcing policies that include, but are not limited to, supplier assessment and selection criteria based on sustainability performance. By working closely with suppliers that share their commitment to sustainability, companies can foster improvements in environmental, social, and economic outcomes across their supply networks.

Enhancing transparency is another key strategy. When supply chains are opaque, risks multiply. Companies should strive for complete visibility to monitor and manage the sustainability of their supply chains more effectively. This heightened transparency can provide deeper insights into areas such as carbon footprint, water usage, and labor conditions.

Increasingly, collaboration across supply chain stakeholders is found to be essential. Companies can no longer act in isolation but must work with suppliers, customers, NGOs, and governments to address complex sustainability challenges comprehensively and collectively.

Embracing circular economy principles within supply chain operations represents another transformative approach. By designing out waste and promoting the reuse and recycling of materials, businesses can not only reduce the environmental impact, but also optimize resource use and uncover new business opportunities.

Investing in training and capacity building for both internal staff and external partners ensures all participants in the supply chain understand the importance of sustainable practices and are equipped to implement them effectively.

Demand planning and efficient use of resources are critical for managing environmental impacts and maintaining resilience in the face of fluctuating market conditions and natural resource scarcity. Predictive analytics and sophisticated demand forecasting can enhance supply chain responsiveness and reduce waste.

Supply chain management software with sustainability modules can help in tracking and managing the environmental footprint across different stages of the supply chain. The integration of such systems into business processes can lead to the automation of sustainability reporting and facilitate continuous improvement.

Alternate sourcing strategies, such as local sourcing, can contribute to sustainability by reducing transportation emissions and supporting local communities, thus, balancing global efficiency with local responsiveness.

Design for sustainability is another important strategy to consider. When products are designed with their entire life cycle in mind, they can be produced, used, and disposed of or recycled in a manner that minimizes negative environmental impacts and promotes resource efficiency.

The choice of transportation and logistics partners who are committed to sustainability can significantly reduce the carbon footprint of the supply chain. This may involve selecting partners that use low-emission vehicles, optimize route planning, or utilize alternative, greener modes of transportation, such as rail or sea freight over air or road transport.

Risk management strategies must be adapted to include sustainability risks, considering both the probability and the potential impact of events related to environmental, social, and governance factors. Businesses should not only prepare for, but also actively work to prevent, manage, and mitigate these risks.

Finally, engaging end users and consumers in the sustainability conversation can lead to more environmentally friendly product use and disposal, closing the loop on the supply chain. Consumer education campaigns and product labeling that promotes responsible use and recycling are examples of how companies can extend their sustainability influence beyond their immediate operations.

In conclusion, sustainable supply chain management requires a multi-faceted approach that integrates environmental and social considerations at every stage. Companies willing to innovate, collaborate, invest in technology, and engage stakeholders will be at the forefront of sustainability, fostering a future in which the supply chain is not only a conduit for goods and services, but also a catalyst for global sustainability.

Ethical Sourcing and Procurement

In the pursuit of a sustainable supply chain, the practices of ethical sourcing and procurement stand as critical pillars. This section aims to unpack the complexities of ethical sourcing, laying the groundwork for businesses to integrate these concepts into their core strategies. Ethical sourcing extends beyond mere compliance with regulations; it encapsulates the responsibility of businesses to consider the environmental, social, and economic impacts of their purchasing decisions.

At its heart, ethical sourcing is about recognizing the intricate web of human and environmental interdependencies. Companies must ensure their procurement strategies promote the welfare of the people, communities, and ecosystems from which they source materials and services. This approach necessitates a radical shift from traditional cost-centric procurement to value-driven sourcing in which ethical considerations are paramount.

To achieve ethical sourcing, companies must establish clear guidelines that articulate their commitment to responsible practices. These guidelines should embody the principles of fairness, transparency, sustainability, and respect for human rights. A critical component here is the screening of suppliers to ensure they adhere to labor standards that prohibit child and forced labor, and respect workers' rights to fair wages and safe working conditions.

Conducting due diligence is a non-negotiable aspect of ethical procurement. It involves thorough assessments of suppliers' operations, leading to a better understanding of their compliance with ethical standards. Due diligence goes beyond checking certifications; it includes on-site audits, interviews with stakeholders, and continuous monitoring to ensure ongoing adherence to ethical practices.

One of the underlying challenges in ethical sourcing is traceability. Businesses must endeavor to establish traceability within their supply chains to ensure sourced materials are not tainted by unethical practices. Through the use of emerging technologies such as blockchain, companies can create transparent and immutable records of their product's journey from raw material to end user, thus, guaranteeing the integrity of their supply chains.

A connected concern is the environmental cost of sourcing decisions. Ethical procurement must take into account the environmental impacts of products and services throughout their life cycles. This includes assessing carbon footprints, ecosystem damage, and resource depletion. Opting for materials and inputs that can be sourced sustainably or choosing suppliers that invest in renewable energy and waste reduction, reflects a commitment to planetary stewardship.

Joining forces with other organizations can amplify the effects of ethical sourcing initiatives. Through collaborative efforts, such as industry consortia or roundtables, companies can collectively push for higher ethical standards across sectors. These collaborations can also lead to shared learning and the development of best practices that help to elevate the entire industry's performance concerning ethical procurement.

Yet, the transformation to ethical sourcing and procurement is often fraught with challenges. Addressing issues related to cost, accessibility, and the complexities of global supply chains requires innovative thinking. It entails analyzing the Total Cost of Ownership (TCO), which factors in not just the price tag of goods and services, but also the social and environmental costs associated with procurement choices.

Customers and end users increasingly demand transparency, which presents both a challenge and an opportunity for businesses. Companies that openly communicate their ethical sourcing efforts can differentiate themselves in the market and build stronger relationships with their customers. This transparency reassures consumers that their purchases align with their values, further fostering brand loyalty.

Importantly, ethical sourcing is not a static process; it requires ongoing engagement and improvement. Companies must commit to continuous learning and adaptation of their sourcing policies as new information and practices emerge. They must also be willing to engage with suppliers to assist in their development rather than penalizing them for non-compliance, creating a more collaborative and progressive supply chain environment.

Moreover, ethical procurement extends to the procurement of services. Contracts with service providers must include clauses that ensure ethical labor practices, fair treatment of workers, and environmental protection. In this way, ethical sourcing permeates every facet of a business's operations, from the tangible goods to the services that underpin its day-to-day activities.

Particular attention must be paid to risk management within the ethical sourcing framework. Companies need to identify potential ethical risks in their supply chains and develop strategies to mitigate these risks. By preemptively managing risks, companies protect themselves against the reputational and financial damages that can arise from ethical oversights.

The integration of ethical sourcing and procurement within businesses is not merely about risk aversion; it is about taking a leadership role in forging a sustainable future. Those companies that endeavor to set and maintain high ethical standards serve as the future in the marketplace, inspiring others and contributing to a global movement toward sustainable business practices.

In conclusion, ethical sourcing and procurement are essential components of a sustainable supply chain. By adopting these practices, businesses can help ensure their operations contribute to a world that values people and the planet alongside profit. As more organizations embrace these principles, we edge closer to a future in which sustainability is not just an aspiration but a realized practice integrated within the fabric of all business activities.

Logistics and Distribution: Minimizing the Footprint

The pursuit of a sustainable supply chain is a complex and multifaceted goal, one that encompasses not only the ethical sourcing of raw materials, but also the responsibility that comes with distribution and logistics. In this critical phase of the supply chain, the focus is on minimizing the ecological footprint, ensuring products reach their destination with the least environmental impact possible. This section draws attention to the practices and strategies vital for achieving this aim.

As we navigate this portion of the supply chain, it's clear the transportation of goods stands as one of the most significant contributors to carbon emissions worldwide. To combat this, companies are increasingly turning to carbon footprint analysis to understand and mitigate the emissions associated with their logistics operations, and implementing practices such as route optimization, fleet diversity, and modal shifts, which reduce reliance on carbon-intensive transport modes.

Fleet optimization, which involves the use of cleaner vehicles and technologies, promises substantial reductions in greenhouse gas emissions. Investments in fuel-efficient or electric vehicles, along with advanced planning systems to ensure fuller loads and fewer empty return trips, showcase a tangible commitment to sustainability in the logistics sector.

Another key element is the modal shift, which encourages the use of transportation means that have less environmental impact, such as rail or waterways, instead of road or air. However, these changes don't come without their challenges; for many companies, the infrastructural and operational shifts needed are not insignificant. They may require upfront investments, but the long-term benefits can be substantial, both economically and environmentally.

Furthermore, the growth of "last mile" delivery in urban areas poses unique challenges and opportunities for minimizing emissions. The adoption of bicycles, electric vehicles, and even walking couriers for these final steps can dramatically reduce carbon footprints and also alleviate congestion and local pollution in crowded city spaces.

It's also essential to acknowledge the importance of cross-sector collaboration in achieving more sustainable logistics. Efforts such as the Clean Cargo Working Group foster shared standards and methodologies among freight carriers and shippers to measure and reduce environmental impacts. Collaboration offers the promise of scale, turning individual actions into industry-wide advances.

Warehouse operations, too, have a role to play in sustainability. By optimizing storage efficiency and minimizing energy usage, companies can significantly reduce their overall environmental impact. Renewable energy sources, such as solar panels on warehouse roofs, are becoming increasingly common, as are practices such as rainwater harvesting and green roofing.

Embracing sustainability within logistics and distribution also means considering the "circularity" of packaging materials. Initiatives focused on reusable packaging, waste reduction, and recycling programs are not only environmentally sound but can resonate positively with eco-conscious consumers.

Technology, as always, is a great enabler. Advanced logistics software can forecast the most-sustainable routes, while telematics in vehicles can monitor and encourage fuel-efficient driving. The use of drones for delivery may still be nascent but it is a space watched closely for its potential to disrupt traditional delivery methods with its promise of reduced emissions.

It's evident that consumer preferences are shifting, too, with an increased demand for delivery options that are sustainable. Consumers are often willing to wait longer for a product if it means the delivery method is more eco-friendly. This illustrates an essential shift in the demand landscape that companies must acknowledge and adapt to.

In a globalized economy, the international scope of logistics adds layers of complexity, with different regulations and environmental standards across countries. It is critical to navigate these with sensitivity and commitment to not only compliance, but also excellence in sustainability.

As we strive toward a sustainable future, it's essential to recognize the ripple effect of each decision made within logistics and distribution. Reducing packaging materials influences waste management, just as choosing a certain mode of transport impacts energy consumption patterns far beyond the immediate supply chain. The sum of these decisions can lead to a historic transformation in environmental impact.

Moreover, forward-thinking businesses are harnessing the power of partnerships to facilitate sustainable logistics. Companies are developing symbiotic relationships in which logistics needs are pooled to maximize efficiency, leading to fewer trips and less energy consumption.

Transparency in the logistics process is also increasingly non-negotiable. Consumers and stakeholders alike demand visibility of the sustainability practices of companies. This transparency not only boosts brand integrity, but also fosters a culture of accountability and continuous improvement. Data-driven insights into distribution practices are enabling businesses to make informed decisions that support sustainability goals.

Lastly, training and empowering employees to understand and engage with sustainability initiatives is crucial. Their day-to-day actions and innovative ideas on improving efficiency can have a significant impact on the company's overall environmental footprint.

In conclusion, the goal of minimizing the footprint in logistics and distribution is a robust endeavor that requires strategy, investment, and unwavering commitment. By embedding sustainability into every logistical decision, businesses can not only contribute to the protection of the environment, but also ensure long-term viability in a world where consumers increasingly prioritize eco-friendly practices.

Transparency and Traceability Across the Supply Chain

In the complex webs of modern supply chains, transparency and traceability are not mere buzzwords but the pillars of sustainable business practices that respect the environment and human rights. For stakeholders who have grown increasingly conscientious, the provenance of products—their journey from raw materials to end users—holds significant importance. Unwrapping the layers of the supply chain to reveal its inner workings is a daunting yet essential task in the demonstration of ethical stewardship.

To grapple with the opacity that often characterizes supply networks, transparency must be more than an ad-hoc initiative. It demands a systematic approach where information about the products, processes, and policies is not only accessible, but also comprehensible. This means businesses have to adopt a mindset of openness, regularly sharing data regarding their suppliers, materials, labor conditions, and environmental impacts.

Traceability complements transparency by providing the historical data necessary to track products through each stage of the supply chain. It's a form of storytelling, where items carry with them a narrative of their origins to ensure each chapter of their history aligns with ethical and sustainable practices. Stakeholders can then verify the claims of businesses and hold them accountable should they falter in their corporate responsibilities.

These concepts do not operate in a silo; they are interconnected and reinforce each other. For example, sustainable procurement can't be claimed without evidence of traceability that confirms adherence to social and environmental standards at each supply chain stage. Similarly, accountability through transparency is meaningless without the attendant proof provided by traceability mechanisms.

Initiating transparency begins with understanding one's supply chain partners. Firms must conduct thorough due diligence, minimizing risks by engaging with suppliers that share their commitment to sustainable practices. Moreover, periodic audits and certifications can provide external verification of adherence to ethical standards. Companies must be vigilant, ever-watchful for signs that point toward malpractices, and ready to sever ties with partners who violate their ethical precepts.

Embedding traceability within the supply chain often involves implementing systems that monitor and record the path of products. From barcodes to RFID tags, the technology employed varies, but the goal remains constant: to maintain a line of sight on goods as they move across borders and through various stages of production, processing, and distribution.

Digital technologies, notably blockchain, are enhancing these capabilities by providing an immutable ledger where transactions and products' journeys can be stored in a manner that's virtually tamper-proof. Such technology not only aids in substantiating the sustainability claims, but also in increasing efficiency by pinpointing bottlenecks and waste within a supply chain.

The benefits of achieving transparency and traceability are manifold. They include better risk management and enhanced brand reputation, as consumers increasingly make purchasing decisions based on a company's environmental and social performance. Companies that can prove their integrity through clear, accessible supply chain information gain trust and loyalty in the market.

However, such endeavors are not without challenges. Implementing systems that ensure transparency and traceability can be complex and costly. Small and medium-sized enterprises, in particular, may find the initial investment and the operational shifts demanding. Despite these barriers, the move toward more transparent and traceable supply chains is not just an ethical imperative; it is a strategic one that can lead to long-term business value and resilience.

Indeed, with transparency and traceability, businesses can decrease the likelihood of scandals that can emerge from undisclosed labor abuses or environmental harms hidden within their supply chains. By taking precautionary steps, companies can safeguard against the repercussions of being associated with such malfeasance, which can include loss of consumer confidence and legal penalties.

It is crucial for firms to not only implement these principles internally, but also require them of their partners. Pressuring upstream suppliers to adopt similar standards amplifies the impact throughout the entire supply chain, ensuring a consistent approach to sustainability. This shared responsibility model reinforces the ideal that sustainability is not solely the domain of individual companies but rather a collective enterprise.

Moreover, transparency and traceability enable companies to respond swiftly and effectively in the face of controversies. Real-time tracking can help isolate the source of an issue, whether it's a defective batch of products or a supplier's lapse in compliance, allowing businesses to take prompt remedial action.

For transparency and traceability to truly take root in the supply chain, education and collaboration are key. Stakeholders across the spectrum, from suppliers to end users, need to understand the importance and role of these concepts in advancing ethical business practices. Collaborative initiatives and partnerships can serve as platforms for sharing expertise and resources to achieve these goals more holistically.

As we look to the future, companies that pioneer and perfect transparency and traceability in their operations will stand out as leaders of the sustainability movement. Their commitment reflects not only a high ethical standard, but also an understanding that in an interconnected world, the health of one's business is inextricably linked to the well-being of the planet and its inhabitants.

Enlightened businesses recognize a sustainable supply chain is a sound investment—one that pays dividends, not just in financial terms, but in social and environmental benefits too. The collective endeavor to illuminate the supply chain and make its every link traceable is an ongoing journey, one that holds the promise of building a more sustainable, equitable, and trustworthy business landscape.

The Role of New Technologies in Sustainable Supply Chain Management

In the intricate journey from raw materials to the hands of end users, new technologies are pivotal in the orchestration of sustainable supply chain management. Advanced tools are dramatically transforming how companies trace sources, streamline operations, optimize logistics, and prognosticate demand patterns. By intertwining sophisticated software with innovative hardware, enterprises craft resilient networks that not only thrive amidst volatility, but also honor the planet and its people.

The integration of Internet of Things (IoT) devices ensures the efficient use of resources, reducing waste and energy expenditure. Meanwhile, blockchain technology bestows an unprecedented level of transparency and traceability, paving the way for responsible sourcing and consumer trust. Additionally, the harnessing of big data through analytics capacitates firms to anticipate market trends and adjust production accordingly, mitigating environmental impacts by curbing overproduction and spoilage.

As companies adopt these technologies, they're not simply investing in their supply chains; they're sowing seeds for a sustainable and equitable future that aligns with the planet's rhythm and humanity's core values.

The Impact of Blockchain Intelligence on Sustainable Supply Chains

Within the vast nexus of sustainable supply chain management, blockchain intelligence emerges as a transformative tool. This technology, harnessing the power of decentralization and cryptographic security, has the potential to redefine transparency, traceability, and accountability in supply chains. For every stakeholder leaning into the watershed of ethical business practices, the arrival of blockchain is not merely a tool but a harbinger of systemic change.

In the pursuit of sustainable development, the crux lies in ensuring every product that reaches the hands of consumers encapsulates a narrative of environmental stewardship and social justice. Blockchain intelligence validates these narratives by providing an immutable ledger that records every transaction and exchange across a product's journey. This level of meticulous recording can reveal to sustainability professionals the exact environmental impact of products, bolstering efforts to reduce carbon footprints, alleviate resource depletion, and clamp down on exploitative labor practices.

Imagine a world where the ecological imprints of raw materials are readily accessible. As supply chain constituents engage with blockchain platforms, they feed a stream of data that encapsulates everything from the source of raw materials to the factory conditions under which products are made. This data forms an intricate web of information, laying bare the sustainability credentials of each link in the supply chain. Policymakers, environmental activists, and consumers alike can examine these credentials to make informed decisions, driving businesses toward more responsible practices by virtue of market demand.

At the intersection of ecological ethics and business efficacy, blockchain intelligence can remedy some of the opacity that has long shrouded supply chain operations. Firms aspiring to actualize their corporate social responsibility mandates can no longer hide behind abstract promises or superficial sustainability reports. Blockchain's inherent transparency demands action and honesty, galvanizing businesses to honor their moral obligations to the planet and its people.

But the adoption of blockchain technology goes beyond moral edification. It carries the seeds of economic incentive, appealing to a customer base that increasingly prizes ethical sourcing. A reputed sustainability index etched into the blockchain can become a powerful competitive differentiator. It's an invitation to join a leading vanguard that not only preaches sustainability but practices it with unwavering fidelity.

Moreover, by streamlining processes and ensuring tighter compliance with environmental regulations, blockchain can deliver cost savings. The ledger's thoroughness ensures inefficiencies, waste, and duplications are slashed, presenting a leaner, more responsible supply chain. This eco-efficiency speaks to the heart of ecological economics, balancing economic activity with the carrying capacity of the Earth.

However, like all tools, the effectiveness of blockchain intelligence is contingent on its implementation. It requires meticulous planning, robust partnerships, and an unwavering commitment to shift from traditional, linear supply chain paradigms to circular, regenerative models. It is not merely a technological upgrade but a revolution in thinking—a reminder that our collective destiny is woven into the sinew of every product we produce and consume.

While challenges abound, ranging from technical complexities to the need for standardization, the trajectory is clear. Blockchain intelligence is poised to become a staple in the architecture of sustainable supply chains. As businesses gradually awaken to this new dawn, the fusion of blockchain with ethical supply chain management can catalyze an era wherein commerce and conservation coalesce, fashioning a more sustainable and equitable future.

In closing, as we dare to reimagine supply chains through the prism of blockchain intelligence, it is crucial to remember technology alone cannot usher in this new epoch. It is the combination of innovative technology with the unyielding spirit of human resolve and responsibility that holds the key. Together, they can unlock a future in which every link in the supply chain is a bastion of sustainability, teeming with the virtue of ecological consciousness and social equity. And therein lies our collective hope, our shared endeavor, and our boundless possibility.

The Impact of Artificial Intelligence and Machine Learning on Supply Chains

Within the intricate latticework of supply chain management, artificial intelligence (AI) and machine learning (ML) are swiftly becoming indispensable allies in championing sustainability and creating systems that are both resilient and ethically attuned. The transformative infusion of AI into supply chains is altering their very anatomy, allowing for a conduit through which businesses can not only thrive in efficiency, but also stand as a guiding light for environmental and social responsibility.

In the quest to forge supply chains that respect planetary boundaries, AI and ML facilitate the leap from opaque to transparent operations. With techniques sophisticated enough to analyze vast data sets, AI provides unparalleled insights into every link of the supply chain. In this realm, predictive analytics emerge as a game changer, empowering companies to anticipate disruptions and effectively manage resources to mitigate environmental impact, aligning with this book's ethos of sustainability and foresight.

AI-driven algorithms are at the forefront of optimizing routes for logistics, substantially slashing emissions by reducing unnecessary transport. These algorithms don't merely scratch the surface; they delve deep into the intricacies of timing, loading, and fuel economy, thus, crafting a logistics mosaic that resonates with our collective yearning for a greener planet. It's not merely about transfer from point A to B but embodying an ecological conscience with every turn of the truck's wheels.

An essential corollary to sustainability is the minimization of waste, and here ML reveals its prowess. By accurately forecasting demand, avoiding overproduction becomes an attainable reality rather than an elusive mirage. Every product not made saves a whisper of potential waste from ever forming—it's a silent victory, yet monumental in the aggregate.

AI also stands as a pillar for ethical sourcing, with the ability to trace the roots of materials back to their source. Supply chains were previously murky rivers of transactions, but AI and ML can now illuminate them, ensuring ethical practices are upheld from mine to manufacturer. This transparency is not just about compliance; it echoes a deeper moral imperative to respect those whose hands toil for the resources on which we depend.

Digital twinning, an AI application, creates virtual replicas of physical supply chain components. These simulations enable companies to analyze scenarios and their potential impacts on sustainability without tangible trials, preserving resources and reducing environmental footprints before real-world implementation.

In the contextual mosaics of sustainability, the human dimension cannot be forgotten. AI in supply chains holds the key to not only economic efficiency, but also safeguarding human rights. Machine learning algorithms can screen for risks and abuses, thus, upholding the dignity of labor and reinforcing this book's commitment to equitable social structures within commerce.

Yet, with this newfound power comes a blend of ethical concerns. The data that fuels AI and ML embodies a trove of both potential and peril. Mismanagement or misuse of data can upend privacy and lead to unintended consequences. Vigilance and a steadfast commitment to ethical usage of AI are paramount to ensure technology remains in service of humanity and not in subjugation thereof.

The confluence of AI and sustainability within supply chains is more than a narrative of efficiency; it's about composing an ode to the possible. By harnessing these technologies, businesses don't just engage with the present—they architect a future in which commerce and conservation coalesce, nurturing the delicate balance our world so desperately seeks.

The integration of AI and ML in supply chains heralds a torchbearer for responsible business practices, irradiating paths for others to follow. It's a journey where each step taken is a stride toward a legacy that respects the Earth and all its inhabitants, and in doing so, brands itself indelibly upon the ethos of a generation that demands action with authenticity and ambition.

How New Technologies Can Predict Demand and Enhance Traceability and Transparency

In the pursuit of a sustainable future, the integration of cutting-edge technologies within supply chains yields transformational power. These innovations are pivotal in enhancing traceability, ensuring transparency, and creating adaptive models to predict demand effectively. Traceability and transparency are not mere buzzwords but are central pillars that support ethical and responsible business practices, and the ability to accurately forecast demand is critical in reducing waste and optimizing resource use.

Blockchain technology, with its immutable ledger capabilities, is revolutionizing traceability. By securely documenting each step of a product's journey, from raw materials to end user, blockchain ensures all stakeholders can trust the sustainability credentials that businesses claim. This technology eradicates opacity, enabling consumers and regulators alike to verify the ethical origins and handling of products. Real-time, verifiable insight into the supply chain encourages responsible sourcing and combats the exploitation of labor or the environment.

Transparency is not simply the clear disclosure of practices but a willingness to share information that empowers stakeholders. The dawn of the Internet of Things (IoT) has brought about sensors and devices that monitor processes and conditions continuously, casting light upon the supply chain's dark corners. These smart tools not only provide data that resonates with eco-conscious consumers, but also feed back into the business, aligning operations with sustainability goals.

When it comes to predicting demand, artificial intelligence (AI) and machine learning (ML) technologies are groundbreaking. AI analyzes vast amounts of data, understands patterns, and anticipates future trends with an accuracy unattainable by human endeavors alone. This predictive prowess means businesses can optimize inventory levels, preventing out-of-stock situations while avoiding excess that leads to waste and, potentially, environmental degradation.

AI's companion, ML, further refines predictions by learning from real-time data and constantly improving its forecasts. This adaptability is vital in a world where consumer behavior is increasingly driven by awareness of sustainability issues. ML helps to align supply with genuine demand, reducing overproduction and the resultant pressures on resource extraction and waste management.

In a similar vein, advanced analytics tools are processing complex datasets to deliver insights regarding market trends and consumer preferences. These insights guide businesses in making informed decisions about product development and inventory management, accentuating the move away from a mass-production model to a demand-driven, sustainable approach.

Moreover, smart technologies foster a culture of continuous improvement and innovation. As predictive models become more sophisticated, companies can fine-tune their operations, reducing their carbon footprint and environmental impact while enhancing profitability through better asset utilization.

Another way technology aids sustainability is through digital twins— a virtual representation of physical processes or products. This development allows the simulation of supply chain scenarios without incurring the carbon costs of trial-and-error in real life. Efficient logistics become tangible as routing and distribution strategies are ironed out virtually, affording eco-efficiency gains before a single physical move is made.

It must be mentioned, however, that while these technologies have remarkable potential, they also present challenges. Issues related to data privacy, security, and governance require diligent attention. Moreover, ensuring these tools are used equitably and accessibly mandates proactive policymaking and corporate governance.

Integrating these novel technologies aligns with the broader ethos of ethical business conduct by advancing sustainable practices and illuminating industry's commitment to a greener future. They allow companies not only to pledge, but also to prove their contribution to sustainability, building a trust that is underwritten by data.

In sum, as businesses strive toward sturdier sustainability and ethical fortitude, the adoption of advanced technologies in predicting demand and in enhancing traceability and transparency is no longer optional but a fundamental requirement. The intelligent marshaling of these innovations can result in a more resilient, responsive, and responsible supply chain—a win not only for businesses but for the planet and future generations.

Predictive Analytics for Demand Forecasting

In an age in which monumental shifts loom on the environmental horizon, it is necessary for businesses to adapt proactive methods for predicting demands in markets that are ever-more intertwined with the tides of ecological and social responsibility. Predictive analytics stand at the fulcrum of this transformation, offering a data-driven approach to forecast demand that aligns tightly with the objectives of sustainability.

The adoption of predictive analytics for demand forecasting greatly enables companies to optimize their resources while minimizing waste. Encompassing a spectrum of statistical techniques including predictive modeling, machine learning, and data mining, this analytical tool parses historical and transactional data to predict future trends and consumer demands. The foresight provided enables businesses to calibrate production, manage inventories astutely, and distribute goods with precision, thereby reducing surplus and mitigating the environmental impact of overproduction.

Insights gleaned from predictive analytics are the compass by which firms navigate the unpredictable seas of market demand. By understanding consumer patterns, companies can tailor their offerings to the evolving appetites of a public increasingly conscious of their ecological footprint. For instance, by predicting a rise in demand for eco-friendly products, a company can allocate more resources toward sustainable materials and practices ahead of the curve, illustrating a commitment to the planet.

The use of predictive analytics also feeds into a larger strategic loop. As more precise predictions are made and outcomes measured against forecasts, businesses can refine their models for even greater accuracy. This continuous improvement cycle not only sharpens demand forecasting practices, but also manifests an ethos of perpetual adaptation and learning that is essential for businesses operating within the dynamic context of global sustainability.

An exemplary case of the efficacy of predictive analytics in action is the retail industry, where forecasting accuracy can lead to reduced energy consumption and greenhouse gas emissions through optimized supply chain management. Enhanced forecasts mean retailers can better align inventory levels with actual sales, thereby reducing the instances of transportation of goods that may not meet consumer demand.

Indeed, the connection between predictive analytics and sustainable supply chain practices stretches beyond simple inventory control. By collaboratively sharing predictive insights across the entire supply chain, from suppliers to manufacturers to distributors, all stakeholders can work in unison to meet the common goal of environmental stewardship. This could result in collaborative efforts to source materials more sustainably and create products that are kinder to the Earth.

Companies leading the charge recognize integrating predictive analytics into their business models is not merely a fiscally prudent move; it's a critical step toward a holistic approach to sustainability. The technology acts as a backbone to ethical sourcing and procurement strategies, enabling firms to anticipate and respond to shifts in supplier practices and availability of environmentally preferable materials. This intelligence allows businesses to remain agile and resilient in the face of supply chain disruptions, which are increasingly common due to climate change.

It is imperative, however, for businesses to consider the ethical dimensions of data collection and utilization in predictive analytics. Data stewardship is a moral imperative that intersects with the sustainable model businesses must adopt. Ensuring data privacy, securing consent, and practicing transparency are critical components that fortify the trust upon which predictive analytics is built.

In conclusion, predictive analytics for demand forecasting are more than a tool for economic efficiency; they are a catalyst for an evolution toward sustainable business practices. Leveraging this technology allows companies to anticipate market trends, craft eco-conscious strategies, and honor their ethical obligation to protect our planet. The intelligence harvested today seeds the growth of a resilient and sustainable enterprise for tomorrow.

Chapter 8:
The Technological Revolution
and Sustainable Practice

The thread of technological innovation weaves a transformative pattern across the fabric of sustainable business practices. In this chapter, we delve into the heart of this digital metamorphosis, where radical technologies abet concerted strides toward environmental stewardship.

As we unpack the essence of this chapter, we laser-focus on smart, sustainable solutions, highlighting how the fusion of technology and ecological concern can foster an enduring impact. Here, the digital and the sustainable dovetail seamlessly: from supply chain logistics finessed by cutting-edge software to sweeping enhancements in carbon accounting systems that sharpen the precision of environmental audits. In the realm of corporate responsibility, digitalization isn't just a trend but a robust ally, enabling an era in which real-time reporting meets the urgency of ecological imperatives. This enables a virtuous cycle of transparency, accountability, and innovation—a triad that galvanizes industry leaders to not just conceive, but firmly embed sustainability into their core operations.

Through these explorations, this chapter aspires to capture the dynamic synergy of technology as both a catalyst and a bastion for the stalwarts of the green movement, paving a highway to a future in which the balance between progress and planet is not just attainable, but intrinsic to our modus operandi.

Leveraging Technology for Environmental Impact

In the vanguard of the environmental movement, there sits a potent ally: technology. As businesses strive to become stewards of the environment, they increasingly turn to technological innovation as both a bulwark and a spearhead in forging a sustainable future. This juncture presents a pivotal moment of intersection between innovation and ecological concern, offering transformative potential for the world's ecological challenges.

To appreciate technology's role in environmental sustainability, it is crucial to recognize its capacity to heighten efficiency and reduce waste. Across sectors, businesses are adopting smart technologies such as Internet of Things (IoT) devices and artificial intelligence (AI) to monitor energy usage, streamline operations, and minimize resource expenditure. These advancements herald a new era in which resource optimization is not an ancillary benefit but a core objective of technological progress.

Moreover, technology acts as an enabler for transparency and traceability in supply chains. By leveraging blockchain and other digital ledger technologies, companies can track the provenance of materials with unprecedented accuracy, thus, ensuring ethical sourcing and reducing environmental degradation. This visor of clarity empowers consumers to make informed choices, favoring products and services that resonate with their environmental values.

Data analytics, a field concurrent with the digital revolution, offers another avenue for environmental amelioration. Businesses employ advanced algorithms to discern patterns and forecast trends, enabling them to optimize logistics, reduce energy consumption, and manage resources proactively. Predictive analytics, therefore, allows companies to anticipate and remedy inefficiencies before they burgeon into larger issues.

Renewable energy technologies stand at the forefront of the environmental crusade, offering an antidote to the carbon-heavy energy sources of yesteryear. Innovations in solar photovoltaics, wind turbines, and battery storage are propelling a shift toward cleaner energy systems. These technologies are empowering businesses to diminish their carbon footprint and invest in a renewable, sustainable future.

Amidst this technological renaissance, the concept of a "smart grid" is gaining traction. By integrating communication and control capabilities, the smart grid facilitates a more dynamic and efficient electricity supply system. This includes accommodating for variable renewable energy sources and promoting energy conservation amongst consumers.

Crucially, technology also plays a sentinel role in monitoring and protecting biodiversity. Remote sensing, drone technology, and geographic information systems (GIS) enable scientists and conservationists to track environmental changes, protect endangered species, and manage natural resources with unprecedented precision.

Water scarcity, a pressing concern in many parts of the world, can also be addressed through technological innovation. Advanced water purification systems, smart irrigation methods, and water management software are among the tools businesses can deploy to conserve and sustainably manage water resources.

The increasing relevance of urban centers in contemporary life makes the concept of "smart cities" a beacon of green promise. These tech-driven metropolises optimize transportation systems, energy usage, and waste management, weaving an urban fabric that is not only more livable, but also fundamentally sustainable. Technologies such as adaptive traffic signals and automated waste sorting are making this vision a tangible reality.

Agricultural technology, or "agritech," delivers hope for more sustainable food production. Precision farming and vertical agriculture minimize land use and reduce pesticide application while biotechnologies enhance crop resilience and yield. These tools can significantly lower agriculture's environmental impact, ensuring food security in an eco-friendly manner.

The Responsibility

The digital realm also presents considerable potential for environmental engagement and advocacy. Social media platforms, apps, and online portals not only spread awareness, but also catalyze collective action. Crowdsourcing and citizen science projects, for instance, empower individuals to contribute to environmental monitoring and conservation efforts.

Going forward, the horizon of sustainably focused technologies appears boundless. Innovation in materials science promises the development of biodegradable materials and the advancement of the circular economy. Nanotechnology, for instance, plays a growing role in creating cleaner industrial processes and eco-friendly materials.

Concurrently with these technological strides, ethical considerations must remain at the forefront. The design, deployment, and scaling of technologies must be evaluated not just for their potential to advance sustainability, but also for their broader social implications. This requires a commitment to inclusivity and equity in the access to and benefits derived from these technologies.

The technological revolution, if harnessed with intent and ethical consideration, can indeed be the harbinger of a sustainable renaissance. It is incumbent upon businesses, along with policymakers, activists, and consumers, to champion these technologies, integrate them into operations, and shape the future with a conscientious hand. Technology, after all, is a tool—a reflection of the values and visions of those who wield it.

Investing in, developing, and implementing eco-friendly technologies is no mere trend; it is a call for a new business paradigm—a confluence of innovation and responsibility that has the power to catalyze an age of sustainability. It is this vision that businesses must cherish and pursue with passion and purpose.

Smart Technologies and Sustainable Solutions

As we delve deeper into the techno-sustainable landscape, smart technologies emerge as pivotal to crafting solutions that can significantly reduce our ecological footprints. Within the business sector, harnessing these innovations means streamlining processes, cutting waste, and elevating efficiency to new heights, all while fostering a sustainable ethos that touches every aspect of operations.

Groundbreaking advancements such as the Internet of Things (IoT) and advanced biodegradable materials are setting a foundation for companies to minimize resource depletion and remain competitive in a rapidly evolving green economy. These smart technologies are not just a matter of corporate convenience but are revolutionizing the ways in which we perceive and engage with our environment. They offer real-time data to optimize energy use, lower emissions, and promote a closed-loop system that is both regenerative and economical.

The integration of such solutions is compelling evidence of our capacity to marry technological prowess with sustainability and to create a world where business thrives in symbiosis with the planet. The potential for transformation is monumental, as companies begin to see themselves not merely as profit engines but as stewards of the Earth, deploying technologies that can reshape our future into one that is equitable, resilient, and life affirming.

Carbon Accounting Technological Solutions

As our journey toward sustainable practices unfurls, businesses must acknowledge the pivotal role of carbon accounting in environmental stewardship. The rigorous quantification of carbon emissions, essential for effective climate action, has been greatly facilitated by the advent of technological solutions that promise accuracy and transparency. It is these very solutions, capable of transforming intentions into measurable outcomes, that we now turn our gaze toward.

Advanced software platforms serve as the linchpin in this domain, enabling companies to capture emission data across their operations. These platforms provide a holistic approach, integrating data from various sources to offer a comprehensive view of a company's carbon footprint. An example of such innovation is the use of cloud-based systems that allow real-time monitoring and reporting, enabling immediate insights and agile decision-making.

Internet of Things (IoT) devices have carved out a niche as indispensable tools in real-time data acquisition from factories, supply chains, and transportation networks. By harnessing IoT sensors, businesses can derive granular data related to energy consumption and vehicular emissions, and even monitor deforestation activities, allowing them to weave this information into their carbon accounting tapestries.

Artificial intelligence and machine learning algorithms emerge as key allies, processing vast datasets to identify patterns, predict trends, and offer recommendations for reducing emissions. These technologies not only help in sifting through the noise of big data, but also predict future carbon output, aiding in the creation of proactive strategies for emission reduction.

Blockchain technology, too, shows promise within carbon accounting. Its potential lies in immutable record-keeping, enabling the verification of emissions data and providing a trusted basis for carbon credits and trading schemes. This enhances credibility and accountability in reporting, crucial elements to envisage in the collective march toward transparency.

Leveraging geographic information systems (GIS) and remote sensing technology enables meticulous tracking of carbon sequestering efforts, such as afforestation and reforestation. In essence, businesses can use such technologies to corroborate their positive impact—essentially quantifying their ecological contributions with the same rigor as they do emissions.

Mobile applications now afford employees and stakeholders the capability to participate actively in carbon accounting. By democratizing the process, these apps can foster a culture of collective responsibility and engagement, further amplifying the potential of individual contributions to meet overarching sustainability objectives.

Moreover, the integration of carbon accounting into enterprise resource planning (ERP) systems allows for the seamless adoption of sustainability metrics side by side with financial performance indicators. This integration underpins a future in which carbon efficiency is just as critical to a business's success as its profitability.

However, it's not merely about adopting technology but evolving with it. The agility to adapt to newer, more advanced solutions is instrumental in remaining at the forefront of sustainability. Flexibility and a willingness to continually refine systems in line with emerging standards and regulations underpin a forward-thinking business ethos.

In inspiring the leveraging of such technologies, this narrative asserts an unquestionable truth: technological advancements are not only enablers, but also accelerators of sustainable transformation. They arm businesses with the precision and dependability needed to navigate the complexities of carbon accounting, ultimately catalyzing a shift toward responsible environmental stewardship. Hence, the deployment of these innovative solutions is not just a strategic necessity but a moral imperative in our quest for ecological equilibrium and societal justice.

Reporting Technological Solutions

In modern commerce, transparency has transmuted from a commendable trait to a non-negotiable hallmark of sustainable practices. Within this ethos of openness, reporting technological solutions bear significance for businesses striving toward ecological and social responsibility. These platforms and tools act not as inert mechanisms but as dynamic heralds of progress, efficiency, and accountability. With meticulous design, they align the intricate narratives of environmental performance with corporate governance, thereby shaping an interconnected web of sustainability that speaks authoritatively to stakeholders.

Reportage technology has evolved dramatically to serve beyond mere regulatory compliance. In a symbiotic dance with the evolving demands of informed consumerism and stakeholder engagement, these tools now offer robust analytics, real-time insights, and predictive modeling, which enable companies to not just chronicle past exploits, but also to strategize future endeavors. The modern mantra "measure to manage" shines through here, with platforms converting data streams into actionable intelligence—key to forging a path of continuous improvement.

New reporting solutions facilitate integrated reporting, marrying financial data with Environmental, Social, and Governance (ESG) performance. Such integration yields a holistic picture of a company's impact and value creation processes. It hands investors and policymakers a comprehensive chronicle, which is vital for informing sustainable investment decisions and framing public policy.

Futuristic advancements are further championing innovation through blockchain technologies, ensuring transparency and indisputable traceability within sustainability reporting. Indeed, when a business's supply chain efficiencies, carbon footprints, and ethical credentials are immutably recorded, a newfound trust is instilled among consumers and investors alike. This leap forward not only redefines accountability, but also entrenches a brand's commitment to verifiable sustainability.

Software and platforms engaged in sustainability reporting are also increasingly incorporating artificial intelligence (AI) to refine data collection and interpretation. AI's potency lies in its capacity to scour vast datasets to discern trends and anomalies, illuminating pathways toward more sustainable operational practices. Moreover, machine learning algorithms harness this data to predict outcomes and optimize performance—fueling a proactive rather than reactive approach to sustainable business practice.

Emergent reporting technologies cultivate stakeholder engagement by rendering impenetrable data into digestible, interactive formats. Dashboards and apps engage users, affording them the agency to dissect and interpret sustainability metrics personally relevant to their interests or investments. This functionality not only emboldens public scrutiny, but also democratizes access to information—fostering a culture of collective responsibility and informed discourse.

The reported interplay between these technological solutions and corporate sustainability is a powerful demonstration of business's transformative potential. As we reimagine the pillars of corporate reporting, we also reinvent how business values are perceived and propagated in the public sphere. The integrity and efficacy of a company's commitment to sustainability become testaments to its identity and operational essence.

Lastly, the path toward a transparent, ethical business environment is not without its challenges and calls for consistency in both reporting standards and technology implementation. Universalizing reporting methodologies and fostering inter-operable platforms ensure comparability and coherence, essential if these tools are to underpin global sustainability movements with integrity and impact.

In conclusion, technological solutions for reporting are more than mere conduits for information transfer; they are central pillars in the edifice of sustainable business practices. By delivering insight, foresight, and cross sight, they endow businesses with the means to not only communicate their sustainability narratives, but also to coherently integrate these narratives into the fabric of their strategic actions. In their silent, steadfast service, these solutions hold the promise of a future that marries profit with purpose, and commerce with conscience—an endeavor worthy of our collective ambition.

The Digitalization of Corporate Responsibility

The digitalization of corporate responsibility emerges as a cornerstone in the pathway of integrating sustainable practices with the technological revolution. This is not just about leveraging technology to create efficiencies but about embedding ethical considerations within digital strategies to drive a more sustainable future.

At its core, the digitalization of corporate responsibility represents the convergence of information technologies with social and environmental ethics. It is an era wherein data, analytics, and digital processes play a pivotal role in informing and executing responsible business practices. One could say data becomes the lifeblood of the sustainable organization, providing insight and transparency that underpin ethical decision-making.

Efficient resource management has always been a major element of corporate responsibility. Predictive analytics and artificial intelligence empower companies to anticipate trends, streamline resource usage, and minimize waste. The thrust toward precision is now an achievable goal when companies adopt these smart technologies.

Furthermore, digitalized corporate responsibility redefines stakeholder engagement. Platforms for collaboration and communication facilitate dialogue between a company and its diverse stakeholder groups. This not only provides a mechanism for increased transparency, but also expands the potential for stakeholders to participate in corporate governance directly.

In the vein of enhancing accountability, digital tools have allowed for real-time monitoring of environmental impacts. Through Internet of Things (IoT) devices and other smart systems, businesses can capture and analyze data that speak to their footprint, making the necessary adjustments to their operations in the pursuit of sustainability.

Social responsibility, too, benefits from digitalization. Blockchain technology, for instance, has the potential to revolutionize supply chain transparency by making it possible to track the ethical sourcing of materials at every stage of production. This not only fights against labor exploitation and environmental damage, but also contributes to building consumer trust.

Undoubtedly, the rise of corporate social responsibility (CSR) reporting has been instrumental in propelling the discussion of corporate ethics into the public domain. Yet, it is the digitalization of such reporting—through accessible, interactive formats—that has democratized information, allowing stakeholders to assess companies' commitments against their actual performances.

It's important to recognize that digitalization has transformed the very understanding of corporate responsibility. It's no longer seen simply as philanthropy or compliance; it's becoming a driver of innovation where new business models are created in response to sustainability challenges. Companies engaging in this transformation can unlock value that transcends the financial, creating social and environmental dividends.

The empowerment of consumers through information has shifted the dynamics of the marketplace. In the digital age, an informed consumer can hold companies accountable, expressing preferences for sustainable products and services. Thus, corporate responsibility is no longer merely an internal endeavor but one that is increasingly co-created with consumers.

Challenges, however, abound in this new frontier. With an increasing dependency on data, issues such as privacy concerns, the need for robust cybersecurity measures, and the ethical use of artificial intelligence all throw down the gauntlet for tomorrow's sustainable leaders. Navigating these challenges requires a robust ethical framework, one that balances the capabilities of digitalization with the demands of responsible conduct.

Investing in digital literacy for employees, therefore, becomes imperative. As businesses adopt more advanced technologies, employees must be equipped not only with the skills to use these tools, but also with the understanding of how they relate to the larger ecosystem of corporate responsibility.

In considering the impact of digitalization on the environment, we must also contemplate the carbon footprint of digital infrastructure itself. Cloud computing centers, data storage, and the proliferation of electronic devices all contribute to the ecological footprint of the digital sphere. Thus, companies must approach the digitalization of their operations with a holistic perspective that prioritizes sustainability in the deployment of technology itself.

In conclusion, the digitalization of corporate responsibility suggests a future in which technology and sustainability are interlinked aspects of a company's strategy. It's an exciting prospect with the potential to enhance corporate transparency, efficiency, and engagement, thus, propelling businesses toward a sustainable and ethical future. Yet, it requires a thoughtful approach, underpinned by a commitment to learning and the recognition that technology is a powerful tool that must be wielded responsibly in the service of societal and environmental well-being.

As we step deeper into this digital age, corporations can't stand as bystanders to technological advances but must instead be proactive in shaping how these tools are employed. It's through the deliberate and strategic use of digitalization that corporate responsibility will not only adapt, but also thrive in the context of sustainable practice.

Chapter 9:
Ethics of Artificial Intelligence and Data in Sustainability

As we peel back the layers of technological advancement within sustainable business practices, this chapter delves into the complexity of ethical considerations that arise with the integration of artificial intelligence (AI) and extensive data usage. This pivotal chapter, "Ethics of Artificial Intelligence and Data in Sustainability," lies at the heart of the transformative shift we seek, bridging the gap between raw computational power and moral philosophy.

Here, we grapple with the responsibility entwined in harnessing AI to propel sustainable practices forward while safeguarding the integrity and privacy of data. It's a nuanced ballet, where each calculated step toward innovation is weighed against potential ethical ramifications. This delicate balance is paramount as AI systems become stewards of sustainability, shaping decisions that impact the environment and society alike. The chapter ponders, for instance, the implications of predictive algorithms that can preempt resource depletion but may also inadvertently perpetuate biases or infringe upon privacy. Moreover, it contemplates a future in which the amassed data serves as the backbone for eco-centric strategies, yet it must be managed with the utmost respect for confidentiality and ethical use—spearheading a forward-thinking discourse where technology and virtue coalesce to architect a sustainable and equitable future.

The Role of AI in Advancing Sustainable Practices

As we venture deeper into the realm of sustainability, it is crucial to recognize the transformative role artificial intelligence (AI) plays in sculpting a more sustainable future. AI's impact on sustainable practices is significant, cutting across various sectors and enhancing our ability to not only understand, but also to effectively respond to environmental challenges.

In the grand field of sustainability, AI emerges as a formidable ally. Its capacity to process large volumes of data at an unprecedented speed allows us to gain insights into complex ecological systems. With AI, we can monitor deforestation patterns, manage renewable energy resources efficiently, and even predict climate anomalies, all of which are crucial for preserving our planet.

One of the quintessential elements of AI in sustainability is precision agriculture. By leveraging AI, we can significantly reduce resource consumption and unnecessary waste, ensuring water, fertilizers, and pesticides are only used when and where they are needed, thus, minimizing the environmental footprint of agriculture.

But AI's role doesn't stop at eco-efficiency; it also supports the circular economy. Intelligent algorithms help identify materials that can be reused and recycled, not as an afterthought but as a core element of product design and supply chain management. Companies that integrate AI into their circular strategies often find that waste can indeed be transformed into wealth.

Yet, the power of AI isn't merely in its ability to optimize resources. Its predictive prowess allows businesses to anticipate environmental risks and act in a precautionary manner. By implementing AI-driven risk assessment tools, companies can mitigate potential impacts before they materialize, adhering to the adage of being "better safe than sorry."

In the battle against emissions, AI assists in carbon accounting and helps to identify patterns that lead to high carbon outputs, offering strategies to reduce a company's carbon footprint. From suggesting alterations in logistics to enhancing energy efficiency in manufacturing processes, AI-driven solutions are instrumental for businesses looking to tackle climate change proactively.

Another significant contribution of AI is in the domain of smart cities, where AI systems manage traffic flows to reduce congestion and, consequently, urban emissions. AI can revolutionize urban planning by accounting for environmental concerns in the initial design stages, fostering a harmonious balance between urban growth and ecological sustainability.

Within the fabric of corporate entities lies another vital application of AI—the enhancement of sustainable supply chains. AI's ability to provide real-time data and analytics ensures transparency and traceability, enabling companies to maintain ethical standards and reduce their environmental impact throughout their supply chain networks.

Certainly, the integration of AI in sustainability extends to consumer engagement. By harnessing data and predictive analytics, AI can tailor communication about sustainability initiatives to specific audiences, inspiring informed and conscious purchasing decisions. It's not about selling a product; it's about creating a movement for sustainable consumerism.

Despite its many benefits, integrating AI into sustainable practices isn't without its challenges. There are ethical considerations regarding the deployment of AI, especially when it comes to potential job displacement and ensuring AI decisions are transparent and fair. Tackling these issues requires a robust ethical framework in which AI is programmed with a set of sustainable and humane values at its core.

AI also powers the renewable energy sector by enhancing the forecasting of energy production, which can be highly variable and dependent on weather conditions. This allows for a more reliable integration of renewable energy sources into the power grid, promoting a shift away from fossil fuels toward a cleaner and more sustainable energy system.

In the realm of conservation, AI facilitates the analysis of biodiversity data to protect endangered species and manage natural resources effectively. By using AI to monitor and predict the movements of wildlife, we forge a path toward not just protecting these beings, but also understanding them on a deeper, more empathetic level.

To reap the full benefits of AI in advancing sustainable practices, it is paramount that businesses and policymakers collaborate. The implementation of AI must be done responsibly, with considerations for its long-term impacts on society and the environment. Rigorous regulations and standards must be established to guide the ethical use of AI in sustainability efforts.

Moreover, it would be naïve to view AI as a silver bullet for sustainability. It should instead be seen as one of many tools in our arsenal, working in synergy with political reform, corporate responsibility, and public engagement to realize a sustainable future. It is not the tool but the craftsman that will ultimately determine the outcome.

As we forge ahead, it behooves us to not only embrace AI, but also to guide its growth responsibly, ensuring it aligns with the values and goals of sustainability. At the heart of AI must be a commitment to advancing the well-being of our planet and its inhabitants. The ethical deployment of AI can serve as a catalyst, heralding a new epoch in which technology and ecology coalesce to craft a more promising and equitably sustainable horizon.

Data Privacy and Ethics in Sustainability Analytics

The sustainable business movement has seen the exponential growth of data collection and analysis aided by artificial intelligence (AI) and machine learning (ML) technologies. As we venture deeper into this domain, issues of data privacy and the ethics of sustainability analytics become increasingly vital. In this digital age, the capture and utilization of data must respect individual privacy while driving corporate responsibility and the broader global sustainability movement.

Within the realm of sustainability analytics, personal data can uncover patterns in consumer behavior, production efficiencies, and environmental impact, equipping businesses with the intelligence to make more informed decisions. Yet, this remarkable capability brings forth ethical implications. The safeguarding of personal information is not merely a technical endeavor but an ethical commitment to respect individual rights.

In assessing the intersection of data privacy and sustainability analytics, we must confront the trade-offs and negotiate boundaries. Analytics can empower sustainable practice but they cannot operate in a vacuum devoid of ethical considerations. The organizations that harness data must also ensure the maintenance of trust through transparency, consent, and the security of the data they gather.

As sustainability analytics advances, there is a growing need for regulatory frameworks that guide ethical data use. General Data Protection Regulation (GDPR) in the European Union sets a global example, influencing how organizations worldwide approach data privacy. Individuals are stakeholders in sustainability initiatives, and as such, they have the right to understand and control how their data is used.

Data anonymization techniques are commonly employed to protect individual privacy, yet these do not always guarantee anonymity due to advancements in re-identification algorithms. As a result, businesses and researchers must be diligent in constantly updating their methodologies to stay ahead of potential privacy breaches.

Furthermore, the use of data for sustainability initiatives must consider the ethics of consent. Individuals need to be informed about the purposes for which their data is being collected and the potential sustainability outcomes. This emphasizes the need for clarity and openness in data collection practices.

The Responsibility

While data analytics in sustainability can lead to significant benefits such as reduced resource consumption and improved efficiency, it also raises questions of equity and access. There is a potential for data-driven sustainability practices to widen the gap between the affluent and the less privileged, as not everyone has equal access to the benefits of these technologies. Ethical analytics should aim to include and favor all sectors of society, preventing the creation of a data divide.

Bias in data analytics is another ethical concern. AI systems are only as unbiased as the data they are fed, and historical data can often reflect existing prejudices. This can inadvertently lead organizations to make sustainability decisions that perpetuate inequalities. Vigilance in dataset composition and algorithm design is crucial to ensure fair and ethical outcomes.

The question of ownership when it comes to sustainability-related data is also contentious. Communities that contribute data—especially in biodiversity-rich but economically poorer regions—should benefit from sustainability solutions derived from their data. This fairness in data transactions is a key aspect of environmental justice and needs to be upheld within sustainability analytics.

Data analytics in sustainability is also concerned with the well-being of future generations. Implementing privacy and ethical guidelines today will prevent future societal harms and create a model for how data can be harnessed responsibly for the common good. This consideration of future implications aligns with the essence of sustainability and its focus on long-term viability.

Transparency is a linchpin of ethical data practice. Not only does it build trust with stakeholders, it also serves as a check on the use of data, reducing the risk of misuse or exploitation. By proactively offering insights into data collection, algorithms, and decision-making processes, businesses can demonstrate their commitment to ethical standards and societal well-being.

Autonomy, a crucial ethical principle, extends into the realm of sustainability analytics. Individuals must have autonomy over their personal information. This includes the right to opt-out of data collection, access to information about how their data is being used, and the ability to challenge and rectify incorrect or misused personal data.

Finally, we must highlight the collaborative effort necessary to weave ethical principles into the fabric of sustainability analytics. It is not the concern of a single role but a multidisciplinary endeavor. Technologists, ethicists, sustainability experts, and policymakers must come together to outline standards, best practices, and regulations that assure ethical data use within sustainability initiatives.

As the foregoing discussion elucidates, data privacy and ethics in sustainability analytics cannot be overemphasized. The potential to use data analytics for good is immense, yet without a strong ethical foundation, we risk undermining the very goals of sustainability we seek to achieve. The responsibility lies with us to ensure our pursuit of a sustainable future is not tarnished by ethical negligence but ennobled by our commitment to integrity, equity, and respect for individual privacy.

Balancing Technological Innovation with Ethical Considerations

As we delve deeper into the era of artificial intelligence (AI) and data-driven practices, it behooves us to explore the intricate dance between technological progress and ethical imperatives. Within the realm of sustainability, this equilibrium is paramount, marking the intersection where innovation can either flourish with conscience or flounder amidst ethical oversight.

At the vanguard of sustainable ventures, AI and big data analytics present opportunities of vast potential. These technologies, when deployed with discernment, can dramatically reduce energy consumption, optimize resource allocation, and contribute significantly to conservation efforts. However, the accelerating pace at which these technologies evolve necessitates a parallel and robust ethical framework to govern their application.

Consider the implications of algorithmic decision-making. Machine learning algorithms, though adept at pattern recognition, can inadvertently perpetuate systemic biases if not meticulously scrutinized. The ethical quandary arises in ensuring AI systems in sustainability respect the gamut of human values and rights while preventing data-driven discrimination.

Data privacy emerges as another cornerstone of the ethical debate. Here, the concern rests on the collection, analysis, and dissemination of data. The urgency to uphold data privacy and secure trust is pivotal, especially when personal data intersects with environmental performance and sustainability goals.

A conscientious approach to innovation also demands attention to the digital divide. As AI becomes integral to sustainability strategies, we must grapple with the unequal distribution of technological benefits. The commitment to ethical principles calls for bridging these disparities to ensure inclusive progress and to prevent creating new forms of inequity.

In architecting AI systems for sustainability, the application should be tethered to ethical bylaws that prioritize transparency. The notion of explainable AI, where decision-making processes are made understandable to non-expert stakeholders, is not just a lofty goal but an ethical imperative.

Ownership and control over AI technologies bring forth another critical ethical discussion. As businesses adopt AI to enhance sustainability practices, questions about who controls these technologies and to what ends must be addressed. Ensuring AI serves the greater good and not just the financial objectives of a select few stands as an ethical obligation of modern enterprises.

Moreover, the environmental impact of technological infrastructures themselves must not be overlooked. The substantial energy required to power databases, AI algorithms, and networking equipment beckons a sustainable re-examination. Embracing renewable energy sources and optimizing efficiency are vital steps in reconciling technological advances with ecological stewardship.

Engaging in dialogue and collaboration across disciplines is essential in balancing technological innovation with ethical concerns. Technologists, ethicists, environmental scientists, and policymakers must come together to form a synergistic core that continually examines the converging paths of technology and ethics.

The role of corporate policy cannot be understated in this debate. Companies that implement forward-thinking policies that embed ethical considerations within their technological adoptions are rightfully recognized as trailblazers in the sustainable landscape. These policies should cover the life cycle of technologies, from conceptualization to deployment and beyond.

Education and awareness-raising are equally critical components. Businesses must not only understand the importance of ethical AI but be adept at applying it within their sustainability initiatives. This underscores the necessity for ongoing training and the development of specialized skills amongst the workforce.

As we chart the course for sustainability in this digital age, we must remember technology serves as both a tool and a partner. Our respect for its power and potential should be coupled with a cautious optimism, guided by ethical guardrails that ensure the well-being of both our society and our planet.

Within the ethos of sustainability, the threads of ethics and innovation must be woven together with deliberate care. It is an intricate balance, one that challenges us to expand our technological horizons while steadfastly upholding the principles that define our humanity.

In conclusion, the fulcrum upon which technological innovation and ethical consideration balance is not static. It is a dynamic interplay, evolving as new technologies emerge and societal values shift. Businesses at the helm of sustainability must remain vigilant, adaptive, and, above all, committed to the ethical integration of AI and data analytics into their practices. This balance is not just desirable but essential for a future in which sustainable and ethical innovation thrives.

Chapter 10:
Consumerism and Responsibility:
Redirecting Behaviors and Demands

Inextricably woven into the fabric of sustainable development is the role of consumer choice and its shaping force on market dynamics. As we traverse the subtleties of ethical consumption in this chapter, we are reminded that responsibility does not rest solely on industries or policymakers, but also on the individual choices of consumers.

The imperative to redirect consumer behaviors and demands toward sustainability presents a multifaceted challenge, where education, values, and accessibility to sustainable choices converge. Developing an understanding of these behavioral mechanisms is critical for businesses aiming to engage responsibly with their customer base. It involves delving into the psychology that fuels consumption and harnessing that knowledge to foster an environment where making a sustainable choice becomes intuitive and commonplace. Marketers play a pivotal role in this transformation, narrating the sustainability narrative so vividly and compellingly that it resonates deeply with consumers' values and belief systems.

This chapter envisions a symbiotic relationship between ethical business practices and consumer habits, describing a future in which market demands and supply chains mutually reinforce each other in a virtuous cycle of sustainability. By encouraging and facilitating responsible consumption, businesses can not only reflect, but also shape societal values, driving a groundswell of support for a sustainable future in which ethical consideration becomes intertwined with everyday purchasing decisions.

Encouraging Ethical Consumption

In the vibrant mélange of global consumerism, the thread of ethical consumption weaves a compelling narrative of responsibility and change. The catalyst for this transformative shift in purchasing habits stems from an emerging understanding that each transaction casts a vote for the kind of world consumers wish to inhabit. This narrative is not just a call to consumers, but also a charge to companies to foster environments where ethical choices are not only available but are made appealing and actionable.

The emergence of ethical consumption represents an intersection where personal values and purchasing power meet. To encourage this practice, one must present the concept not only as a moral choice but a desirable and empowering lifestyle decision. It is the responsibility of sustainability-focused businesses to support, engage with, and educate consumers on the impacts of their choices—setting a gold standard for what ethical consumption looks like in tangible, everyday terms.

Encouragement of ethical consumption begins with transparency. In a world rife with greenwashing and murky supply chains, businesses must illuminate their operations, offering clear insight into the origins and impacts of their products. This transparency is not just informational; it serves as the foundation for building consumer trust and loyalty. Achieving this necessitates rigorous assessments of product life cycles, fair labor practices, and sustainability measures, as well as communicating these factors clearly.

Engagement is the next layer in promoting ethical consumption. By connecting with consumers through storytelling, businesses can illustrate the tangible benefits of sustainable choices. For instance, a narrative that connects fair trade coffee purchases with the well-being of coffee farmers can convert a mundane morning routine into a potent act of global solidarity.

In fostering ethical consumption, businesses must not only herald the virtues of green products, but also align them with impeccable quality and desirability. Herein lies the opportunity to dissolve the dichotomy between luxury and sustainability, thus, appealing to a broader market who will not compromise on quality or ethics.

Accessibility is a critical element in expanding ethical consumption. Ethical options must become the default rather than the exception. To this end, businesses can integrate ethical choices seamlessly into consumers' lives, offering them at competitive prices and with ubiquitous presence. This strategy has a dual benefit: It makes sustainable products the norm and it concurrently stimulates market innovation and competition.

Consumer education is indispensable in fostering this shift. It's not enough to present an ethical product; consumers must be informed about why it matters. Sustainability literacy can empower consumers to make informed choices and can engender a sense of agency with each purchase. This education can take many forms—from labels that explain the benefits of the purchase to campaigns that articulate the broader social and environmental impacts.

A personalized approach to ethical consumption is another avenue for encouraging responsible purchasing. By leveraging data analytics, companies can curate recommendations that align with an individual's values and past behavior, thus, simplifying the process of making ethical choices and reinforcing the personal relevance of sustainability.

Collaboration with influencers and thought leaders who exemplify sustainable lifestyles can also serve to make ethical consumption aspirational. These public figures can bring ethical consumption to the forefront of popular culture, elevating it to a status symbol and source of inspiration.

The Responsibility

Loyalty programs and incentives can be reimagined to support ethical consumption trends. Rewards for choosing sustainable options or for customer advocacy of ethical practices can help ingrain these behaviors, turning occasional choices into lifelong habits.

The digital space offers vast opportunities for retailers to employ innovative platforms and apps designed to aid ethical consumption. Features such as carbon footprint calculators linked to product choices, or the ability to track the journey of a product from raw material to retail, can imbue the shopping process with informative and game-like elements that encourage deeper engagement.

In considering the regulatory environment, businesses committed to fostering ethical consumption can advocate for policies that favor sustainable products and practices. While such advocacy is a longer-term strategy, it creates a regulatory framework that incentivizes ethical choices from both consumers and producers.

Businesses must also lead by example, practicing what they preach by making ethical decisions within their own operations. Allocating resources toward sustainability initiatives, investing in renewable energy, and adopting circular economy practices are all indicative of a genuine corporate commitment to ethical consumption and planetary stewardship.

The fabric of consumer society must be rewoven so sustainability is not just a fringe feature but the cornerstone of consumption. It is here, in converting the narrative of responsibility into a suite of appealing, intuitive, and rewarding choices for consumers around the globe, that the creative force of business can most effectively mobilize.

Ultimately, the call to encourage ethical consumption is an invitation to partake in a shared journey toward a more sustainable, equitable future. It's a collective endeavor where each step forward and each ethical choice made signals a deeper societal commitment to nurturing the planet and its inhabitants—a testament to our collective power to shape the mercantile world anew.

Marketing Sustainability: Engaging the Responsible Consumer

The urgency of our ecological situation demands businesses not only innovate responsibly, but also engage consumers in sustainability. The pivot requires a confluence of vision, ethics, and strategic marketing. Ethical consumerism, a rising force propelled by awareness and concern for the future of the planet, presents a fertile ground for cultivating sustainable practices that respond to, and also help shape, consumer demands.

Developing meaningful connections with the conscious consumer, however, demands authenticity. The modern consumer can't be underestimated; with information at their fingertips, they seek out brands whose actions align with their values. This discernment calls for marketers to present transparent and earnest narratives regarding their sustainable practices to avoid skepticism.

Marketing sustainability is not a superficial change in advertising but rather a substantial shift in how a company conducts its business. The responsible marketer recognizes the need to embed sustainability in every touchpoint of the brand experience, from product development to after-sale service. This holistic approach not only reinforces a brand's commitment to sustainability, but also encompasses an array of initiatives that collectively impact consumer behavior.

Educating consumers is paramount. While many express a desire to make responsible choices, the complexities of sustainability can be daunting. Brands must play an informative role, simplifying the complexities into digestible messages that empower consumers to make sustainable choices.

Consumers also respond to emotional narratives that illustrate the impact of their purchase decisions. Storytelling can be a potent tool. When wielded with care, it connects the personal with the global and the individual action with collective impact. This narrative approach can turn mundane purchasing decisions into expressive acts of environmental stewardship.

Incentivization is another powerful strategy. Harnessing rewards for sustainable consumer behavior encourages positive reinforcement—whether through loyalty programs, discounts, or recognition. These incentives can transform good intentions into action, fostering habits that contribute to a more sustainable future.

Critical to these endeavors is collaboration. Partnerships with non-profits, government entities, and other corporations can amplify a brand's sustainability message and facilitate greater reach and credibility. Building a community around shared environmental values unites consumers and brands in pursuit of common goals.

Technological integration marks another frontier in marketing sustainability. From augmented reality that reveals a product's life cycle to apps that track individual carbon footprints, technology can bridge the gap between knowledge and action, fostering an informed and engaged consumer base.

Amidst these strategies lies the challenge of avoiding greenwashing. In their earnestness to appeal to responsible consumers, businesses must tread carefully to ensure their claims are substantiated. Accusations of greenwashing not only undermine consumer trust but can also bring about legal and reputational repercussions.

Moreover, businesses should embrace the principle of co-creation with consumers. In an era in which feedback loops are instantaneous, brands can harness consumer insights to continuously refine their sustainability initiatives. Such an approach not only enhances the product offering, but also fosters a sense of ownership among consumers—it's their brand that is shaping a responsible world.

Adopting a local focus within global marketing initiatives can also resonate with consumers. Localization not only addresses the unique sustainability challenges and priorities of specific communities, but it also fosters a sense of connection and relevance global messaging may lack.

The notion of exclusivity should be revisited. Sustainable products and services need to be accessible to a broader audience to allow for a democratization of sustainability. By integrating sustainable choices across all price points, businesses can engender inclusivity in responsible consumerism, which serves to broaden the market impact and acceptance of sustainable products.

Finally, as traditional advertising mediums evolve, so too must the venues for sustainability marketing. The rise of social media influencer marketing, for example, allows for a more personalized consumer engagement strategy. Leveraging influencers who are passionate about sustainability can provide a voice that resonates with like-minded consumers.

In conclusion, the intersection of ethical leadership in business and eco-conscious consumer demand provides a promising path forward. The call to action is clear: businesses must harness the tools of marketing not just to sell a product but to advocate for a sustainable lifestyle. This is not mere marketing; this is mobilization for change, where every transaction is a vote for the future we aspire to create.

Marketing sustainability, then, becomes a transformative act—a confluence of persuasion, education, and social evolution. The engaged, responsible consumer is a partner, ally, and co-creator in this journey toward a more sustainable and equitable tomorrow.

Understanding Consumer Behavior, Values, and Beliefs

Delving into the heart of consumerism, we encounter a complex web of behavior, values, and beliefs that dictate the myriad choices individuals make each day. It's within this nuance where businesses must understand and navigate if they are to foster responsible consumerism and drive the sustainability movement forward. This understanding is not merely about market segmentation or demographics; it stretches into the deep recesses of psychological patterns and ethical considerations that influence purchasing decisions.

The act of consumption isn't a mere transaction; it's a reflection of one's identity, upbringing, cultural background, and philosophical outlook. Consumers are not a monolithic group that responds uniformly to market stimuli. They are diverse, and their consumption patterns are shaped by how they perceive themselves and wish to be perceived by others. When sustainability enters this conversation, we appreciate that consumers don't just buy a product for its utility, but also for the values it represents.

The entrenchment of responsible consumer behaviors begins with an exploration of values—the deep-seated principles that guide people's judgments and actions. In the realm of sustainable consumption, values such as social equity, environmental stewardship, and responsibility toward future generations come to the forefront. Businesses that align with these intrinsic motivations are better positioned to connect with and inspire their customer base.

Beliefs, while closely related to values, are the acceptance that certain ideas or statements are true or real. They are often based on moral, cultural, or religious grounding and can greatly influence consumer choices. For instance, the belief in the importance of conserving natural resources can lead consumers to prioritize products with minimal packaging or products that are reusable and recyclable.

The intersection of personal and societal beliefs with consumer behavior is where businesses can catalyze change. Encouraging ethical consumption begins with understanding the driving forces behind consumer choices, which often trace back to belief systems. Companies that comprehensively engage with these belief systems in their marketing and operational strategies can harness the power of consumer convictions to set new industry standards in sustainability.

Consumer behavior is also heavily influenced by perceived norms and societal expectations. What others do—and the approval or disapproval of those actions—plays a significant role in shaping individual behaviors. For example, as community recycling initiatives become normalized, individuals are more likely to engage in recycling behaviors. Businesses can leverage this by creating a perception that sustainable behavior is not only expected but is the prevailing norm within society.

Ongoing research consistently indicates that heritage, culture, and national identity impact consumer behaviors toward sustainability. Consumers are often more likely to embrace sustainability if they can relate it to their cultural customs or national pride. This cultural lens is critical, as companies must understand how sustainability initiatives can resonate with, or potentially disrupt, cultural norms and traditions.

Understanding consumer behavior goes beyond what people buy; it encompasses the entire consumer journey, including how they use and dispose of products. These usage and post-usage phases are instrumental in closing the loop on a truly sustainable life cycle. Here, it's important to consider the rational and emotional factors that govern how consumers interact with products throughout the product's lifespan.

Rational factors are practical considerations such as cost, convenience, and accessibility. Emotional factors may include the pride one feels in making an ethical choice or the sense of belonging to a community of like-minded individuals. A business's role, therefore, in nudging consumers toward sustainable behaviors includes addressing both the rational and the emotional, creating a path that makes sustainability the most logical and fulfilling choice.

When businesses overlook the importance of consumer education and empowerment, they miss a crucial component of driving sustainable behavior. Educated customers make more informed decisions and are better equipped to discern between genuine sustainability and greenwashing. Education efforts can take many forms, from straightforward and transparent product information to more engaging marketing campaigns that tell a story about the company's sustainability journey.

The Responsibility

Economic theories suggest consumers are inherently rational and seek to maximize their self-interest. Yet, contemporary studies reveal a more nuanced picture in which ethical considerations can override the pursuit of self-interest. People are often willing to pay a premium for ethical goods or make personal sacrifices for the greater good if they believe in the cause.

The concept of social responsibility itself has evolved in consumer minds. It's no longer seen as an altruistic side-note but is now weaving itself into the fabric of expected business practice. Consumers recognize the influence their spending habits exert on business behavior, and many are utilizing their purchasing power to mold corporate practices in more sustainable directions.

The notion of responsibility extends to the acknowledgment of interconnectedness. In an increasingly globalized world, consumers are beginning to understand the far-reaching impacts of their consumption choices, from the local community repercussions to international environmental effects. When they recognize this interconnectedness, their sense of responsibility often strengthens, which can motivate a shift toward more sustainable behaviors.

Unveiling the motivational drivers behind sustainable consumer behaviors reveals factors such as self-efficacy, personal relevance, and the desire for positive change are significant. When consumers believe their individual choices make a difference, they're more likely to engage in pro-environmental behaviors. This self-efficacy must be reflected through business practices that reinforce consumer impact, demonstrating the tangible outcomes of their choices.

Translating this understanding of consumer behavior into actionable business strategies requires a sophisticated balance of empathy, ethics, and economics. As scholars and business leaders, we are at a pivotal moment in which the fusion of these elements can direct the markets toward a sustainable equilibrium, where consumer demands drive responsible business practices just as much as those businesses inform consumer expectations. By prioritizing an intimate comprehension of the values, beliefs, and behaviors of consumers, businesses can lead the charge in establishing a new paradigm—one where sustainability is not just a feature but the foundation of consumerism.

The Psychology of Sustainable Choices

The conversation about sustainability often focuses on what needs to be done at an organizational or systemic level, yet individual consumer choices play a crucial role in driving demand for sustainable products and behaviors. To promote a shift toward a more sustainable world, we must understand the psychological drivers behind consumer decision-making. At the core of this investigation is the recognition that psychology can provide insights into how to encourage ethical consumption patterns that support environmental and social well-being.

Research in environmental psychology suggests values, beliefs, and attitudes significantly influence sustainable decision-making. Values are core aspects of our psychological makeup that guide our behavior in consistent ways. Individuals who place a high priority on biospheric values, for example, are more likely to engage in behaviors that benefit the environment. Therefore, these intrinsic values can be leveraged to foster more ecologically conscious consumer choices.

Beliefs also play a critical role in sustainable choices. When consumers believe their individual actions can make a difference, they're more likely to undertake efforts to behave sustainably. This sense of self-efficacy and belief in collective-efficacy can drive substantial change in consumer markets, guiding individuals toward products and services that are aligned with their desire to positively impact the environment.

Attitudes, inclusive of cognitive and affective components, are another psychological facet influencing our choices. Positive attitudes toward sustainability can result in a higher willingness to pay for green products and adopt new behaviors that reduce environmental footprints. Effective communication strategies that reinforce these positive attitudes can nudge consumers toward making choices that align with these attitudes.

However, while values, beliefs, and attitudes are significant, they sometimes contrast with actual behavior. Known as the attitude-behavior gap, this phenomenon illustrates consumers do not always act in accordance with their professed beliefs. Overcoming this gap is vital for businesses seeking to market sustainable options effectively and for policymakers aiming to encourage ethical consumerism.

The theory of planned behavior (TPB) adds a valuable framework to understand the mechanics behind sustainable consumer behavior. TPB posits that intention, influenced by attitudes, subjective norms, and perceived behavioral control, predicts behavior. By understanding these predictors, we can design interventions that not only inform, but also engage and empower consumers in making sustainable choices.

Emotional investment is another potent motivator behind sustainable choices. When individuals feel connected to nature and empathetic toward other beings, they are more likely to engage in sustainability. Marketers and educators can tap into this emotional connection, cultivating a sense of empathy and personal responsibility that acts as a strong driver for making sustainable choices.

Social norms provide cues for how to behave in certain situations, and when society values sustainability, individual behaviors are likely to follow. By creating a culture where sustainable choices are seen as the norm, we increase the likelihood that individuals will adopt those behaviors. This can be achieved through community-driven campaigns, influencer figures promoting sustainable lifestyles, or policies that shape public perception of sustainability as a valued norm.

The importance of habit in shaping sustainable consumer patterns cannot be ignored. Many unsustainable behaviors are habitual, carried out with little conscious thought. Developing new, sustainable habits can be challenging but is crucial for lasting change. Interventions that make sustainable choices more convenient and rewarding can help in creating new, long-term sustainable habits.

Additionally, framing of information influences consumer choices. Effective framing can highlight the benefits of sustainable behavior in a way that aligns with the consumer's self-identity and values. Framing products and practices in terms of their health benefits, cost savings, or alignment with ethical self-image can guide consumers toward choices that are beneficial for both themselves and the environment.

Furthermore, understanding the barriers to sustainable choices is essential for creating strategies that circumvent these challenges. Factors such as perceived inconvenience, lack of information, or higher costs can deter consumers from choosing sustainable alternatives. By identifying and addressing these barriers, businesses and policymakers can make sustainable choices more accessible and appealing.

Psychological research also points to the significance of mental accounting in sustainable choices. Consumers often categorize money into different mental accounts, which can affect their willingness to spend on sustainable goods. Understanding how people mentally budget for sustainability-related expenses can help in structuring pricing and payment plans that encourage greener purchasing decisions

In the realm of sustainable choices, the role of messenger is as important as the message itself. Credible and trustworthy sources are more effective in influencing consumer behavior. Marketers and leaders advocating for sustainability must establish trust and demonstrate a genuine commitment to environmental values to effectively sway consumer choices.

Finally, the concept of moral licensing can sometimes undermine sustainable consumption. After making a sustainable choice, individuals may feel licensed to make a less-sustainable choice later on, negating the positive effects. Awareness and messaging that encourage consistency in sustainable behaviors can mitigate this psychological phenomenon.

The Responsibility

The integration of psychological insights into marketing strategies, policymaking, and educational initiatives can be transformative. By understanding the psychological mechanisms that drive sustainable choices, we have the potential to create a culture that not only encourages, but also rewards and sustains ethical consumption, thereby fostering a more equitable and sustainable future.

Chapter 11:
Societal Expectations and Business Responses

As the winds of change sweep across the globe, demanding a more sustainable approach to the way we live and conduct business, a poignant discussion emerges in "Societal Expectations and Business Responses." Society is no longer a silent bystander in the realm of corporate operations; instead, it has risen as a formidable voice in shaping business ethics and sustainability practices. Enlightened by a mounting awareness, stakeholders today seek companies that not only promise profitability, but also show an unwavering commitment to environmental stewardship and social welfare.

Forward-thinking businesses have begun to recognize the path forward requires a delicate balance—and indeed, a synthesis—between delivering value to shareholders and honoring their duties to communities and ecosystems. Through an intricate dance of pragmatism and idealism, these companies are finding ways to turn societal expectations into innovative strategies that propel them toward a position of leadership in the sustainability movement. They're not merely reacting to external pressures but rather actively redefining their corporate identities to align with a societal paradigm that cherishes responsibility as deeply as it does reward. In doing so, they set a new standard for what it means to succeed in business—one that heals and nurtures rather than depletes and exploits, at once securing their legacy and ensuring a more equitable and thriving world for generations to come.

Understanding and Meeting Stakeholder Demands

In today's business environment, a company's ability to understand and respond to stakeholder demands is paramount. Stakeholders include not only shareholders and customers, but also employees, suppliers, communities, governments, and society at large. As the bedrock of ethical business, meeting these demands necessitates a deep comprehension of what diverse stakeholders value and require.

Divergent stakeholders often have distinct interests, needs, and definitions of success, meaning businesses must navigate a complex matrix of expectations. These demands range from financial profitability to socio-environmental impacts, reflecting a social fabric that is increasingly sensitive to the ethical dimensions of commerce. Hence, stakeholders seek a higher degree of transparency and accountability from businesses.

To address this, companies are institutionalizing stakeholder engagement as a strategic tool. They hold consultations, involve stakeholders in decision-making processes, and adjust business models to integrate these insights. Engaging with stakeholders allows businesses to predict and adapt to evolving societal expectations.

A critical aspect of meeting stakeholder demands lies in embracing the concept of value creation beyond financial metrics. This concept has been integral to shaping business strategies that consider social and environmental dimensions as indistinguishable from economic value. It's about crafting a shared value proposition that serves all parties.

Such holistic responses to stakeholder expectations have necessitated rethinking of organizational purpose to include sustainability goals. The modern enterprise is expected to not only turn profit, but also contribute to the welfare of communities, preservation of the environment, and overall human flourishing. It is an imperative that calls for embedding ethical considerations into the core corporate strategy.

Businesses actively mapping their stakeholders' concerns onto their strategies often find themselves ahead in fostering innovation and resilience. They recognize sustainability-driven innovation can unlock new markets, drive growth, and differentiate their brand. A purpose-driven innovation agenda caters to stakeholders' expectations while pursuing commercial success.

There's also a growing acknowledgment of the "license to operate"—the notion that businesses must continually earn the right to operate in society. This license is granted through meeting or exceeding societal expectations in areas such as environmental stewardship, social equity, and economic inclusion.

However, identifying what stakeholders value is an ongoing challenge. It is a dynamic task, as what is deemed important can shift due to factors such as technological advancements, shifting cultural norms, and regulatory changes. To stay aligned, companies often employ tools such as materiality assessments to pinpoint where to focus their efforts.

Furthermore, progressive businesses are not only reactive to societal expectations, but also proactive in shaping them. They work to influence norms and policies in favor of sustainable practices. This proactive stance doesn't merely respond to demands but helps in forming them, positioning such businesses as leaders in the sustainability realm.

Effective stakeholder engagement also means grappling with trade-offs. Saying "yes" to certain stakeholder groups may mean saying "no" to others. The ability to navigate these ethical dilemmas without losing sight of the larger sustainability goals is crucial. It requires a deep moral compass and a nuanced understanding of the interplay between varied interests.

Transparency is paramount in meeting stakeholder demands. Stakeholders are increasingly concerned with not only what businesses do, but also with how they do it. Initiatives such as sustainability reporting and third-party certifications have become important methods of demonstrating a company's commitment to ethical practices and its progress toward sustainability goals.

To synthesize these views, it's necessary to recognize the strategic value of stakeholder theory, which asserts stakeholder interests are part and parcel of the firm's interests. A firm that strategically manages its stakeholder relations is more likely to obscure the traditional boundaries of the business and become a cohesive part of society's fabric.

In conclusion, understanding and meeting stakeholder demands is a dynamic and complex task, requiring a dedicated and strategic approach. It involves ongoing dialogue, integration of feedback, and a willingness to adapt and innovate. Businesses that excel in this will not only thrive, but also drive the transformative shift toward a more sustainable, equitable future. This is the essence of ethical business in our changing world, where the lines between profit and purpose are increasingly intertwined, and success is measured by the positive impact on all stakeholders.

Balancing Profit and Purpose

In the ever-evolving landscape of business ethics and corporate responsibility, modern companies face a compelling challenge: the need to balance profit generation with their societal and environmental purpose. This pursuit is not merely a trend; it has become a necessity. In this intricate dance, corporations can no longer afford to prioritize shareholder value at the expense of their broader stakeholder community.

The proposition that businesses should be solely profit-driven artifacts of capitalism is fading into obscurity. A transformation is at hand, where value creation is measured not just in financial terms but in social and environmental impact as well. The impetus for this change is fueled by increasing societal expectations, which demand businesses contribute positively to the world.

Understanding financial success and responsible conduct are not mutually exclusive is the cornerstone of this segment. Indeed, the harmonization of profit and purpose can lead to resilient business models that thrive in an era of conscious consumerism and intense regulatory scrutiny. The question is no longer whether businesses should integrate ethical considerations into their core strategy but rather how they can do so effectively while remaining competitive.

One of the primary mechanisms for achieving this balance is the incorporation of Environmental, Social, and Governance (ESG) criteria into business operations. ESG represents a set of standards for a company's operations that socially conscious investors use to screen potential investments. These criteria help businesses navigate the complexities of sustainability and provide a framework for measuring their ethical efforts.

Innovative companies are redefining their corporate mission to reflect a broader array of objectives that include community well-being, environmental stewardship, and fair labor practices. This shift toward a more holistic understanding of purpose often starts with a reevaluation of corporate values and a recalibration of business activities to ensure alignment with these values.

Stakeholder theory posits that the success of a business is dependent on its relationships with all stakeholders, including employees, suppliers, customers, and the communities in which it operates. Stakeholder engagement, therefore, becomes a critical component of balancing profit and purpose. By actively listening to stakeholders, businesses can identify material issues and opportunities for positive impact that also ensure long-term profitability.

However, the integration of ethical objectives into a company's profit strategy can present unique challenges. Tensions may arise between short-term financial goals and long-term sustainability commitments. Overcoming these challenges requires leadership that is both visionary and grounded, capable of making decisions that benefit the company without comprising ethical responsibilities.

Collaborative approaches involving cross-sector partnerships are essential for tackling issues that extend beyond the reach of any single organization. Public-private partnerships, for instance, can facilitate the sharing of resources, knowledge, and expertise, leading to sustainability outcomes that no entity could achieve alone.

Transparent reporting and communication are critical in the balance between profit and purpose. Stakeholders expect companies to be forthright about their efforts, successes, and failures in sustainability. Such transparency fosters trust and accountability, offering a competitive edge to businesses that consistently demonstrate their commitment to sustainable practices.

Moreover, businesses that integrate purpose into their core are finding this approach drives innovation. When companies invest in sustainable practices, they often uncover new product lines, services, or processes that not only benefit society and the environment, but also lead to unanticipated profit streams.

Consumers, particularly the younger generations, are increasingly aligning their purchase decisions with their values, opting for products and services from companies they perceive to be responsible. Thus, purpose-driven businesses often enjoy increased customer loyalty and resilience in the face of market volatility, as their core principles resonate with a growing demographic of conscious customers.

An ever-growing body of research illustrates purpose-oriented companies can outperform their profit only–focused counterparts in the long run. These companies often have more engaged employees, lower turnover rates, and higher levels of innovation, all of which contribute to a sustained competitive advantage.

Indeed, the reconciliation of profit and purpose is not about diminishing returns but about reimagining the role of business in society—treating profit as a vital means to a more significant end. The end being a thriving civilization where businesses play a critical part in building sustainable and just economies.

In summary, with the right strategic vision and commitment to ethical practices, businesses can transform challenges into opportunities, fostering a more sustainable and equitable future for all. This balance becomes imperative, not only for survival but for the flourishing of both business and society in the complex, interdependent world we share.

Chapter 12:
Ethics in Marketing and Advertising

As we progress through our exploration of sustainable business practices, we turn our focus to the role of marketing and advertising—the front lines of corporate communication. Here, the imperative for ethical conduct cannot be overstated. These channels not only shape consumer perceptions, but also manifest the values to which a company aspires or feigns allegiance.

Within this domain, promoting sustainability through ethical communication involves a judicious blend of transparency and responsibility. It's about purpose-driven marketing, which resonates with both the heart and the intellect of a discerning public that no longer just buys what they need but invests where they believe.

Corporations find themselves at a critical juncture, where combating greenwashing and misleading claims is not just a regulatory compliance but a moral imperative. A brand's integrity is its currency in the marketplace of trust. Building that integrity through authenticity means dispelling illusions and embracing the substance of truthful representation of products, services, and the company ethos. In doing so, businesses not only align with the emergent ecological consciousness, but also foster a more durable and reciprocal relationship with consumers, ultimately driving the global movement toward sustainability and an equitable future.

Promoting Sustainability Through Ethical Communication

In the realm of modern business, the essence of communication can't be underestimated, especially when it is wielded as a tool to promote sustainability. Employing ethical communication strategies is a cardinal approach for businesses looking to champion sustainability effectively. The impact of such communication echoes through the pillars of trust, transparency, and authenticity, which are integral to engaging stakeholders and consumers in the sustainability narrative.

Ethical communication in the context of sustainability goes beyond mere information dissemination. It seeks to build a bridge of mutual understanding and respect between companies and their audiences. No longer can businesses afford to overlook the implications of their messages or the mediums they choose. The call, instead, is for being purpose-driven in the crafting and sharing of sustainable visions and practices.

Companies that embed ethics into their marketing and advertising strategies not only respect the intelligence of their audience, but also honor the urgency of the environmental challenges we face. It is not just about telling a story that resonates; it is about telling a story that is firmly rooted in truth and commitment. A narrative that doesn't just scratch the surface with dazzling imagery or clever slogans, but one that dives deep into the practical measures being undertaken to make a tangible difference. An ethical approach to communication, thus, is not only amenable but necessary for businesses aiming to contribute to the global sustainability movement.

An organization's communication strategy should reflect its environmental values and practices. This means aligning marketing materials, advertisements, employee communications, and public relations efforts with sustainable principles and ensuring all forms of communication mirror the underlying eco-friendly ethos for which the company stands. This alignment not only garners respect, but also fosters a sense of accountability within the organization.

To actualize this, businesses must promote a culture of transparency. Openness about sustainability initiatives, their outcomes, and the areas that need improvement is crucial. Customers are more discerning than ever; they possess an acute ability to spot discrepancies and are quick to call out organizations that fail to walk their green talk. In this light, sustainable messaging should be clear, consistent, and comprehensive.

Moreover, ethical communication necessitates inclusivity. Inclusivity in the sense that it doesn't just speak to a privileged few who can afford to make sustainable choices; it speaks to all segments of society, encouraging and empowering them to partake in sustainable behaviors. This approach requires marketers to understand the diverse barriers different communities face and mold messages that resonate and mobilize these diverse audiences.

Pivotal to ethical communication is avoiding greenwashing at all costs. Greenwashing undermines trust and misguides consumers, thus, derailing the very foundation of sustainability efforts. Authenticity—including substantiated claims, factual accomplishments, and realistic aspirations—must be at the core of sustainability messaging. Firms must provide evidence of their sustainability claims through certifications, reports, and independent assessments to build credibility and confidence.

The language employed in sustainable communications should be considered with care. It should not instill fear or guilt but inspire positive action and hope. Companies have the opportunity to evoke emotions that motivate change and demonstrate the positive impacts of sustainability, leading not only with facts, but also with compelling storytelling that captures hearts and minds.

At the intersection of ethics and communication lies the power of dialogue. We're not just broadcasting messages but inviting consumers, stakeholders, and the wider community to engage in conversations around sustainability. Open dialogues showcase a company's willingness to listen, learn, and grow—a fundamental step toward achieving a more sustainable future.

Strategically leveraging social media platforms also plays a significant role in amplifying sustainable practices and initiatives. These platforms offer an immediacy that can be harnessed to showcase real-time progress, share consumer stories, and engage audiences in environmental advocacy.

A commitment to ongoing education should be another pillar of ethical communication. As consumers become more environmentally conscious, they seek out knowledge about sustainable practices and products. Businesses, therefore, have a golden opportunity—and a responsibility—to educate their audience about environmental issues and the impact of their choices.

Nevertheless, ethical communication in sustainability is not just outward-facing; internal communication within companies is just as critical. Establishing internal narratives that underscore the importance of sustainability initiatives can engender a culture of environmental responsibility amongst employees, who can, in turn, become ambassadors of the company's sustainability ethos.

Finally, ethical communication must also look beyond marketing and advertising. It should be embedded in policy advocacy, stakeholder engagements, and partnerships. Businesses owe it to their stakeholders, and to the larger community, to champion policies that support sustainability, further enriching communication with actions that speak louder than words.

In conclusion, promoting sustainability through ethical communication is as much about framing the narrative as it is about embodying it within all aspects of business operations. It's a robust exercise in integrity, responsibility, and foresight—one that requires effort, consistency, and a heart firmly planted in the present with eyes on the future of our planet. As businesses continue to harness the power of ethical communication, they not only contribute to the sustainability movement, but also pave the way for a flourishing Earth, one message at a time.

Purpose-Driven Marketing

In the quest for a more sustainable and equitable world, businesses face not only the challenge of internal practices, but also the crucial task of how they communicate their values to the world. Purpose-driven marketing emerges as more than a strategic addition of value, it is an ethical imperative that reshapes the landscape in which companies interact with the environment, society, and consumers.

At its core, purpose-driven marketing refers to the alignment of a company's advertising and promotional activities with its broader mission to contribute positively to societal and environmental outcomes. This alignment goes beyond traditional profit-centric motives to encapsulate a holistic view of business success—one that prioritizes the well-being of all stakeholders.

The integration of altruistic purpose into marketing strategies creates a symbiotic relationship between ethical values and brand strength. Consumers are increasingly seeking out brands that demonstrate a commitment to the greater good. By responding authentically to this demand, companies can cultivate deeper connections with their customers and differentiate themselves in a crowded marketplace.

When businesses adopt a purpose-driven marketing approach, they commit to transparency as a foundational principle. This transparency enables consumers to see through the veil of marketing rhetoric and assess the actual impact of a company's actions on the environment and society.

It is crucial for businesses to recognize purpose-driven marketing is not an exercise in charity or mere corporate social responsibility. Instead, it is a strategic framework that inherently integrates a company's sustainable and ethical practices into its brand narrative, enabling consumers to align their values with their purchases.

However, the journey toward authentic purpose-driven marketing is fraught with potential pitfalls, such as the temptation to engage in greenwashing (making misleading claims about a product's environmental benefits). This unethical practice undermines trust and can cause long-term damage to brand reputation. It is, therefore, imperative for companies to ensure their messages are not only engaging, but also accurate and honest.

Moreover, the responsibilities of purpose-driven marketing extend to all touchpoints of customer interaction. This means not only should the promotion of products or services be ethically sound, but the entire customer experience, from packaging to post-purchase support, should reflect the organization's core values.

The cultural impact of purpose-driven marketing is significant; it has the capacity to influence social norms and consumer behavior. When effectively implemented, it can act as a catalyst for widespread change, encouraging consumers to make more sustainable and ethical choices in their day-to-day lives.

Marketing that is rooted in purpose also invites a new level of stakeholder engagement. When companies communicate their commitment to social and environmental objectives, they encourage stakeholders—from employees to investors—to participate in a collective effort toward sustainability. This inclusive approach not only strengthens internal morale, but also fosters a sense of community and shared mission.

It is important to note purpose-driven marketing is not a one-size-fits-all solution. Each company must define its unique purpose based on its values, culture, and business model. This personalized approach ensures the marketing strategy resonates authentically with both the company's internal stakeholders and its external audience.

As the globe becomes increasingly digitized, the digital realm offers an expansive canvas for purpose-driven narratives. Utilizing social media, content marketing, and other digital channels, companies can amplify their ethical messages and engage with consumers on a deeper level. The interactive nature of these platforms also allows businesses to receive direct feedback, promoting an ongoing dialogue around sustainability and ethics.

In light of the rise of global issues such as climate change, economic inequality, and social injustice, purpose-driven marketing is fast becoming an essential tool for businesses to demonstrate leadership and commitment to a better future.

The ultimate goal of purpose-driven marketing is to embed the sustainability agenda within the DNA of the brand. When this is accomplished, marketing no longer serves merely as a tool for driving sales but as a force for positive change that reinforces the company's role as a steward of the planet and advocate for social progress.

In conclusion, purpose-driven marketing represents a powerful intersection of business acumen and ethical imperative, providing companies with an opportunity to lead by example in the era of sustainability. It is a potent reminder that businesses can—and should—be a force for good, fostering a world where economic growth and environmental stewardship go hand in hand.

Combating Greenwashing and Misleading Claims

In an age in which the environment is at the forefront of global conversation, the marketing landscape has transformed significantly. Companies, aware of the growing consumer demand for sustainable and eco-friendly products, have necessarily had to adjust their marketing strategies. However, this wellspring of eco-consciousness has also given rise to a critical challenge for ethical marketing and advertising: the practice of greenwashing and spreading misleading claims about environmental benefits.

Greenwashing is a deceptive practice in which a company exaggerates or fabricates the environmental benefits of its products or services. It's a form of misinformation that can erode public trust and impede genuine efforts for sustainable progress. As environmental awareness increases, consumers are becoming ever-more vigilant in scrutinizing brands that claim to be "green." Thus, companies that engage in greenwashing can incur not only reputational damage, but also consumer backlash and legal repercussions.

To confront greenwashing and misleading claims, the first step is to develop a robust understanding of what constitutes ethical environmental marketing. This understanding must be rooted in transparency and accountability. Companies must not only make genuine efforts to reduce their environmental impact, but also accurately report these efforts. Honesty, including avoiding vague language and unverifiable assertions, should be the cornerstone of all environmental claims.

Ensuring veracity in environmental marketing requires adopting stringent internal review processes for sustainability-related messages. This can involve multi-departmental checks or third-party verifications to ensure compliance with environmental advertising standards. For instance, certifications such as the Ecolabel or Energy Star serve as shortcuts that help consumers make informed choices while protecting them from unfounded claims.

Laws and regulations play a critical part in deterring companies from engaging in greenwashing. The Federal Trade Commission's Green Guides provide businesses with guidance on making legitimate environmental claims in their marketing in the United States. Such regulations help outline what is permissible, making it easier for companies to communicate their green initiatives transparently and for consumers to trust the claims they see.

Beyond regulation, educating consumers about environmental issues and what constitutes realistic and significant green initiatives can empower them. Knowing how to distinguish between authentic and hollow claims helps consumers hold companies accountable. For example, understanding the meaning behind labels such as "biodegradable" and "recycled content" enables consumers to make more responsible choices.

Collaboration with environmental experts and NGOs can help businesses refine their marketing campaigns to ensure they are not misleading. These entities can lend their expertise to validate claims, offering an additional layer of credibility to marketing campaigns. Such collaborations not only strengthen ethical marketing strategies, but also demonstrate a company's commitment to real environmental stewardship.

Recognition of the importance of authenticity should lead marketing professionals to direct their creativity toward honest storytelling. Instead of fabricating green credentials, brands can share their journey toward sustainability, including the challenges and incremental improvements they've made. This approach invites consumers to engage with the brand's sincerity and progress rather than be dazzled by potentially false claims.

Digital media and social networks have drastically changed the landscape of marketing and are powerful tools in combating greenwashing. Brands can use these platforms for transparent communication, answering consumer inquiries, and providing detailed information about their sustainability efforts. Moreover, social media can be leveraged to invite customer participation and feedback, creating a community around shared environmental goals.

Another promising approach is incorporating actual environmental impacts into product design and marketing. This concept, termed "product greening," involves emphasizing reductions in resource consumption, energy use, and emissions in both product development and advertising. By making sustainability integral to the product and the marketing of it, the company can reduce the possibility of misleading consumers.

Marketing and advertising professionals must be educated and encouraged to uphold ethical standards in their work. In-house training and professional development can instill a deep understanding of eco-friendly practices and the gravity of misleading environmental claims.

With knowledge comes the responsibility to engender marketing campaigns that reflect true environmental benefits.

The importance of independent watchdogs and consumer advocacy groups in exposing greenwashing cannot be overstated. Their investigative work and reporting illuminates cases of misleading marketing, forcing corrections in the industry. They act as a necessary balance to corporate interests, ensuring consumers receive trustworthy information.

The active role of policymakers in creating a framework that nurtures ethical marketing and advertising is indispensable. This goes beyond merely enacting regulations to include offering incentives for businesses that consistently demonstrate genuine and effective sustainable practices in their operations and marketing.

Finally, to foster an ongoing and dynamic conversation about green marketing ethics, academia can contribute substantially through research and public discourse. By publishing studies on effective ethical advertising practices and the impact of greenwashing, academia can provide critical, evidence-based insights for businesses, policymakers, and the general public.

Tackling greenwashing and misleading claims is a multifaceted endeavor that necessitates a synergistic approach across all sectors. It involves regulatory frameworks, consumer education, industry self-regulation, and the vigilant oversight of independent bodies. Only through such concerted efforts can we hope to cultivate an environment where ethical marketing fosters genuine sustainable development and advances the global sustainability movement.

Building Brand Integrity Through Authenticity

In the quest for corporate sustainability, one cannot overlook the essential role that marketing and advertising play in transmitting authentic messages to the consumer. Authenticity forms the bedrock upon which brand integrity is built and sustained, particularly in an era in which consumers are increasingly vigilant about the environmental and social footprints of the brands they support.

Brand integrity is not merely about the image a company projects but about the congruence and alignment of stated values with actions. A brand that advocates for sustainability must not only voice this commitment but demonstrate it through every facet of its operation. Hence, ethical marketing champions the truthfulness of claims and the transparency of processes.

Authenticity in marketing and advertising demands a brand's messages are not only honest, but also verifiable. When sustainability is at the forefront of a brand's messaging, the claims must stand up to scrutiny. This requires a thorough vetting of supply chains, sustainability initiatives, and the potential impact on diverse stakeholders.

Moreover, to maintain brand integrity, companies must avoid the trap of greenwashing—the practice of disseminating deceitful information to present an eco-friendly public image. It's an ethical pitfall that not only tarnishes brand reputation, but also undermines the entire sustainability movement.

The authenticity of a brand is enhanced when it engages in dialogues with its audience, rather than imparting one-sided messages. Open and honest communication about successes, as well as challenges faced in meeting sustainability goals, resonates with stakeholders' increasing expectations of transparency.

Customer engagement through storytelling can be a powerful tool for brands to convey their commitment to ethical practices. Stories that highlight tangible sustainability efforts, when shared with humility and without exaggeration, can invigorate trust and reinforce a brand's authenticity.

Authentic marketing also calls for a holistic approach where sustainability is integral to the brand and not just an add-on for promotion. When sustainability principles are embedded in the organizational culture, marketing efforts naturally reflect this ethos.

Feedback loops are crucial in fostering brand integrity. Actively seeking consumer input and responding with substantive action demonstrates a genuine commitment to upholding sustainable and ethical values within business practices.

In an age dominated by social media, authenticity in marketing is scrutinized in real time. Companies are compelled to operate in a milieu where information is disseminated rapidly, and feedback from stakeholders can significantly sway public perception. This dynamic environment necessitates vigilant self-regulation and a readiness to address concerns promptly and genuinely.

Authenticity is multifaceted and extends beyond environmental claims. A brand that seeks integrity must also ensure social aspects, such as fair labor practices and human rights, are addressed within their marketing narratives. This comprehensive approach conveys a more thoughtful understanding of and commitment to sustainability.

Additionally, brands with authentic sustainability profiles are poised to foster better customer relationships, loyalty, and, ultimately, a competitive edge. The enhanced credibility that arises from genuine environmental and social efforts can translate into increased consumer trust and may lead to stronger financial performance.

Employee advocacy is another key aspect of authentic marketing. Employees who genuinely believe in their company's sustainability ethos can become passionate brand ambassadors. Their genuine stories and experiences provide a human touch that can bridge the gap between brand rhetoric and consumer reality.

Finally, in the drive for marketing authenticity, the nexus between the brand's core values and society's needs must not be overlooked. When a brand's purpose aligns with social or environmental well-being, it not only resonates deeply with consumers, but also contributes to the upliftment of the communities and ecosystems it touches.

In conclusion, building brand integrity through authenticity is not simply a marketing exercise but a strategic imperative. It is a coherent blend of genuine representation, ethical practice, and an enduring commitment to sustainability that amplifies a brand's respect and standing in the eyes of all stakeholders. The future indeed belongs to those who can build and maintain an authentic and ethically responsible brand identity and, in so doing, contribute to a more sustainable, equitable world.

Chapter 13:
Measuring Impact:
Metrics and Standards for Ethical Business

To navigate the transformative shift toward environmental and social responsibility, businesses must not only commit to ethical practices, but also demonstrate their impact through quantifiable measures. This chapter delves into the realm of assessment, where the ardor for sustainability is not just articulated, but also substantiated with metrics and standards that are robust, transparent, and universally recognized.

An ethical business meticulously tracks its Environmental, Social, and Governance (ESG) performance—these are not just checkboxes for annual reports, but diligent reflections of a company's societal and environmental footprints. Leaders in the movement recognize the vital role of setting benchmarks, they champion the development of Sustainability Key Performance Indicators (KPIs) that align with global standards and expectations.

As we refute greenwashing with accountability, the future of sustainability reporting gleams on the horizon—a future in which businesses become the meticulous custodians of data that inform impactful decision-making and foster a more sustainable, equitable future.

Pushing beyond complacency, this chapter catalyzes an examination of an organization's core—ensuring every claim of sustainability is not just an echo of good intentions but a clearly defined, measurable outcome that resonates with integrity throughout the global economy.

The Role of ESG in Business Valuation and the Global Economy

In modern enterprise, Environmental, Social, and Governance (ESG) considerations have become indispensable threads woven intricately into the fabric of business valuation and global economics. The consciousness of a company's impact on the environment, its roles and responsibilities within society, and the quality of its governance no longer sit peripherally in strategy meetings—they are core of the ideals and practices that determine a business's place in the new global market. This proliferation of ESG criteria represents a seismic shift in not only how businesses are appraised, but also how they operate within the broader economic ecosystem.

At its essence, ESG encapsulates an investment ethos that goes beyond the traditional financial considerations. It represents a methodology for discerning a business's robustness and potential for long-term success considering imminent global challenges. The integration of ESG into business valuation cannot be overstated; it is a barometer for future sustainability and a predictor for enduring profitability. This section examines how a commitment to ESG principles is reshaping business landscapes and becoming an imperative valuation tool.

It is increasingly clear that environmental concerns are not isolated phenomena but are deeply tethered to the heart of economic survival. Climate change, resource depletion, and loss of biodiversity represent just as much a risk to the balance sheet as they do to planetary health. Strategies that involve sustainable resource management, reduction in carbon footprint, and investment in green technologies now have definitive implications for valuation. Companies that proactively embrace these practices tend to see a fortification of their brand equity and market valuation.

The social aspect of ESG delves deeper into corporate responsibility, beyond the enterprise gate. It scrutinizes how a company nurtures its workforce, the extent to which it goes to foster diversity and inclusion, and its impact on the communities where it operates. Practices such as fair labor, community engagement, and customer satisfaction can result in enhanced productivity, innovation, and customer loyalty that fundamentally increase a company's value.

Good governance is no less pivotal in this trinity. It encompasses the systems, controls, and procedures that govern corporate affairs, safeguarding stakeholder interests and ensuring accountability. Robust governance structures can reduce risk, prevent scandals, and promote a solid market reputation, which in turn sustains investor confidence and supports a higher valuation.

Financial markets and investors have taken note of ESG's significance. ESG investments are witnessing massive inflows, reflecting a growing recognition that these factors translate into financial performance. Yet, it's not merely about values aligning with value; it's an acknowledgment that businesses do not operate in a vacuum. The ripple effects of their operations reach far and wide, and the traditional mentality of profit at any cost is giving way to a more holistic view, where financial success is intrinsically linked to positive global impact.

Furthermore, ESG metrics provide a vital lens through which to assess business resilience. Companies with strong ESG performances are perceived to be better at navigating long-term risks, which is critical in a volatile world economy. This risk mitigation attribute makes ESG a crucial component not only for business valuation but for predicting a firm's durability within an ever-changing global marketplace.

As consumer awareness and demands for ethical business conduct rise, ESG compliance also becomes a competitive advantage. Companies with a strong ESG proposition often experience a customer base that is increasingly loyal and willing to pay a premium for goods and services provided in an ethical and sustainable manner, driving up valuation and market share.

The interplay between ESG and regulations is also significant. Governments worldwide are imposing stiffer regulations relating to environmental protection and social responsibility, adding layers of compliance that can potentially impact a company's profitability. Businesses that align their strategies along ESG principles may find it easier to navigate these regulatory waters, whereas those that lag may face penalties, restrictions, or even litigation.

One of the notable advancements aided by ESG integration is the shift in narrative from short-term earnings to long-term sustainability. Companies that prioritize ESG guidelines are likely building steadier platforms for future growth, with investment decisions anchored on sustainability and ethical considerations. This approach is proving crucial in securing funding, particularly as investors place an ever-greater emphasis on sustainable growth paths.

Uniting the global economy and ESG is the shared understanding that long-term success is increasingly contingent upon a company's ability to adapt and thrive within planetary boundaries and social expectations. The entwining of these factors into a company's fabric is not merely a charitable nod to societal pressures; it's a strategic imperative for survival and relevance.

The pervasive narrative is clear—businesses can no longer afford to ignore ESG criteria within their valuation. This paradigm shift is empowering businesses that take stances on pertinent issues by assisting them in differentiating themselves in crowded markets.

There is, however, a persistent challenge in standardizing ESG metrics and reporting, which complicates comparative valuation and full integration into investment decisions. The success of ESG in valuation processes is predicated upon transparency and comparability, which is only as achievable as the uniformity of measurements and reporting.

In this evaluation of ESG's role in business valuation and the global economy, it is clear integrating ESG principles into business strategies is no longer optional for companies wishing to remain competitive. ESG is transforming markets, altering investor preferences, and recasting the very foundations upon which businesses are judged and valued. The tide has turned, and ESG is directing companies toward a future in which profit aligns with the planet and its people.

Corporate Impact of ESG

In a world riddled with environmental challenges and social disparities, businesses must confront the essence of their impact through the lens of Environmental, Social, and Governance (ESG) criteria. The pragmatic embrace of ESG principles reflects a transformative journey toward corporate responsibility and sustainable growth. It is the centerpiece for businesses intent on navigating the intricate dance of profit-making and planetary well-being. ESG metrics stand as a compass, orienting corporate strategies toward sustainability while mollifying shareholders' concern for long-term value.

Companies diligently integrating ESG are tailoring resilient operations that weather economic and environmental storms. The proactive adaptation to these non-financial factors culminates in enhanced risk management, inciting investor confidence and enabling access to capital at favorable terms.

ESG's ripple effect does not stop at fiscal performance; it recalibrates brand identity, attracts talent keen on ethical association, and solidifies customer loyalty in an era increasingly defined by conscientious consumption.

Thus, ESG emerges not only as a barometer for navigating the risks and opportunities inherent in the twenty-first-century business landscape but as the forge where a company's legacy is tempered, ensuring their narrative is both profitable and purposeful in the annals of time.

Impact of ESG on Public Companies

The advancing dialogue surrounding Environmental, Social, and Governance (ESG) has undoubtedly reached the core of corporate strategy for public companies. The adoption of ESG principles signals a recognition that long-term value is inexorably tied to social welfare, environmental stewardship, and sound governance. Today, public companies are no longer evaluated solely on short-term financial outcomes; their societal impact—far-reaching and momentous—commands an equal share of attention.

Public companies face intense scrutiny regarding their role in the larger ecosystem of the planet. Their monolithic production capabilities can yield remarkable environmental consequences. As custodians of significant human and natural resources, they must navigate the responsibility to minimize ecological devastation while fostering biodiversity and sustainability. Environmental stewardship, therefore, is not merely an ethical imperative but is increasingly seen as a determining factor in a company's resilience and potential for long-term growth.

Social considerations, including labor practices, community engagement, and human rights, weigh heavily on the operations of public firms. Transparency in addressing these issues has become a minimum standard, with investors and consumers alike favoring businesses that transcend mere compliance and aspire to actively enhance societal well-being. Promoting equality, diversity, and inclusion, whether within the workforce or the broader society, has become a potent impetus for positive brand differentiation.

Corporate governance, the G in ESG, influences every other aspect of a public company's sustainably responsible journey. Governance encompasses corporate ethics, compliance, accountability, and board diversity. Ethical business practices, robust management structures, and proactive shareholder advocacy define the governance quality that can mitigate risks and contribute to sustainable economic growth.

The financial implications of ESG factors for public companies are significant. Enhanced ESG practices can mitigate operational risks and secure competitive advantage. ESG-driven investment is accelerating; funds are increasingly channeled into companies demonstrating robust sustainability practices. This "green" capital not only facilitates projects that are environmentally responsible, but also grants access to a growing base of investors prioritizing sustainable investment opportunities.

Regulatory pressures, too, are shaping the landscape. Governments around the globe are introducing legislation mandating ESG disclosures, thereby enforcing companies to reckon with their societal footprint. Such demands for transparency induce public firms to adopt systemic changes to reporting practices, which, in turn, reflect upon their brand equity and market positioning.

Indeed, ESG metrics offer a blueprint for companies to drive innovation. The necessity to adhere to sustainability regulations often begets novel approaches to product development, operational efficiency, and supply chain management. Public companies thereby find themselves at the vanguard of transformative eco-friendly innovations that bear the dual fruit of regulatory compliance and value creation.

Yet, one cannot overlook the fact that the integration of ESG principles confronts companies with formidable challenges. Establishing reliable, consistent ESG metrics; grappling with the intricacies of sustainability reporting; and aligning disparate interests between shareholders and stakeholders are tasks demanding deft management and visionary leadership.

Concurrently, reputational risk is a notable concern for public companies in the ESG realm. In an interconnected world where information travels instantaneously, any misstep pertaining to sustainability can lead to significant brand damage, customer churn, and investor divestment. Herein the ghastly specter of greenwashing looms large, but misleading claims of environmental virtuosity can backfire spectacularly when uncovered.

However, the benefits of comprehensive ESG integration extend beyond risk mitigation. Companies with strong ESG credentials frequently witness enhanced employee morale, attraction of talent, and increased innovation capabilities. Engaged employees, aligned with the company's ethical practices, can drive productivity and contribute creatively toward sustainability goals.

Furthermore, the court of public opinion now sits in perpetual session, holding firms accountable for their ESG performance. A positive public perception can lead to brand loyalty and customer retention, as consumers increasingly make purchasing choices aligned with their own values. This consumer advocacy translates into tangible profitability for companies leading the charge in sustainability.

Finally, as the call for corporate responsibility amplifies, ESG considerations take on even greater significance for public companies in the context of global challenges such as climate change and social inequality. Enterprises that proactively address these challenges position themselves as leaders in forging a sustainable future, thus, attracting support from like-minded investors, consumers, and policymakers.

In sum, the impact of ESG on public companies encapsulates a diverse array of considerations—from operational to reputational, regulatory to financial. The integration of Environmental, Social, and Governance factors is not simply an act of corporate benevolence but a strategic imperative embedded in the quest for enduring profitability and societal contribution.

Impact of ESG on Private Companies

In the landscape of contemporary business, Environmental, Social, and Governance (ESG) criteria have emerged as crucial determinants of a company's ethical footprint and operational ethics. For private companies, these considerate practices, though often not mandated by public regulation, are essential for fortitude in market resilience and reputation. Private companies, unbound by strict shareholder expectations, have the latitude to prioritize long-term benefits over short-term gains, creating fertile ground for integrating ESG principles deeply into their business model.

Central to understanding the impact of ESG on private companies is the role of investor appeal. As modern investors seek more than financial returns, they gravitate toward companies with robust ESG standards. These entities are often seen as better positioned to navigate the fluctuations of global markets and societal demands, thereby reducing investment risk. Moreover, this assurance of stability extends beyond investors to other stakeholders, including customers and employees, who desire association with ethically run businesses.

Furthermore, ESG initiatives allow private companies to attract and retain top talent. Members of today's workforce, especially those from younger generations, seek workplaces that align with their values. Companies that demonstrate a commitment to environmental and social issues enjoy enhanced employer branding, turning into magnets for individuals aspiring to work for purpose-driven organizations. This talent draw correlates with higher innovation, motivation, and, ultimately, improved business performance.

Another aspect where private companies feel the impact of ESG practices is risk management. ESG considerations help in identifying potential risks such as environmental disasters related to climate change or social unrest due to unethical labor practices. Addressing these issues proactively can protect companies from reputational damage and associated financial losses. Furthermore, ESG-sensitive risk assessment and mitigation are gradually becoming a benchmark for investment decisions, urging private firms to refine their risk management approaches.

Private company governance also takes on a new dimension under the ESG umbrella. Good governance fosters trust among stakeholders, providing a framework for accountability and transparency. ESG criteria bring governance into sharp focus, promoting ethical leadership, robust internal controls, and compliance strategies that can thwart corruption and fraud while endorsing sustainable corporate strategies.

Supply chain sustainability has become another critical area for private companies. By including ESG criteria in procurement and sourcing policies, these businesses can influence their entire supply chain to minimize environmental and social impacts. This often necessitates new levels of collaboration and support for suppliers in meeting ESG standards, resulting in a ripple effect throughout the sector that reinforces the industry norms in ethical business practices.

Private enterprises adopting ESG principles may also find an enhanced ability to innovate. The constraints posed by sustainability challenges often spur creativity, resulting in products and processes that not only comply with ESG standards, but also pave the way for market differentiation. This vanguard approach can open new business opportunities and markets, particularly within the burgeoning realm of green technology and services.

However, it's not just a matter of internal processes and innovations; ESG also affects how private companies engage with the communities where they operate. Community engagement and social investment can drive grassroots-level change, building strong bonds that may buffer companies against local opposition and bolster their social license to operate. Such initiatives present companies as responsible citizens, fostering goodwill that can be intangible but is a considerable community asset.

Regulatory compliance, albeit less stringent for private entities, is another realm where ESG can have a meaningful impact. While private companies may not be subject to the same disclosure requirements as their public counterparts, aligning operations with ESG best practices can prepare them for potential regulatory shifts. It also provides a competitive advantage when dealing with institutions or public companies that require their vendors to maintain high ESG standards.

The impact of ESG transcends operational maneuvers; it can also serve as a driving force in shaping company culture. An ESG-forward company culture can influence every decision and action taken within the organization. By deeply embedding these principles, private companies can foster a workforce that is vigilant, engaged, and aligned with the core tenets of sustainability and ethical practice.

For those private companies considering an exit strategy, be it an initial public offering (IPO), a merger, or an acquisition, adopting ESG principles can significantly impact their valuation. Enhanced ESG performance conveys to potential buyers or investors that the company is not only a responsible steward of environmental and social resources, but also sophisticated in its strategic planning and risk assessment.

Conversely, deficiencies in ESG measures may raise barriers for private businesses. Difficulty attracting financing, increased operational costs due to inefficient practices, or the pitfalls of negative externalities may erode profitability. A company's lack of ESG foresight can become a critical liability in a transformative economic era that demands environmental cognizance and sociocultural sensitivity.

While the role of ESG in public companies is often highlighted due to regulatory pressures and shareholder scrutiny, the potential for private companies is substantial. Moving from an optional "nice-to-have" to a "must-have," implementing ESG strategies can catalyze innovation, improve resilience, and yield a sustainable competitive edge for private companies in a global economy increasingly aligned with ethical stewardship.

In essence, ESG is not just a matter of compliance or a marketing ploy; it represents a foundational pivot in the operational psyche of private companies. Through ESG, private businesses can participate in crafting a more sustainable, equitable future, converting challenges into pathways for innovation and growth. Companies that recognize and embrace this shift can carve out a role as leaders in the global sustainability movement and shape the business ethos of the twenty-first century.

Seeing through the lens of pragmatic optimism, it becomes evident that the impact of ESG is a crucial narrative in the story of private sector evolution. Through conscientious governance, environmental accountability, and social integrity, private companies stand at the helm of effectuating genuine transformative shifts, heralding an era in which profitability synchronizes with planetary and societal well-being.

Criticism of ESG

Environmental, Social, and Governance (ESG) criteria have emerged as ethical business practices, aspiring to link the financial success of companies with their ecological and social footprints. While ESG's principles are often seen as a necessary evolution in modern business, they do not escape criticism. By examining these critiques, companies can refine their approaches to truly embody the transformative shift toward environmental and social responsibility this book champions.

One of the most pertinent criticisms arises from ESG's complexity and lack of standardization. Despite numerous frameworks and reporting standards, the practical application of ESG criteria can be inconsistent and confusing. This disparity can make it challenging for investors and stakeholders to evaluate and compare company performances accurately, potentially undermining the efficacy of ESG as a tool for driving corporate accountability.

Moreover, critics argue ESG metrics can be manipulated to present a favorable image of a company's sustainability efforts, a practice known as greenwashing. This can lead to a focus on superficial changes that benefit a company's image more than they contribute to substantial environmental or social improvements. Without rigorous verification processes, there is a risk that ESG standards could be utilized more for public relations than impactful change

Additionally, while ESG aims to align with broader societal values, there is a critique that it imposes a one-size-fits-all approach that may not be culturally sensitive or applicable across different global contexts. What may be considered socially responsible or environmentally sound in one region can be seen quite differently in another, complicating the global implementation of ESG principles.

Another critique concerns the dominance of large companies in shaping ESG standards, which can inadvertently marginalize the voices and needs of smaller enterprises, local communities, and Indigenous populations. This may entrench the power imbalances ESG seeks to rectify, ultimately contradicting its own mission.

Detractors also point to evidence that ESG does not always lead to improved financial performance. While there have been examples of ESG-aligned companies outperforming their less-sustainable peers, the relationship between ESG practices and financial success is not universally substantiated. This raises questions about using ESG factors as a proxy for company quality or resilience.

Another line of criticism comes from a perceived overemphasis on governance at the expense of environmental and social components. Although governance is undoubtedly vital for a well-run organization, it can often be quantified and managed more easily than environmental or social impact, which may lead businesses to prioritize it disproportionately.

There is also a delicate balancing act between holding businesses accountable for their ESG performance and allowing them the flexibility to innovate and adapt to changing sustainability challenges. Critics warn that overly prescriptive or rigid ESG criteria could stifle innovation and distract from adaptive strategies that could lead to more significant environmental and social benefits.

In view of these critiques, it is crucial to recognize not only does ESG face practical limitations, but its philosophical underpinnings are also challenged. Critics argue ESG is still deeply rooted in the capitalist system that often gives rise to the environmental and social issues it aims to address. Amid this context, there is skepticism about whether ESG can genuinely foster the necessary transformative change or simply serve as a modest adjustment within an unsustainable status quo.

ESG's focus on current stakeholder engagement can also be criticized for not fully considering the rights and needs of future generations. Sustainable development principles emphasize we must meet our current needs without compromising the ability of future generations to meet theirs. ESG standards may need to develop further to embody genuinely long-term thinking and responsibility.

Finally, there is a growing discussion about the moral foundation of ESG. Some suggest that by focusing on quantifiable metrics, ESG may commodify ethical considerations, reducing moral questions to data points that can be traded and measured, rather than engaging with more ethical deliberations.

To navigate these critiques and enhance the efficacy of ESG, it will be essential for companies to undertake rigorous internal assessments and engage a wide range of stakeholders in their ESG strategy development. By acknowledging these criticisms, businesses can evolve their practices beyond mere compliance and toward stoking the fires of a transformative shift that embeds ecological and social ethics deep within their operations, fostering a brighter and more sustainable future for all.

Developing and Implementing Sustainability KPIs

In the strategic quest for a more sustainable, equitable future, harnessing the power of metrics stands as a critical component. Key Performance Indicators (KPIs), especially those centered on sustainability, provide a tangible way for organizations to measure the efficacy of their environmental and social efforts, thereby implementing change that is both significant and observable.

The first step in developing meaningful sustainability KPIs is to align them with the core values and strategic objectives of a business. This realignment makes the intangible tangible, transforming broad company visions into precise points of focus. Sustainability KPIs should not only resonate with a company's mission, but also inspire actionable steps toward that mission's realization.

It's imperative to engage stakeholders—employees, customers, suppliers, and community members—in the development of these KPIs. The inclusion of varied perspectives not only cultivates a sense of shared purpose, but also enhances KPI relevance across diverse interaction points within the company's ecosystem.

Setting SMART (Specific, Measurable, Achievable, Relevant, and Time-bound) sustainability KPIs is the cornerstone of effectuating genuine change. Be it reducing energy consumption, minimizing waste, or enhancing labor practices, KPIs should be clear-cut and quantifiable. Such precision enables continuous progress tracking and ensures accountability.

Well-defined KPIs must strike a balance between ambition and practicality. Setting the bar too low will not drive the necessary change, whereas excessively aspirational goals may result in demoralization if they're perceived as unattainable.

Data collection for these KPIs can't be an afterthought. It requires an initial establishment of reliable data sources and rigorous methodologies to prevent any distrust or skepticism about the integrity of performance reporting.

The integration of sustainability KPIs extends beyond internal processes and into the supply chain. It necessitates businesses to work closely with suppliers to establish KPIs that reflect the sustainability values upheld throughout the entire production cycle.

Implementing sustainability KPIs often mandates modifications in business processes. These changes must be managed skillfully to minimize disruption while maximizing positive outcomes. This often means fostering a culture that supports continuous improvement and innovation.

Additionally, consistency in KPI reporting is vital. The metrics should be revisited regularly to reflect changes in the company's strategy, market conditions, and regulatory environment. This dynamism ensures KPIs evolve alongside the business, maintaining their relevance and effectiveness.

Transparency in communication about KPIs and their performance is key for building trust and credibility among stakeholders. Businesses should openly share both successes and areas for improvement. Celebrating milestones stimulates morale, while acknowledging shortcomings provides valuable lessons for future endeavors.

Moreover, the comparability of sustainability KPIs is crucial for benchmarking against industry peers. This allows businesses to understand their performance in the broader context and drives industry-wide competition for sustainability excellency.

Technology plays a pivotal role in tracking and managing KPIs. Digital tools facilitate a seamless flow of information, ensure accurate data collection, and enable real-time performance monitoring. This technological leverage is a game changer for comprehensive sustainability management.

Businesses need to remain cognizant of the limitations of KPIs. While they serve as powerful tools for measurement and accountability, they cannot capture every nuance of sustainability. Qualitative assessments and narratives are indispensable companions to KPIs, providing the context and stories behind the numbers.

Ongoing education and training ensure all employees not only understand the KPIs, but also recognize their role in achieving them. When an organization's human capital is mobilized toward common sustainability goals, the likelihood of accomplishing them multiplies exponentially.

In conclusion, the thoughtful development and diligent implementation of sustainability KPIs catalyze the transformative shift toward a more responsible business paradigm. These KPIs are not just measures of performance, but also instruments of change—scaffolding the business journey toward a sustainable and regenerative future.

Patience and persistence in this endeavor are prerequisites, as the fruits of these labors will not only redefine the essence of success, but also rewrite the relationship between business and the biosphere.

The Future of Sustainability Reporting

The context of business is transforming, with the nexus of sustainability and ethics reshaping the corporate world. As we focus on the future of sustainability reporting, it's essential to contemplate not just where we are, but where we need to go. Evolving from traditional sustainability reporting, businesses are now on the brink of adopting more dynamic, integrative, and strategic reporting frameworks that accommodate the rapid changes in our Environmental, Social, and Governance (ESG) landscapes.

The emerging future demands businesses go beyond mere compliance and proactively demonstrate their commitment to ethical practices and sustainability. Dynamic sustainability reporting serves as a communication tool that reflects an organization's journey toward sustainable development, while also capturing its impact on the global sustainability movement.

Currently, there are several established sustainability reporting standards, such as the Global Reporting Initiative (GRI), the Sustainability Accounting Standards Board (SASB), and the Task Force on Climate-related Financial Disclosures (TCFD). However, as the landscape evolves, we are beginning to see a convergence of these standards into a unified framework that holds the potential for more cohesive and comparable reporting.

Future sustainability reporting must accommodate the increasing sophistication of data analytics and the incorporation of digital technology. The integration of artificial intelligence (AI) and blockchain into reporting mechanisms will enhance accuracy, consistency, and traceability of reported data, thus, providing stakeholders with more reliable information.

Another important facet is the shift toward forward-looking sustainability disclosures. Stakeholders are not only interested in what companies have done, but also their future sustainability targets and how they plan to achieve them. This includes their responsiveness to climate risks and their commitment to innovation that supports the transition to a low-carbon economy.

Reports will start to reflect not just financial information, but also how companies affect—and are affected by—natural, human, and social capital. This shift to integrated reporting will be vital for businesses to convey a truly comprehensive view of their operations, ethics, and contributions to sustainability.

Transparency will remain a cornerstone of sustainability reporting. However, the need for transparency will drive deeper connections between what a company reports and what it does. Meaningful stakeholder engagement and public scrutiny will continue to pressure companies to match their reporting with genuine action, thereby fostering accountability and trust.

The future will also see a stronger regulatory push for sustainability reporting. Governments around the world are beginning to mandate non-financial disclosures, and this trend will likely intensify, leading to more standardized and enforceable reporting guidelines. It's also possible the cost of not participating in sustainability reporting will increase, be it through regulatory penalties, investor actions, or public opinion.

Materiality in reporting will also evolve, with companies needing to navigate the changing definitions of what is material—not just to the business but to a broader set of stakeholders, including the environment and society at large. Material issues will not only encompass current impacts, but also consider long-term effects, requiring companies to take a more far-sighted approach to their business strategies and reporting practices.

One of the most-significant transformations in the realm of sustainability reporting will be the enhanced focus on societal outcomes.

Businesses will increasingly be expected to report on how their sustainability efforts contribute to societal goals, such as the Sustainable Development Goals (SDGs). This illustrates a company's broader purpose and its role in supporting a sustainable and equitable future.

Furthermore, the role of the auditor and assurance services in sustainability reporting will expand, lending more credibility to sustainability disclosures. Assurance can provide stakeholders with confidence that the sustainability information presented by companies is accurate, complete, and reliable. This trend will likely drive improvement in reporting quality over time.

Additionally, cross-sector collaboration will impact the future of sustainability reporting. Businesses, standard-setters, academics, and non-governmental organizations will need to work together to refine reporting measures, ensuring they are meaningful, manageable, and drive progress toward sustainable practices.

Finally, the way businesses report on sustainability must embrace inclusivity and diversity, ensuring the voices of all stakeholders are heard and represented. This will not only enrich the reporting process, but also reinforce the ethical dimension that underpins the entire sustainability endeavor.

In summary, the future of sustainability reporting is set to be more integrated, predictive, and aligned with the transformative shift in business practices. As we look ahead, it is clear sustainability reporting will continue to be an essential tool for businesses to demonstrate their commitment to ethical and sustainable operations, thereby influencing the global sustainability movement positively.

Chapter 14:
Government Policies and Corporate
Accountability

A
s we delve into the critical interface between governmental frameworks and corporate conduct, this chapter disentangles the complex web that binds regulatory measures to corporate accountability. Government policies are not just enforcers of compliance but can serve as a catalyst for igniting the spark of ecological and social responsibility within the corporate fabric.

The call for a symbiotic relationship between public regulators and private entities can't be overstated; it has the potential to transform the landscape of sustainable business practices. Regulation, though often viewed as a barrier, can be designed creatively to incentivize transformative corporate behavior, thus forging pathways for companies to align with the greater good. Harmonizing these policies with corporate strategies involves leveraging public-private partnerships that pool resources, knowledge, and influence toward shared sustainability goals.

Additionally, firms carry a weighty responsibility to advocate for policies that do not merely protect their bottom lines but sustain the planet and its inhabitants. As agents of change within their industries, companies have the clout to drive policy change, leading to a future where corporate advocacy reflects a commitment to the environmental stewardship and societal well-being. This chapter challenges corporations to rise to the occasion, not as reluctant followers of governance but as proactive champions of an ethic that marries profitability with planetary preservation.

Regulation and Incentives for Sustainable Business Practices

In the quest for a harmonious balance between economic growth and environmental stewardship, governmental regulation and incentives emerge as pivotal instruments. As the tide of public opinion turns increasingly toward finding solutions to our ecological crisis, governments around the globe are compelled to lay down the gauntlet: legislation and frameworks that hold corporations accountable for the environmental impact of their operations.

Regulation takes many forms, from mandating transparent reporting of greenhouse gas emissions to enforcing limits on resource extraction. Such laws serve as the guardrails on the highway of commerce, ensuring business pursuits do not veer off into unsustainable practices. Despite the perception of regulations being burdensome, they are essential to leveling the playing field and compelling industry leaders and laggards alike to adhere to minimum sustainability standards.

However, the role of government isn't merely to regulate; it is also to inspire and facilitate the adoption of sustainable practices. Incentives such as tax benefits, subsidies, and grants are powerful tools that can encourage businesses to innovate and integrate sustainability into their core strategies. They function as catalysts, accelerators of progress in the realm of ecological and social ethics within the corporate landscape.

One of the most-significant incentives for businesses is the capacity to enhance their reputation and brand value. Companies that lead in sustainability often enjoy a more positive public image, which can translate into customer loyalty and increased market share. Moreover, aligning with sustainable principles can foster greater employee satisfaction and attract top talent, further strengthening a company's competitive advantage.

The Responsibility

In recent years, there has been a surge in Environmental, Social, and Governance (ESG) criteria, forming a cornerstone for investment decisions. This shift in investor sentiment underscores the need for solid regulatory frameworks and incentive systems that reward organizations for prioritizing sustainability and ethics.

Effective government policies can also promote sustainable innovation. By setting ambitious yet attainable targets, such as renewable energy goals or waste reduction milestones, businesses are pushed to rethink their processes and products from the ground up. The result is often a blossoming of creativity, leading to breakthroughs that may have otherwise remained dormant.

The intersection of regulation, incentives, and voluntary corporate sustainability initiatives can create a potent mix for transformative change. Case in point, the advent of carbon pricing mechanisms in certain jurisdictions puts an explicit cost on carbon emissions, encouraging companies to decrease their carbon footprint. It showcases a model where regulatory measures and market-based instruments can conjure a financially tangible rationale for businesses to invest in cleaner technologies.

However, the path is not without obstacles. The complexity of global supply chains and divergent international regulations can result in a patchwork of standards, sometimes leading to confusion and compliance difficulties. This highlights the urgency for not just national but global consensus on the fundamental principles of sustainability law.

Furthermore, the onus is on governments to ensure incentives are not merely short-term sweeteners but part of a long-term strategic vision. It's about creating an economic environment where sustainability is not just viable but is the most-sensible business decision.

Another dimension is the role of public-private partnerships (PPP). These collaborations can drive sustainability into sectors traditionally seen as resistant to change. By sharing expertise, risk, and rewards, PPPs can execute large-scale projects with sustainability baked into their DNA, from infrastructure to energy solutions.

For local economies, incentive programs tailored to sustainability can stimulate job creation in emerging industries such as renewable energy, while also addressing social issues such as income inequality and access to education. These programs offer a blueprint for a more inclusive economic model that integrates the well-being of both people and planet.

As we look toward the horizon, the role of legal frameworks and incentives in shaping a sustainable future cannot be underestimated. Governments and policymakers bear a weighty responsibility to craft policies that not only protect our environment, but also unleash the innovative potential of businesses striving to do good.

Ultimately, the success of these policies will be judged by their impact. Do they lead companies to alter their trajectory toward a more sustainable and equitable future? The answer lies in a delicate balancing act—one that demands foresight, adaptability, and an unwavering commitment to the ethical imperatives at the heart of sustainability.

Public-Private Partnerships: Collaboration for the Common Good

As we delve into the heart of corporate accountability within the sphere of government policies, the role of public-private partnerships (PPPs) cannot be overstated. These collaborations, formed between government entities and private sector companies, are instrumental in advancing a common good, a premise deeply embedded in sustainable development and environmental stewardship. The essence of such partnerships stems from the acknowledgment that no single entity holds all the keys to the complex challenges we face in sustainability.

Historically, PPPs have navigated infrastructure projects and service delivery with varied success. Today, these partnerships are increasingly seen as pivotal in driving large-scale environmental initiatives that require the innovation and agility of the private sector as well as the regulatory powers and broad reach of public institutions. A functional and ethical PPP model can lead to shared value—benefiting not just the partners involved but society at large.

The ethical dimensions of PPPs are particularly potent. When governments and businesses unite with a shared vision, the implicit social contract is reinforced. Each party must act not only on behalf of its immediate interests, but also for the welfare of the community they serve. This means integrating social and environmental considerations into project planning, execution, and beyond, ensuring sustainability is not just a byline, but a core objective.

For businesses, engaging in PPPs is an opportunity to transcend the traditional corporate boundaries, showcasing a commitment to not just profit, but also responsibility toward the planet and its inhabitants. These collaborations strengthen corporate accountability by aligning business operations with public welfare goals, creating transparency and fostering trust. Companies involved in such partnerships are often subject to heightened scrutiny, motivating them to adhere to rigorous ethical standards.

From a policy perspective, governments can leverage PPPs to meet their environmental and social targets, delivering outcomes that may be beyond their capabilities when working in isolation. By harnessing private sector competencies in technology, management, and finance, public agencies can accelerate environmental programs and conservation efforts, moving toward the realization of international agreements such as the Paris Climate Accord.

One inspiring example of a successful PPP is the collaboration between government agencies and renewable energy companies to transition toward low-carbon economies. These initiatives have not only reduced greenhouse gas emissions, but also demonstrated the economic viability of sustainable energy solutions, incentivizing further private investment in this domain.

Yet, PPPs are not without their challenges. Concerns, such as the alignment of objectives, equitable risk-sharing, and ensuring the public's interests are paramount, have to be navigated with diligence. Structured dialogue and clearly defined agreements are fundamental to address these issues and to demarcate responsibilities and benefits transparently.

Monitoring and evaluating the impact of PPPs is another critical aspect. Accountability metrics must be established at the onset, allowing for the assessment of environmental performance and social outcomes. This assessment enables both parties to measure progress, make informed adjustments, and celebrate achievements in a structured manner.

Furthermore, PPPs should strive for inclusivity, engaging with communities and allowing for local perspectives to inform project development and implementation. Such engagement can lead to improved project outcomes, greater local economic development, and enhanced community support for the initiatives underway.

To incentivize PPPs, governments often deploy supportive frameworks, including tax incentives, subsidies, or guarantees that mitigate some of the financial risks for private sector participants. These incentives should be judiciously crafted to ensure they effectively promote sustainable practice while maintaining fiscal responsibility and accountability.

Technology, too, plays a crucial role in contemporary PPPs. Innovations in areas such as carbon capture, sustainable infrastructure, and waste management are frequently at the center of such collaborations, with both government support and private expertise critical to their advancement.

In conclusion, the potential of PPPs in the realm of sustainability is immense. As the demand for corporate responsibility intensifies, PPPs stand out as collaborative potential. Their capacity to align government policy with corporate practice in pursuit of shared environmental and social goals makes them an unparalleled catalyst for positive change.

As we embrace partnerships that foster the common good, the benchmark of success for any PPP should be the extent to which it contributes to a sustainable and equitable future. For businesses, this translates into a critical evaluation of their long-term strategies, ensuring partnership opportunities are utilized to reinforce their commitment to ethical, environmentally conscious operations.

Ultimately, the synergy between public agencies and private organizations can lead to transformative outcomes, creating legacies that transcend the lifespan of individual projects. By embracing the power of collaboration, we edge closer to the vision of a harmonious coexistence with our planet, securing the well-being of generations to come.

Corporate Advocacy and Policy Influence

Corporations have risen to a level of influence in society that was perhaps unimaginable a century ago. Today, their impact extends beyond economics, reaching deep into the political and social spheres. Given the urgency of the sustainability challenges we face, understanding and guiding this influence toward positive change is not just beneficial but essential. Corporate advocacy can and should be a critical tool for molding the policy landscape to foster environmental stewardship and social responsibility.

The ability of corporations to influence policy is largely predicated on their significant economic contributions and the jobs they create, which grant them an attentive audience among policymakers. However, with great power comes great responsibility. Indeed, how corporations engage with government policies can play a pivotal role in either hastening or hindering the march toward a more sustainable future.

Advocacy, when ethically conducted, can enhance the government's capacity to address complex issues by providing expert knowledge and resources. Conversely, policy influence that serves only the narrow interests of a corporation can lead to regulatory capture, where the welfare of the broader public is subordinated to corporate profit.

Corporations can advocate for sustainability by supporting regulations that protect the environment and voluntarily exceeding compliance standards to demonstrate the feasibility and benefits of such regulations. These actions send a powerful message that fiscal health need not come at the expense of environmental integrity.

Another avenue for ethical advocacy involves corporations taking a stand on social issues that resonate with their values and mission. Through lobbying efforts, businesses can push for progressive policies on topics such as renewable energy, equitable labor practices, and human rights protections, thereby aligning their corporate ethos with broader societal benefits.

However, the advocacy landscape is riddled with challenges. The risk of greenwashing—wherein a company's policy influence is merely a facade for improving its public image, rather than signifying genuine commitment to sustainability—is an ongoing concern. Credible corporate advocacy must be backed by transparent and consistent actions that reflect the company's public statements and policy positions.

Moreover, aligning corporate incentives with long-term societal and ecological well-being requires a reevaluation of the company's performance metrics. Sustainability must be embedded into the core strategy of the corporation, with clear and quantifiable accountability measures. By doing so, advocacy efforts become a demonstration of the company's core values and a strategic investment in its long-term viability.

Collaboration across sectors, including meaningful partnerships with non-governmental organizations (NGOs), can enhance the effectiveness and legitimacy of corporate advocacy. NGOs can provide invaluable knowledge, grassroots support, and ethical credibility to corporate policy initiatives. This collaboration is particularly impactful when targeting broad, systemic changes that resonate across multiple stakeholder interests.

Corporations should focus not only on advocating for beneficial policies, but also on defending against regressive measures that threaten sustainability progress. Resistance involves not just passive objection but proactive engagement in shaping the policy discourse and educating stakeholders about the benefits of sustainable practices and the risks of inaction or backsliding.

To influence policy responsibly, companies must engage in dialogue with a wide range of stakeholders, including those who may be adversely affected by proposed policies. This inclusive approach ensures policy advocacy accounts for diverse perspectives and mitigates any negative outcomes, upholding the company's commitment to ethical practices and social responsibility.

Public trust in corporate advocacy is contingent upon a record of genuine, verifiable contributions to sustainability goals. This trust is fundamental to the efficacy of any advocacy effort. Companies that transparently report their environmental and social performance, and then link these reports to their policy positions, help build and maintain trust with the public and within the policymaking community.

Ultimately, corporate advocacy for sustainability needs to be long term and consistent, rather than fluctuating with market trends or political cycles. A deep commitment to societal and environmental needs must transcend short-term gains and reflect a vision for a planet where both business and nature can thrive symbiotically.

To summarize, corporate advocacy is an indispensable tool in guiding public policy toward sustainability. However, its value is inherently tied to the authenticity and transparency of the corporation's commitments and practices. The challenge lies not in whether corporations will influence policy but in how and to what end they choose to wield that influence.

Realizing a sustainable future is an ambitious journey filled with immense challenges, but also with remarkable opportunities for visionary corporations that are willing to lead the way. As such, corporate advocacy must evolve to become a proactive, collaborative, and principled voice in the policy landscape, contributing to a legacy that future generations will look back on with gratitude.

Chapter 15:
The Role of NGOs and Universities in Shaping Business Sustainability

As the narrative of sustainability in business practices unfolds, it's become increasingly evident NGOs and academic institutions play pivotal roles in sculpting the contours of corporate responsibility. These organizations, often driven by altruistic goals, provide a deep well of knowledge and a formidable counterbalance to the profit-centric paradigms that have traditionally dominated the corporate world.

It can't be overstated how the contribution of NGOs, with their grassroots insights and activist leverage, are sparking transformative thought across boardrooms by acting as catalysts for ethical policy development and implementation. Their partnerships with businesses aren't just superficial collaborations but are often deeply integrated endeavors that push companies to adopt more ecologically sound and socially just practices.

Universities, with their hallowed halls of learning and research, pour forth a constant stream of innovative solutions, sustainability frameworks, and future thought leaders. They not only critique the ways in which businesses interact with the planet and its inhabitants, but also shape the sustainability discourse, empowering students—who are future professionals—with the tools to enact change within various industries.

The synergy between academia and organizations that refuse to let profit mute their responsibility can't but guide businesses through the uncharted territories of sustainable practice. Thus, these entities are not only educators and watchdogs, but also collaborators and innovators in the vital quest to embed sustainability into the very DNA of modern business practice.

NGO-Business Partnerships for Change

In a world where the challenges of sustainability grip the global consciousness, it's paramount we explore conduits for change that are not just effective, but also innovative. One such conduit is the synergistic relationship between non-governmental organizations (NGOs) and the business sector, which has emerged as a transformative force in pushing the boundaries of ethical and sustainable practices.

NGOs, with their grassroots connections and comprehensive understanding of social and environmental issues, provide invaluable insight into the complexities of sustainability. These organizations often drive progress as they catalyze change, drawing upon deep wells of expertise and advocacy. On the other hand, businesses hold the keys to implementation; their resources and reach can translate ideals into tangible outcomes. The convergence of these two spheres, therefore, sets the stage for partnerships that can address the multifaceted challenges of our time.

NGO-business collaborations bring a multitude of benefits. For NGOs, partnering with industry leaders can amplify their impact, ensuring sustainability efforts scale beyond niche interventions to affect mainstream business practices. Conversely, businesses can leverage NGO partnerships to navigate ethical quandaries, tapping into the social consciousness needed to align with societal expectations and stakeholder demands.

At the heart of impactful NGO-business partnerships lies a shared value principle, which transcends traditional philanthropic gestures such as corporate social responsibility programs. Instead, these partnerships strive for deeper integration of sustainability into the core business strategy, fostering mutual benefits in both social and economic terms.

This approach, however, requires a sea change in typical corporate behavior. It asks businesses to engage authentically, committing not just funds, but also a willingness to reevaluate and potentially overhaul operations, supply chains, and business models to align with sustainability goals.

Take, for instance, NGOs that work to protect marine ecosystems partnering with seafood companies to create sustainable fishing practices. Such alliances have led to the development of certification programs that ensure responsible sourcing and have a ripple effect across the industry, benefiting the environment, fisher communities, and end consumers.

Further examples can be found in partnerships that tackle the pressing issue of climate change. Businesses, in collaboration with environmental NGOs, are increasingly investing in renewable energy projects, contributing to a reduction in dependence on fossil fuels and accelerating the transition to a cleaner energy future.

Education is another realm where NGO-business collaborations have cultivated groundbreaking results. Initiatives to promote sustainability within academic curricula are flourishing, with businesses often providing real-world case studies, funding research, and facilitating internships. Such initiatives prepare the next generation of business leaders to prioritize and adeptly manage sustainability issues.

However, successful NGO-business partnerships don't materialize without challenges. One such challenge is balancing the often-differing organizational cultures and objectives. NGOs are primarily driven by their mission, while businesses focus on profitability and shareholder value. Finding common ground requires negotiation, transparency, and a shared understanding of the desired outcomes.

Moreover, there is a necessary deliberation over accountability and reporting. Ensuring progress is measurable and communicated effectively is key in maintaining trust, not just between partners, but also with the public, stakeholders, and policymakers. This is where the implementation of rigorous metrics and standards for sustainability, discussed in later chapters, becomes crucial.

Building on the intersection of trust and transparency, another pivotal area is the fight against greenwashing. As companies seek to portray their sustainable practices, partnerships with NGOs can lend credibility by substantiating claims and providing a framework for genuine, verifiable environmental stewardship.

The role of technology, particularly the emerging fields of blockchain and artificial intelligence, can enhance these partnerships by offering new tools for tracking and validating sustainability efforts. Innovations in this space have the potential to create a transparent, immutable record of a business's environmental and social impacts, laying bare the truth of their sustainability assertions.

Yet, the ultimate measure of an NGO-business partnership's success is its real-world impact. Whether it's improving livelihoods, safeguarding biodiversity, or contributing to the global fight against climate change, the true testament of these partnerships lies in the tangible changes they effectuate. These changes feed into global sustainability initiatives such as the Sustainable Development Goals (SDGs), offering a pathway to a more equitable and sustainable future.

To encapsulate, NGO-business partnerships are not just a hopeful strategy but an imperative one for achieving sustainability in an era of global interconnectivity and shared challenges. Embodying the ethos of combining the "head and the heart," they are a force that can, and should, be harnessed to steer us toward a resilient and conscientious business landscape.

Influencing Corporate Policies Through Activism

The relentless push for progress in business sustainability owes much to the concerted efforts of NGOs and universities, but it is also increasingly driven by powerful activism that targets corporate policies directly. Activism operates across multiple platforms—from peaceful demonstrations to social media campaigns—and has become a critical force in steering corporations toward more sustainable practices.

As movements for environmental and social justice gain momentum, they challenge companies to evolve beyond traditional business models. It's not simply about improving the bottom line; it's about acknowledging businesses hold a central role in creating a just and sustainable future. They're being called upon to take responsibility for their part in addressing pressing global issues, from climate change to social inequality.

Activists have honed in on corporate governance as a pivotal domain for change. Shareholder activism is one strategic avenue where investors leverage their stakes in a corporation to influence its behavior. More and more, socially conscious shareholders are using their voice and vote to push for corporate action on sustainability. These investors are not just large institutional players, but also individual shareholders who collectively can sway the direction of corporate policies.

The rise of social media has given activists a robust tool for wider outreach and mobilization. Digital campaigns can rapidly raise public awareness, shape perceptions, and apply pressure where it's most effective. By tapping into the connectedness of the digital age, activists amplify their cause and rally support on platforms that can make a corporate brand viral for the right—or wrong—reasons.

NGOs often take up the mantle in influencing corporate changes by crafting campaigns that inform, inspire, and mobilize public participation. Their work frequently entails exhaustive research to unearth corporate practices that undermine sustainability, leading to compelling evidence that backs their campaigns.

Universities are influential as well, contributing a wealth of knowledge and informed critique of corporate practices. Academics bring forward rigorous analyses and independent perspectives that can underscore the urgency of corporate policy change. Their research often feeds into the foundations of activist campaigns, providing the credible data necessary to ground calls for action in fact.

Successful activism harnesses the power of collective will by enlisting consumers, who are pivotal to changing corporate behavior. Consumer boycotts and "buycotts" can directly impact a company's bottom line, demonstrating the public's will to support brands that align with their values and to reject those that don't.

Furthermore, corporate social responsibility (CSR) has ceased to be a peripheral concern; it is now often a core strategic element shaped by external pressures from activists and civil society organizations. Companies are finding proactive engagement with activists can offer insights and pave the way for meaningful policy changes.

There are also collaborative efforts where activists work alongside companies to foster sustainability initiatives. These partnerships can lead to transformative changes within industries that cascade down supply chains, effecting wide-reaching improvements in sustainability.

Activism also leads to transformation through the legal and regulatory frameworks. Campaigns often target policymakers to enact legislation that compels companies to adopt sustainable practices. By influencing policy, activism ensures sustainability becomes not just an option but a mandate for corporate compliance.

Direct action is another influential tactic where activists physically intervene to prevent environmentally destructive practices. While this method can entail legal risks, it often brings vivid attention to issues that may otherwise remain under the radar of public discourse.

Corporate policies are increasingly informed by the principles of environmental justice, which assert the equal right of all to a healthy environment. Activism rooted in these principles champions sustainability not only for the sake of the environment, but also for the welfare of communities disproportionately impacted by corporate practices.

As conversations around sustainability evolve, there is a growing acknowledgment of the role of emotional engagement in activism. Campaigns that tell the human stories behind the statistics, particularly when those stories involve vulnerable populations, resonate powerfully with both the public and corporate leaders.

Some critics, however, warn against the dangers of performative activism, where companies adopt sustainability language without actual policy change. This concern only underscores the importance of vigilant and continuous activist engagement to ensure corporate shifts toward sustainability are genuine and not merely superficial branding exercises.

In the end, influencing corporate policies through activism is a dynamic and multifaceted endeavor. It draws upon the collective passion for a sustainable future, harnessing the power of the crowd to drive the change that no single entity could achieve alone. It is through these concerted efforts that corporations are being reshaped, reflecting a growing awareness that business and ethics can—and must—coexist.

Sharing Expertise: NGO Contributions to Sustainability Knowledge

Non-governmental organizations (NGOs) have emerged as pivotal players in the evolution of sustainability knowledge, bridging the gaps between academia, corporations, and civil society. NGOs contribute to the sustainability discourse not merely by providing a voice for the marginalized, but also acting as repositories of specialized knowledge and expertise. They harness their unique position to advocate for the environment, influence corporate practices, and enable knowledge sharing on a global scale.

Their role in sustainability is multifaceted, often starting with research and data collection. NGOs invest substantial resources in understanding complex environmental issues, from climate change impacts to biodiversity conservation. This research is then translated into actionable intelligence businesses can use to align their operations with sustainable principles. NGOs serve as sense-makers, distilling technical environmental data into comprehensible insights for company stakeholders.

Armed with evidence-based research, NGOs engage in awareness-raising initiatives. By sensitizing the public and private sectors to the nuances of ecological degradation and social inequities, they create a groundswell of demand for sustainable business practices. These efforts are not just about spreading information; they are designed to elicit a strong emotional commitment to sustainability, which further galvanizes change.

One example of how NGOs share knowledge is through creating sustainability benchmarks and guidelines. Tools such as the Global Reporting Initiative (GRI) or the Carbon Disclosure Project (CDP) have been influential in providing frameworks that assist businesses in measuring and reporting on sustainability performance. Utilizing such benchmarks allows companies not only to evaluate their progress, but also to communicate their achievements in a credible and standardized manner.

Additionally, NGOs are adept at fostering collaboration among various stakeholders. By convening forums that bring together industry leaders, policymakers, and academics, NGOs facilitate the exchange of sustainability best practices. This allows for the cross-pollination of ideas and leads to innovative solutions that may not have been developed in institutional silos.

Knowledge-sharing by NGOs also extends to providing training and education to corporate employees. They recognize for businesses to become sustainable, there must be a workforce that is knowledgeable and skilled in sustainability concepts and practices. NGO-led workshops and seminars play a critical role in upskilling and reskilling employees to navigate the complexities of sustainable business.

In shaping public opinion, NGOs employ compelling narratives that encapsulate the urgency and ethical imperatives of sustainability. They harness storytelling as a powerful tool to promulgate sustainability knowledge, making the abstract tangible and the global local. Through these stories, they connect individual actions to larger environmental and social impacts, thus, sparking collective action toward a sustainable future.

Furthermore, NGOs provide technical assistance to companies seeking to embed sustainability into their operations. This involves helping businesses conduct environmental impact assessments, develop sustainability strategies, and implement corporate social responsibility (CSR) initiatives. This hands-on approach ensures sustainability is not just theoretical but operational within business contexts.

Their role extends beyond just advising businesses; they hold corporations accountable for their social and environmental impacts through various means, including campaigns, reports, and direct engagement with corporate boards. By doing so, they play a vital role in ensuring transparency and pushing businesses toward more ethical practices.

NGOs also serve as incubators for sustainable innovation, supporting research and development efforts that may be too risky or unprofitable for businesses to undertake independently. They provide a testing ground for new ideas and approaches, helping to catalyze breakthroughs in sustainable technologies and business models.

Beyond merely focusing on environmental aspects, NGOs also emphasize the social dimensions of sustainability. They advocate for inclusive business practices that respect human rights, labor standards, and community development. Their influence has been instrumental in bringing social concerns to the forefront of the corporate sustainability agenda.

In a globalized world, NGOs help businesses understand and navigate the complexities of international sustainability standards and protocols. They assist companies in complying with policies such as the United Nations Sustainable Development Goals (SDGs) and the Paris

Agreement, ensuring business strategies are aligned with global sustainability efforts.

Lastly, NGOs themselves often act as examples of sustainable practice. Many operate based on principles of environmental stewardship and social equity, providing a living blueprint for businesses seeking to transition toward sustainability. Their operational models and governance structures often reflect the ideals they champion, serving as proof of concept for sustainable enterprise.

In conclusion, NGOs play an indispensable role in sharing sustainability knowledge. Through their research, advocacy, and collaborative efforts, they catalyze the integration of sustainable practices in the business sector. By continuing to share their expertise, NGOs not only influence today's business operations, but also shape the sustainability leaders of tomorrow, fostering a more sustainable and equitable world.

Chapter 16:
Sustainable Finance: Investing in a Better Future

n the previous chapter, we explored the vital role of NGOs and universities in sculpting the contemporary sustainability landscape. Now, we pivot to unveil the transformative potential embedded within the financial sector in "Sustainable Finance: Investing in a Better Future." Here, money is more than a medium of exchange; it's an influential engine for change, propelling businesses and individuals toward an ethical future.

As the threads of social responsibility, environmental stewardship, and sound governance weave together, a combination of sustainable finance arises, constructed by green bonds and buoyed by impact investing. Investors are no longer mere bystanders but actively engage with their capital, aligning their monetary strategies with moral objectives, mitigating risks, and inaugurating new opportunities for growth. This visionary paradigm eclipses traditional investment logic, prompting a recalibration of financial mechanisms to champion eco-efficient and equality-driven outcomes.

In the pursuit of profit, the quintessence of investment agility is, thus, redefined, intertwining financial acumen with a noble directive: to safeguard our planet's future while fostering prosperity. For society to thrive and natural systems to rejuvenate, embracing these principles of sustainable finance is not just a choice—it's an imperative call to action, resounding with clarity and a surge of hope for the well-being of people and the environment alike.

Understanding Sustainable and Responsible Investing

Sustainable and responsible investing represents a powerful avenue through which capital can not only seek financial return, but also drive transformative progress toward environmental stewardship and social integrity. This investment philosophy extends beyond traditional financial analysis to include ethical considerations, thereby aligning investor values with broader societal goals. Through the incorporation of Environmental, Social, and Governance (ESG) criteria, investors can influence corporate behaviors, pushing them toward greater ecological sensitivity and social responsibility.

Indeed, sustainable investing challenges corporations to recognize their influence on the world's pressing issues, from climate change to social inequality, and to act responsibly in their pursuit of profit. Studies further demonstrate companies with robust sustainability practices may enjoy financial outperformance, presenting a compelling case for the integration of ESG factors as a prudent aspect of risk management and a catalyst for potential long-term outperformance. As this field evolves, investors play an increasingly pivotal role in shaping the future, not just in term of market trends, but in our global community's well-being and ethical progress.

Impact Investing

As we delve deeper into the correlation among ethics, sustainability, and profitability, one can't help but consider the burgeoning field of impact investing. This concept has swiftly moved from the periphery to the mainstream of financial discourse, representing a pivotal shift in the allocation of capital toward endeavors that provide tangible social and environmental benefits alongside financial returns.

Impact investing challenges the traditional financial assumption that social and environmental issues should be addressed by philanthropic donations and that market investments should focus solely on achieving financial returns. Instead, it posits that the two can be synergistically linked. Investors are increasingly seeking opportunities that reflect their values, and firms that can measurably contribute to social or environmental outcomes are becoming attractive investment targets.

The underpinnings of impact investing rest on the belief that businesses have a significant role to play in solving critical global issues. This aligns with the broader ethos where corporate responsibility and sustainability are seen as cornerstones for modern business practices. Companies attuned to this approach are not merely embracing it for altruism; they are invariably positioning themselves for long-term growth and resilience by addressing the root causes of social and environmental challenges.

Often, impact investments are directed toward sectors such as renewable energy, sustainable agriculture, healthcare, education, and social housing. These projects are not just profitable; they offer solutions to the pressing global problems highlighted in international agendas such as the United Nations Sustainable Development Goals (SDGs). By contributing to these goals, businesses and investors can drive progress on a wide scale while creating a positive legacy of change.

In a world where consumer consciousness is rising, businesses that ignore their broader impact risk alienating not only potential investors, but also customers. A brand aligned with positive impact can tap into a growing demographic that values ethical consumption. It's no longer merely about the product or service; it's about the story behind it, the people involved, their well-being, and the environmental footprint left by its creation.

The financial instruments utilized in impact investing are diverse, including, but not limited to, private equity, public debt, venture capital, and fixed-income products. What distinguishes these instruments is not their form, but their intent; they are designed with terms that reflect the measurable success of the impact alongside financial returns. As such, they may include features such as revenue-sharing agreements that benefit a community, or environmental credits generated by green operations.

For an investment to be genuinely impactful, it cannot sacrifice due diligence and profitability. Impact investments aren't charity; they are rooted in the stringent analysis of market trends, local community needs, and long-term sustainability. Investors leverage a variety of metrics and standards to assess the potential impact, as well as the financial viability, of their investments. Businesses that understand and can quantify their impact in clear terms will find themselves ahead of the competition when it comes to attracting investment.

However, the field of impact investing does come with its complexities. Measurements of impact are inherently challenging given their qualitative nature and the long-time horizons involved. Implementing a standard framework for quantifying social and environmental impact remains a topic of active discourse among academics and practitioners alike. Although various standards and metrics exist, such as the Global Impact Investing Network's IRIS+ system, there is still work to be done to establish universally accepted methodologies.

Risk management is another critical aspect within impact investing. As with any other type of investment, impact investments come with their specific risks related to market, political, and social factors, among others. Investors need to understand these risks fully and develop strategies to mitigate them, ensuring both impact and financial return objectives can be realized.

Collaborative efforts are essential in advancing the impact investing field. Investors, businesses, non-profits, and governments must work together to create conducive environments for impact investments to thrive. This could involve developing supportive policies, creating tax incentives, or providing guarantees to mitigate certain risks for investors. Public-private partnerships can also serve as powerful vehicles for scaling up impact investing and addressing the funding gaps for crucial projects.

The growth of impact investing reflects a broader societal call for transparency and accountability. Shareholders and stakeholders increasingly demand evidence of ethical business practices. Through impact investing, businesses and investors can demonstrate their commitment to these principles, not just in word but in deed, by tangibly improving communities and preserving the planet for future generations.

The future of impact investing appears vibrant. As both the demand for and the supply of impact investment opportunities grow, so too will the sophistication of the methodologies and instruments involved. Investors and companies that embrace this trend early on will likely have a competitive edge—they will be the shapers of a new business landscape, where success is measured not purely by financial metrics, but also by the positive impact woven into the fabric of their operations.

In conclusion, while challenges are inherent in anything worth pursuing, the trajectory of impact investing is set on a positive course. Its principles align with an ethical and sustainable future, holding the promise of a more equitable world where finance becomes a powerful force for good. The evolution of this movement will prove to be one of the most-telling indicators of our progress toward an authentically sustainable economy.

Socially Responsible Investing

Socially responsible investing embodies the spirit of our times, where the flux of ethical consciousness is seeping into the marrow of financial decision-making. In a world gasping for breath amidst environmental degradation and social inequities, a clarion call resonates—urging investors to look beyond mere profit and toward the impact of their capital.

At its core, socially responsible investing (SRI) is not a novel concept—its roots spire deep into historical substrates where religious and moral edicts screened investments incompatible with ethical values. As we stand at the crossroads of a paradigm shift, however, the modern incarnation of SRI unfurls as a multifaceted strategy integrating environmental, social, and corporate governance criteria into investment decision-making processes.

SRI endeavors to align personal or institutional values with investment portfolios, constructing a financial landscape that, in its growth, nourishes the soil from which it sprouts. The philosophy here is simple yet transformative: capital can be a catalyst for positive change. It advocates for investing in companies that exhibit a strong commitment to environmental stewardship, social justice, and ethical management— essentially, those that are poised to propel us into a sustainable future.

As readers embarking on this journey from various disciplines, the integration of SRI into the sustainable business narrative offers a converging point. The strategy forwards the premise that businesses should be accountable not just to shareholders but to a wider constituency—including workers, communities, and the very environment that sustains us all.

What is crucial to understand is that SRI is far from being a charitable sideshow—it is a robust financial tool that shapes the contours of the market itself. Studies have illuminated that portfolios calibrated with Environmental, Social, and Governance (ESG) principles can compete with and even surpass traditional investments in terms of financial returns. In essence, ethical and financial considerations are not mutually exclusive; they are complementary forces that, when harnessed together, conjure a powerful momentum for change.

Discerning investors engage in SRI by utilizing various approaches: negative screening to exclude industries such as tobacco or firearms; positive screening to identify industry leaders in sustainability; and thematic investments focusing on specific issues such as clean energy or humane working conditions.

Yet, alongside its financial appeal, SRI serves a much grander vision. It's an act of defying traditional paradigms that equate success solely with financial gain. It's a contribution to a world wherein companies thrive by heeding the call of environmental sanity and social equanimity. It's a testament to the belief that one's investments can echo one's values, sending forth ripples that mend a ruptured world.

The burgeoning interest in SRI is quantifiable; assets managed under responsible investment strategies have seen a substantial upsurge, ballooning into trillions of dollars globally. This swelling tide is not just a wave of transient enthusiasm; it hints at a restructuring of investor psyche and a redefinition of what constitutes a desirable investment.

What firms must come to terms with is that investors are increasingly interpreting corporate performance through the prism of ethical lenses. The rise of shareholder activism signifies a more proactive stance where investors are not merely passive purveyors of capital but are engaged and vocal participants demanding ethical conduct and transparency in operations.

For businesses maneuvering through these evolving landscapes, integrating SRI principles means attracting a wider pool of investors, fortifying reputation and brand value and, often, preempting the regulatory curve that bends inexorably toward sustainability. It represents an alignment with a progressive societal ethic—one that treasures not just economic vitality but the pulsating life of communities and the natural world. It's an investment in continuity—the continuity of the planet, of human societies, and of businesses themselves.

In the orchestration of SRI strategies, myriad challenges arise. The paucity of standardized, reliable ESG data can hinder informed investment decisions. The onus, thus, falls on regulatory bodies to cultivate a transparent environment where ESG reporting is systematic and comparable across industries. Furthermore, a compelling narrative must be maintained to persuade the investment community that long-term value is inextricably linked to sustainable practices.

This evolving nature of SRI taps into our innate desire to forge a legacy that outlives us. Investors are steadily recognizing that through the mindful allocation of capital, they have the extraordinary power to sculpt the economic terrain to reflect deeper human values. It is an evocative blend of pragmatism and idealism, a union of financial acumen with a moral compass—a sanctuary where the heart of investing beats in tandem with the heartbeat of global sustainability.

In conclusion, socially responsible investing stands as an indomitable pillar within the edifice of sustainable business. It harnesses the vigor of markets to chart a course toward a world where financial gain does not come at the expense of social equity and environmental integrity. The ascendancy of SRI is not a mere trend; it's a reflection of an awakening— a sign that we're inching closer to endorsing a more inclusive definition of prosperity, one where the wealth of the common good is the greatest dividend of all.

ESG Investing

As we dive deeper into the transformative shift toward sustainability, we encounter a burgeoning financial strategy that bridges the gap between ethical concerns and profit motives: ESG investing. This investment approach evaluates corporations not only on financial metrics, but also on how they perform in environmental stewardship, social responsibility, and governance integrity. It's here, within these layers of analysis, that investors can align their wealth with the well-being of people and the planet.

Environmental, Social, and Governance (ESG) criteria offer a lens through which investments can be scrutinized for their sustainable impact. Environmentally, this includes a company's energy use, resource conservation, and pollution management. Socially, it considers labor practices, product responsibility, and community relations. In terms of governance, it examines board composition, audit committee structure, and transparency. These criteria don't simply filter out the bad actors; they highlight the organizations leading the charge toward a sustainable future.

The Responsibility

Sustainable investing is rapidly growing, and ESG funds are now a prominent part of the financial markets. The allure of ESG investing lies not only in the social and environmental benefits, but also in the financial returns, which have often matched or even exceeded traditional investments. This challenges the outdated belief that ethical considerations come at the expense of profit, proving these dynamics can coexist harmoniously.

For the sustainability professional, understanding ESG is crucial. It's a language of valuation that translates eco-friendly and ethical actions into quantifiable data investors can understand. Gone are the days when the social impact was unmeasurable. Today, a range of tools and services exist to evaluate a company's ESG performance, integrating such data into mainstream investment analysis.

Yet, ESG investing is not without its critics. The complexity and variability in how criteria are applied lead to concerns about standardization and greenwashing—the practice of over-emphasizing or overstating a company's eco-friendly initiatives. Transparency and credibility in reporting practices are of utmost importance and they serve as the bedrock against which greenwashing is measured.

Another challenge faced by ESG investing is the dynamic nature of what constitutes sound social or environmental practice. As our understanding of sustainable business evolves, so, too, must the metrics that define ESG. The rigidity of some reporting frameworks may lag behind innovative sustainability practices; thus, investors must remain agile and informed to ensure their investments genuinely reflect current best practices.

Corporate advocacy plays a significant role in the ESG narrative. Companies active in policy discussions about sustainability may both influence and get ahead of regulatory changes. Engaging with these issues at a policy level demonstrates a deeper level of commitment to corporate responsibility, one that ESG-minded investors find appealing.

Further compounding the growth of ESG investing are the societal shifts toward sustainability, particularly amongst younger generations. Millennials, for example, are twice as likely to invest in companies targeting social or environmental goals. As these generations accrue wealth and investable assets, the demand for ESG options will likely continue to expand.

This growing interest in ESG investing is more than a trend; it is part of a larger cultural shift in which the public expects businesses to play a positive role in society. The realm of investing, once siloed from moral considerations, is joining the broader movement toward a sustainable and equitable future.

As we progress through this era of corporate change, a compelling argument for ESG investing emerges: companies integrating sustainable practices are positioning themselves for success in a changing global economy. Climate change, resource scarcity, and shifting societal values are creating new market realities. Investors now seek to mitigate risks associated with these macro trends by choosing companies that are proactively addressing them.

One of the key elements in the advancement of ESG investing has been the development of reporting standards and frameworks. Organizations such as the Global Reporting Initiative (GRI) and the Sustainability Accounting Standards Board (SASB) lay out comprehensive reporting guidelines that enable comparability among companies and industries. The standardization of ESG reporting facilitates informed decision-making for investors.

Additionally, ESG investing champions the concept that firms can generate competitive financial returns while accelerating positive social or ecological outcomes. It's the confluence of pragmatic financial decisions and altruistic intentions. As ESG investment strategies mature, they will continue to reshape the contours of finance and investment for a more sustainable world.

Ultimately, the success of ESG investing is contingent upon a commitment to continuous improvement and adaptation. As methodologies evolve and awareness grows, ESG investing will not only reflect the ethical stance of investors, but also undeniably shape the trajectory of corporations worldwide.

The grand narrative here is that ESG is more than an investment criterion; it's a catalyst for the integrated thinking necessary in a world where business impacts every aspect of society and the environment. Embracing ESG investing is part of embodying the change we wish to see, channeling capital to support not only fiscal growth but the health of our communities and the Earth itself.

Therefore, let us be unwavering in our conviction that business, when conducted with foresight and humanity, can and should be a force for good. ESG investing is a voyage toward an inclusive, sustainable economy that nourishes not just our portfolios but our shared future as well. This is the paradigm shift we uphold—an investment not just in stocks or bonds but in the moral fabric of society, in the stewardship of the planet, and in the legacy we leave for generations to come.

The Growth of Green Bonds and Impact Investing

In the quest for a sustainable financial ecosystem, two powerful instruments have risen to prominence: green bonds and impact investing. These tools not only augment ethical business practices, but also provide a tangible pathway for investors to foster a sustainable and equitable future. The increased interest in green bonds demonstrates the financial sector's growing commitment to environmental stewardship, while impact investing redirects capital to ventures that generate social and environmental benefits alongside financial returns.

Green bonds, an exciting subset of fixed-income securities, have surged in popularity over recent years as a means to finance projects with environmental benefits. These bonds function similarly to traditional bonds, but their proceeds are exclusively applied to projects that have a positive impact on the environment, such as renewable energy infrastructure or sustainable water management. Their growth reflects not only the investors' appetite for responsible investments, but also the underlying shift toward valuing long-term ecological sustainability over short-term gains.

The issuance of green bonds is an open invitation for institutions to join in the creation of a low-carbon economy. These instruments offer organizations the means to raise capital explicitly earmarked for green initiatives. The transparency inherent in green bonds ensures investors are acutely aware of the positive environmental impacts their investments are facilitating. This clear linkage between investment and outcome helps align investors' financial goals with their ethical principles.

Impact investing, a close kin of green bonds, delves even deeper into the ethical investment realm. Unlike traditional investing, which often prioritizes economic return above all, impact investments intentionally target ventures that generate measurable environmental or social impacts while still providing financial gains. This dual-purpose strategy is particularly appealing for sustainability pioneers who seek not only economic success, but also a more significant societal contribution.

The true measure of impact investing lies in its intangible benefits, which ripple through communities and ecosystems. When investors engage with firms that prioritize societal welfare, they power a virtuous cycle of improvement and innovation that can shape the landscape of industries. These investments can potentially lead to groundbreaking technologies that minimize environmental impact or social programs that address systemic inequalities.

Understanding the nuances of both green bonds and impact investing is crucial for their effective deployment. Green bonds usually have specific environmental achievements as their target, providing an excellent vehicle for investments with a pinpointed environmental focus. On the other hand, impact investing can cast a wider net, addressing a broader range of social and environmental issues, such as education, healthcare, and social housing, alongside green projects.

A distinguishing feature of impact investments is their emphasis on tracking and reporting the social and environmental performance and progress, which are not typically part of traditional financial analysis. This level of accountability is paramount for investors who are equally vested in the ethical dimension and the financial return of their ventures.

The recent growth of green bonds and impact investing has been remarkable. It's a clear signal of a significant sector within finance that is stepping up to tackle environmental degradation and social challenges. This transition demonstrates the financial industry's inevitable gravitation toward a more deeply interconnected view of capital and its ability to instigate substantial change.

Yet, with this growth comes the responsibility to ensure these instruments deliver on their promises. That means not only continued vigilance over the deployment of funds from green bonds, but also the meticulous assessment of the actual societal impact of investments. While the inherent desire to contribute positively is commendable, thorough due diligence is essential to safeguard against well-intentioned investments that fall short of their impactful targets.

The scalability of green bonds and impact investing is another facet of their potential. Initially in the domain of pioneering institutions and investors, these instruments have now attracted a broader array of market participants. Large institutional investors, pension funds, and insurance companies have joined the movement, spurred by the demand for investments that support a transition toward sustainability.

Governments and municipalities are also playing an important role in promoting the growth of green bonds by issuing their own to fund local green initiatives or by providing incentives for their issuance. This governmental engagement is a testament to the collaborative effort between the public and private sectors required to drive the sustainability agenda forward.

Yet, despite their growth, green bonds and impact investments represent a relatively small portion of the overall investment landscape. It is an indicator that, while progress has been made, there remains substantial room for expansion and innovation within the field of ethical finance.

Future advancements in the sector may hinge on finding a balance between standardization and innovation. Too much rigidity could stifle the creativity required to tackle complex sustainability challenges, while too little could lead to confusion and ambiguity about what truly constitutes a "green" or "impact" investment.

As the worlds of finance and ethical sustainability continue to converge, it is crucial to educate and engage with investors about the importance and potential of green bonds and impact investing. This is not just a trend; it's the emergence of a new paradigm wherein our financial decisions reflect our values and our determination to invest in the health and well-being of our planet and its inhabitants.

By embracing the growth of green bonds and impact investing, we make a clear statement: finance can be a force for good. Our investments can build a resilient infrastructure, support communities in need, and catalyze innovations that safeguard resources for future generations. The onus lies with us, as stewards of capital, to harness these instruments effectively and ethically, enshrining a legacy that extends beyond wealth to well-being.

Aligning Financial Strategies with Ethical Goals

As we venture deeper into an era in which sustainability is not just a preference but a pressing necessity, the investment climate is undergoing a remarkable transformation. Steering this change are financial strategies that not only promise returns, but also encompass broader ethical goals. A key challenge businesses face today is marrying their financial ambitions with their ethical pursuits to create value that extends beyond the balance sheet.

The Responsibility

Historically, the pursuit of profit has often overshadowed the impact business activities have on the environment and society. The rise of sustainable finance is a testament to a growing recognition that financial success can, and should, go hand in hand with positive social and environmental outcomes. However, aligning financial strategies with ethical goals requires a deliberate shift in how investments are made, evaluated, and accounted for.

Impact investing—where investors actively seek out opportunities that generate a measurable beneficial social or environmental impact alongside a financial return—emerges as a shining example of this alignment. Through this lens, the traditional view of a trade-off between profit and purpose is challenged, suggesting financial performance need not be compromised for ethical goals to be achieved. It's a much-needed narrative that reshapes investor psychology and market dynamics.

Similarly, the burgeoning interest in Environmental, Social, and Governance (ESG) factors as integral to investment decisions reflects a broader understanding of risk and return. Incorporating ESG factors into financial analysis is quickly becoming standard practice, with evidence suggesting companies with robust ESG practices may enjoy better financial performance and lower risks. This trend underscores the interconnectedness of ethical performance and long-term corporate viability.

As businesses navigate the complexities of sustainable finance, they must address the crux of ethical dilemmas. Can they avoid investments that, while potentially profitable, contravene sustainability goals or social values? It's a question of drawing boundaries and standing firm on a set of principles, even if doing so may forego immediate gains.

Critical to this discussion is the concept of shareholder versus stakeholder value. The traditional focus on shareholder returns is giving way to a stakeholder-oriented approach that considers the interests of all parties affected by business activities—including employees, communities, and the environment. The stakeholder model aligns naturally with ethical goals, as it compels businesses to consider a more holistic set of outcomes in their financial strategies.

Green bonds offer another pathway for aligning financial strategies with ethical goals. These bonds, specifically earmarked to fund climate or environmental projects, allow investors to contribute directly to sustainability initiatives. The rapid growth in the issuance of green bonds indicates robust investor appetite for environmentally focused financial instruments.

Despite the opportunities, obstacles remain in creating full alignment. Take ambiguity in data and measurement, for example. While efforts to quantify the social and environmental impact of investments are improving, inconsistencies in metrics and reporting can lead to skepticism and limit broader participation in sustainable finance.

Furthermore, there is often a need for short-term sacrifices for long-term gains. Businesses must be willing to reevaluate timelines and return expectations to accommodate the sometimes-slower, yet more beneficial, pace of sustainable growth. In this light, patience becomes an asset, and foresight a necessity.

Transparency, too, is a central pillar in the alignment of financial strategies and ethical goals. Stakeholders demand clear information on how funds are used and the impact they generate. This calls for companies to adopt higher levels of disclosure and for the investment industry to standardize reporting practices around sustainability metrics.

Moreover, the collective action problem poses a unique challenge—while individual firms may strive to align their financial strategies with ethical objectives, the broader impact hinges on widespread adoption across the industry. Herein lies the role of collaborative efforts, industry standards, and regulatory frameworks. Collective action ensures the alignment between finance and ethics evolves from a competitive advantage to standard practice.

Although the process of aligning financial strategies with ethical goals is intrinsically complex, it is not insurmountable. It begins with the recognition of finance as a tool for transformation—a means to catalyze positive change within the boundaries of business. When wielded with foresight, intention, and ethical consideration, finance becomes a powerful ally in the pursuit of sustainability.

In the grand mosaic of sustainable finance, every thread—from green bonds and impact investing to ESG integration and stakeholder management—works in harmony to create a picture of a better future. As businesses and investors stitch together these threads, they craft financial strategies that support the vision of a world where ethical goals are not adjunct but integral to economic success.

In astonishing ways, the alignment of financial strategies with ethical goals presents a compelling case for businesses to be not just agents of wealth creation but champions of global sustainability. It showcases the potential of the financial sector to become a driving force for good, pushing the boundaries of what is profitable and what is beneficial for all.

Ultimately, the transition to sustainable finance reflects a deeper, fundamental shift in societal values and priorities. It embodies the conviction that the economic engines powering our progress must be recalibrated to acknowledge the finite nature of our planet and the shared destiny of its people. Only by aligning financial pursuits with ethical commitments can businesses truly invest in a better future for generations to come.

Risk Management in Sustainability Investment

In the landscape of sustainable finance, a crucial component that steers investment decisions toward fruition is risk management. Not merely a peripheral task or a compliance formality, risk management in sustainability investment is a proactive approach to ensuring the longevity and efficacy of every injected capital with an eye for environmental and social outcomes. This chapter delves deep into the nitty-gritty of managing risks associated with these noble initiatives, aligning financial resilience with the unwavering quest for a better future.

When investors or funds channel their resources into sustainable projects, they are inherently exposed to a unique set of risks, be it Environmental, Social, and Governance (ESG), or financial. The identification, assessment, and prioritization of such risks form the bedrock upon which strategies are built. Companies and investors alike must unveil potential pitfalls in projects not just at their inception but consistently throughout their life cycle.

Risk assessment must start with thorough due diligence, extending beyond traditional financial analysis to integrate ESG criteria. Investments wreathed in sustainability carry inherent uncertainties, such as regulatory changes, technological advancements, and shifts in consumer behavior—all of which can drastically affect a project's feasibility and outcome. The pursuit of sustainability must not neglect the scrutiny of these factors, lest we stumble into well-intentioned follies.

Environmental risks are especially pivotal elements to consider. They include the potential impacts of climate change, resource depletion, or pollution incidents, which may not only harm the environment, but also damage the financial stability of an investment. The challenge lies in projecting these risks under the influence of dynamic ecological systems and gauging their potential disruption to investment returns.

The social angle of risk in sustainable investments touches directly on the pulse of human welfare and social justice. From safeguarding labor rights to ensuring community consent, social risks, if mismanaged, can lead to intense public scrutiny and backlash. A robust risk management strategy must firmly ground itself in ethical human relations, aligning investment success with community progress highlights the significance of incorporating social considerations into risk assessment to enable sustainable outcomes for both investors and communities.

Governance risks are often more insidious in nature, as lapses in corporate governance, bribery, or lack of transparency can undermine an investment from its foundations. Ethical governance practices are a keystone of sustainable investment, fostering trust and ensuring accountability. Investors who meticulously assess these risks demonstrate commitment not only to financial returns, but also to the integrity of their operations in the sphere of sustainable finance.

Financial risk management in sustainable investment stretches beyond the customary balance sheet analysis. It acknowledges ESG factors can drive shifts in market trends and investor sentiments, thus, demanding a broader perspective that incorporates non-financial parameters as equally significant. Tools such as scenario analysis and stress testing against environmental or social upheavals can prepare investors for the capricious nature of the market with a sustainability focus.

Another risk is the so-called "impact dilution," where the proliferation of sustainability claims leads to a marketplace crowded with unsubstantiated or exaggerated sustainability credentials—a situation that can diminish the meaningful impact of truly committed sustainable investors. This risk calls for an unequivocal clarity in communication, underpinned by verifiable data and a transparent reporting paradigm that serves both the conscientious investor and the socially attentive consumer.

Liable as well to political risks, sustainable investments must navigate the tides of changing policies and government priorities. The support for sustainable projects can be heavily influenced by political will and regulatory frameworks. Investors must be agile in adapting to new laws and incentives while anticipating potential shifts in policy that could parlay into significant risks or opportunities.

The mitigation of these myriad risks is not without its tools and methodologies. Portfolio diversification remains a timeless strategy, particularly poignant when considering investments with differing ESG factors. Legal contracts and insurance mechanisms also play a central role in allocating and mitigating risks throughout the investment chain, ensuring investors are not left exposed to sudden unsustainable turns.

Yet, risk management in sustainability investment is not just about defense; it's equally about identifying opportunities where sustainable practices mitigate traditional risks. Investment in renewable energy, for example, skirts the volatilities inherent in fossil fuel markets and regulatory risks associated with carbon emissions—providing a stark example of how sustainability and risk aversion can walk hand in hand.

Engagement with stakeholders—communities, consumers, local governments—also informs risk management by providing insights into the concerns and expectations surrounding an investment. Transparency and dialogue can unearth potential risks before they manifest while concurrently building stakeholder trust and investment buy-in.

Innovation in financial instruments tailored for sustainable investment, such as green bonds and sustainability-linked loans, allows for the alignment of financial products with ESG objectives, creating mutually beneficial outcomes while managing risks. It anchors investor confidence not only on financial returns, but also on the tangible advancements in sustainability.

At its core, risk management in sustainability investment is an exercise in foresight and innovation. It demands we adapt traditional financial rigor to the imperatives of a world in ecological and social flux, a world that calls for shrewd investment not just as an economic engine, but as a vehicle for positive change.

Adopting these advanced risk management strategies propels sustainable finance from a niche endeavor to a cornerstone of mainstream investment portfolios. By critically analyzing and preempting the risks in sustainable investment, the financial sector can play its part in stewarding the Earth and its inhabitants toward a more secure, just, and flourishing future.

Chapter 17:
Education for Sustainability:
Raising Awareness and Building Skills

I n the quest to mold enterprises that are as conscious of their environmental impact as they are of their balance sheets, we hit a cornerstone: education. It's not enough to retrofit industries with the latest green tech; it's about nurturing a mindset that questions the status quo, looks to the long view, and prioritizes the planet's health as a measure of true success.

"Education for Sustainability: Raising Awareness and Building Skills" doesn't merely suggest we sprinkle some lectures on eco-friendliness into a corporate retreat. It's a deep-rooted call to thread sustainability through the very fabric of our learning institutions, corporate training programs, and continuous professional development arenas. We're talking about equipping people with not just the knowledge of why sustainability matters, but also the how-to of integrating sustainable practices wherever they may have influence. It's about instilling competencies that enable individuals to innovate, adapt, and lead in the face of a changing climate and resource constraints.

By constructing curricula that breathe sustainability, businesses can build a workforce that's robust in the capacity to foster ecological integrity and social equity—pillars of a society that can endure and thrive through the waves of challenges we're poised to face. The endgame is a collective of critically-thinking, skilled professionals who don't just implement someone else's sustainability plan but are empowered to be the architects of their own.

Integrating Sustainability into Corporate Training

The journey toward corporate sustainability is continuous and dynamic, requiring a shared language and understanding across all levels of an organization. To create a holistic approach that permeates every aspect of business operations, sustainability needs to be ingrained in corporate training programs. Integrating sustainability into corporate training is not only about enhancing employees' knowledge and skills, but also about fostering a transformative mindset that drives change.

Corporate training programs that focus on sustainability seek to impart the principles of environmental stewardship, social equity, and economic viability in a manner that aligns with a company's mission and values. This is essential, as a company can't make meaningful progress in sustainability without the commitment and understanding of its workforce.

Firstly, it is crucial to integrate sustainability into leadership development programs. Leadership at every level must understand their role in leading the change toward sustainable practices. By doing so, sustainability becomes a strategic priority steered by capable leaders who inspire their teams to follow suit. This echoes the belief that sustainable development demands leadership with the foresight and dedication to engage with complex, long-term issues.

Next, sustainability training must be tailored to the various functions within an organization. For example, procurement teams need training on ethical sourcing and environmental considerations, while marketing teams require knowledge on greenwashing and sustainable communication strategies. The relevance of the training to the everyday tasks of employees maximizes engagement and the application of sustainability principles within their job roles.

To contextualize sustainability, training programs should reflect on current global challenges and the impacts businesses have on environmental and social systems. Understanding the interconnectedness of business operations with broader societal issues is a critical step in recognizing the importance of making sustainable choices and the positive effect they can have.

Scenario-based learning can be a powerful tool in sustainability training. Presenting employees with real-life dilemmas and encouraging them to apply sustainable frameworks helps in developing critical thinking and ethical decision-making skills, which are fundamental to navigating the complex landscape of present-day business challenges.

Moreover, involving employees in the development of corporate sustainability policies and practices can enrich the training experience. This participatory approach can lead to a deeper organizational knowledge base and a more empowered and engaged workforce.

Active learning strategies, such as project-based learning, can support the practical application of sustainability learning objectives. When learners can engage in projects that bring positive, real-world impact, it reinforces the benefits of sustainable practices for people, the planet, and the business.

Measuring the impact of sustainability training is as important as the training itself. Companies must establish clear metrics to evaluate changes in employee behavior, improvements in sustainability practices, and the overall impact of these changes on the business and its stakeholders.

Technology plays a critical role in modern corporate training, enabling scalability and accessibility. Online learning platforms and simulation tools offer opportunities for employees to learn at their own pace and revisit complex subjects as needed, thereby reinforcing understanding and retention.

The success of sustainability training also hinges on its ongoing nature. Rather than being a one-off event, it should be a continuous learning journey that evolves with new sustainability insights and business standards. This lifelong learning approach ensures employees remain current with the latest sustainability trends and regulations.

Engagement in sustainability training should go beyond the walls of the corporation to include collaboration with external stakeholders. By creating partnerships with environmental organizations, NGOs, and academic institutions, businesses can enrich their training programs with external expertise and credibility while also aligning corporate and societal sustainability goals.

By embedding sustainability in corporate training, companies can foster a culture of continuous improvement. Employees become agents of change, equipped to initiate and support sustainability initiatives within and beyond their roles.

As corporate training programs regarding sustainability education continue, employees become more confident in integrating sustainable thinking into daily decision-making processes. This empowers them to actively contribute to the company's sustainability mission and helps build a more resilient and adaptable organization prepared for the future's inevitable shifts and pressures.

Finally, creating diverse and inclusive learning environments within sustainability training is important. Such spaces encourage a wide range of perspectives, leading to innovative approaches to complex problems. Diversity in thought and experience is a vital asset in navigating the multifaceted nature of sustainability challenges.

In conclusion, integrating sustainability into corporate training is not only a wise investment for future-proofing businesses, but also for contributing to the global movement toward a more sustainable and equitable society. Effective training equips individuals with the knowledge, skills, and mindset to drive positive change, making businesses not only more competitive, but also aligned with the ethical imperatives of our time.

Collaborating with Academic Institutions

Education for sustainability isn't an isolated endeavor; it thrives on the interconnectedness of academic institutions, businesses, and communities. The collaborative effort between universities and corporations can serve as a dynamic incubator for sustainable practices, nurturing the academic roots of environmental stewardship and injecting practical, actionable strategies into the business world. This partnership proves invaluable in educating future leaders equipped with the skills and knowledge necessary to spearhead the transformation toward a more sustainable society.

Academic institutions possess immense intellectual capital, rigorous research methodologies, and a tradition of critical inquiry—all fundamental elements in addressing complex sustainability challenges. By teaming up with businesses, they can transpose theoretical concepts into real-world applications, ensuring sustainability isn't just a set of principles but a practiced and measurable outcome. Collaborations can manifest in joint research projects, innovation labs, and think tanks that address both current and emerging environmental issues.

Moreover, embedding sustainability into the curriculum across disciplines can produce a new cadre of professionals who understand the intricate balance between economic success and environmental preservation. Universities have the opportunity to refine the competencies of students by incorporating sustainability across subjects, such as engineering, economics, law, and the arts, to foster a holistic understanding of the topic.

Internship programs established through the symbiotic relationships between academia and industry provide students with hands-on experience in sustainability initiatives. These practical engagements allow students to apply academic insights to solve real-life challenges while offering businesses a fresh perspective and an infusion of innovative ideas.

Extracurricular activities, such as sustainability-focused competitions, hackathons, and case studies developed in collaboration with businesses, encourage proactive learning and problem-solving skills. These platforms can showcase the ingenuity of students and faculty while providing tangible solutions businesses can implement.

Academic conferences, workshops, and speaker series that bring together scholars, industry leaders, and policymakers can serve as a breeding ground for transformative ideas, practices, and policies in sustainability. These events can foster a shared language and conceptual framework for sustainability, ensuring alignment among education, corporate activities, and public policy.

Businesses can also benefit from the cutting-edge research conducted by universities. By funding academic research, companies not only gain access to innovative sustainable solutions, but also contribute to the public knowledge base and demonstrate their commitment to corporate responsibility. Such research collaborations can shape the direction of new products, services, and business models that prioritize sustainability.

Service-learning and community outreach programs developed jointly by universities and businesses encourage students to engage with local communities. This engagement helps students learn the importance of social dimensions in sustainability while providing communities with support and resources to improve their environmental practices.

Centers for sustainability within universities act as hubs that can unite interdisciplinary research, education, and action. These centers can partner with industry to translate sustainability science into best practices, incorporating the iterative feedback from applied practices back into the research and teaching cycles.

To ensure collaborations are successful and mutually beneficial, open channels of communication and joint governance structures are necessary. They help maintain clarity in objectives, milestones, roles, and responsibilities. Regularly assessing the outcomes of partnerships through both qualitative and quantitative measures ensures joint projects are not only reaching their goals, but also progressively evolving to meet new sustainability challenges.

Peer-reviewed publications and white papers stemming from these partnerships are invaluable contributions to the global discourse on sustainability. They help bridge the gap between academic knowledge and practical execution, presenting a unified front in the struggle for a more sustainable future.

In these partnerships, challenges such as divergent goals, cultural differences, and intellectual property rights must not be overlooked. A clear agreement, built on mutual trust and understanding, that outlines each party's expectations and objectives can preempt many potential conflicts.

Global sustainability challenges such as climate change demand a collaborative and interdisciplinary approach. With their international networks, academic institutions have the potential to spur global collaborations, thereby amplifying the impact of sustainability practices across borders.

In conclusion, collaborations between businesses and academic institutions in sustainability education are not just advantageous; they are imperative. They provide an avenue for both theoretical exploration and practical application—an educational duality that can foster an ethical, environmentally conscious, and socially responsible future workforce with the potential to make meaningful change.

This partnership model presents an exciting realm where the passion for knowledge meets the ambition of industry, creating a synergy that is pivotal for the educational renaissance required to address the environmental and ethical challenges of our time.

Lifelong Learning for Sustainable Development

The concept of lifelong learning is pivotal not only to personal growth, but also to the sustainable development of societies and economies. In an era characterized by rapid change and complex environmental challenges, the need to continuously acquire new skills and knowledge extends far beyond the traditional classroom. Lifelong learning for sustainable development encompasses an ongoing process of education that enables individuals to contribute to sustainable practices in every facet of life, from professional circles to personal decisions.

As we confront the necessity for a sustainable future, businesses have a unique and crucial role in fostering lifelong learning. By encouraging and facilitating continuous education, businesses can help develop a workforce that is not only skilled, but also conscious of the environmental, social, and economic dimensions of their work. Investing in employee development is not only a strategy to enhance productivity, but also a testament to a company's commitment to sustainability.

Moreover, it is critical to understand education for sustainability should not be confined to the dissemination of factual knowledge alone. It needs to cultivate critical thinking, problem-solving, and the ability to engage with complex ethical decisions. This integrative approach helps professionals to anticipate and mitigate environmental impacts while also navigating the ethical considerations implicated in these actions.

One of the core tenets of lifelong learning for sustainable development is the alignment of personal values with professional practices. Individuals must see the connection between their roles in the workplace and the broader impacts on the environment and society. This awareness can foster a sense of responsibility that propels individuals to practice and support sustainability initiatives within and beyond the organizational context.

Collaboration with academic institutions plays a vital role in expounding this knowledge and in shaping a curriculum that addresses the skill gap in sustainable practices. Such partnerships can create learning platforms that are responsive to the latest sustainability challenges and can align with professional competency requirements.

Interactive learning environments, workshops, and innovative learning tools are indispensable for encouraging an active engagement with sustainability concepts. Simulation games, scenario planning, and project-based learning offer experiential insights that can aid in understanding the systemic nature of sustainability challenges.

A culture of learning within organizations can also be promoted through mentorship programs, where experienced personnel guide newer employees on sustainability principles and practices. This allows for a transfer of tacit knowledge and values that are fundamental to shaping a sustainable corporate culture.

The digital era has facilitated access to a wide array of online courses, webinars, and platforms where professionals can acquire sustainability-related skills at their convenience. Digital literacy, thus, becomes an important aspect of lifelong learning, enabling individuals to tap into global knowledge repositories and online communities of practice. This access supports a democratization of learning by removing barriers to education.

However, lifelong learning for sustainable development isn't solely the bailiwick of the employed or those in corporate environments. It extends to all societal sectors, including governments, NGOs, and the general public. Public awareness campaigns, community workshops, and local initiatives play a significant role in raising the collective consciousness about sustainable living practices.

An individual's capacity to affect change should not be underestimated. Through informed choices and actions—such as responsible consumption, waste management, and community engagement—lifelong learners embody sustainability principles in their daily lives, amplifying their impact on a sustainable future.

Finally, recognition and certification mechanisms can be employed to motivate ongoing education and the application of sustainable practices. Such systems not only reward individuals, but also spur industry-wide standards that promote lifelong learning as a cornerstone of professional development.

The urgency of these times calls for a transformational approach to education and skills development. Businesses, as stewards of societal progress, must foster environments where continual learning is both valued and expected. This will not only enhance their competitiveness, but also their capacity to address the intricate sustainability challenges of our age.

In conclusion, lifelong learning for sustainable development demands an alignment between knowledge acquisition, personal growth, and engagement in sustainable practices. It requires a collaborative effort across multiple sectors, an openness to new technologies, and, most importantly, a commitment to integrating sustainable development into the fabric of our learning and working lives.

As we forge ahead in this era, we must remember each of us has the potential to influence the trajectory to a more sustainable future. Lifelong learning for sustainable development is not merely an educational concept; it is a personal and collective journey toward a more responsible, equitable, and environmentally conscious civilization.

Chapter 18:
The Green Workplace:
Creating Sustainable and Healthy Environments

Within the heart of the corporate machine, the workplace emerges as a pivotal frontier in the quest for sustainability, where the design of spaces intertwines with human well-being and ecological sensibility. Efforts to foster green workplaces go beyond the mere installation of energy-efficient lights or recycling bins. It's a transformative journey where businesses reimagine the very fabric of their operational environment.

The convergence of efficiency and well-being in this movement isn't incidental; it's the pulse that sustains the vitality of a truly sustainable office culture. Green policies ripple through the veins of organizations, catalyzing behavioral change among employees and encouraging them to act as eco-ambassadors within and beyond the office walls. Such initiatives ground themselves in the proven benefits of clean, well-ventilated, and naturally lit environments that not only lower carbon footprints, but also uplift the spirit and productivity of the workforce.

The embodiment of green workplaces manifests not just in the infrastructure, but also in the daily rituals and shared values that collectively bear the fruit of innovation for a healthier planet. This shift isn't just about cutting costs or meeting benchmarks—it's about creating a symphony of eco-conscious actions that harmonize the orchestra of commerce with the melody of nature's limits, setting a new standard for workplaces that cradle both the economy and the Earth.

Designing for Efficiency and Well-being

Within the expansive realm of sustainability, the concept of a green workplace often focuses on environmental metrics, yet the true sustainability of a workplace encompasses both ecological responsibility and the well-being of its inhabitants. Designing for efficiency is not merely about reducing resource consumption and waste, but also creating workspaces that foster productivity, health, and happiness.

At the intersection of architecture, interior design, and environmental science lies a potent strategy for designing work environments that are both energy-efficient and conducive to well-being. Key to this multidisciplinary approach is the understanding of biophilic design principles, which assert humans have an innate connection to nature. Incorporating natural lighting, green spaces, and organic materials into office design can significantly reduce energy costs and improve employee morale and cognitive function.

The office layout is a canvas for efficiency. Open-plan designs are lauded for their flexibility and the stimulation of collaboration but they must be implemented thoughtfully to mitigate noise pollution and distractions. Quiet zones and nature-rich breakout areas can provide solace and rejuvenation, optimizing the balance between cooperative work and solitude that is necessary for thoughtful contemplation and productivity.

Smart technology integration is fundamental in realizing the potential of a green workplace. Energy-efficient appliances, automated lighting systems, and intelligent HVAC units are capable of drastically reducing a building's energy footprint while maintaining a comfortable working environment. Furthermore, these systems can provide data for ongoing adjustments, further enhancing the sustainability of the workplace.

A critical component of designing for efficiency involves considering the air quality within indoor environments. Research indicates indoor air quality can be significantly worse than outdoor air, with implications for employee health and cognitive function. Advanced ventilation systems and the use of non-toxic building materials can vastly improve the air employees breathe, thereby elevating their overall well-being.

Acoustic design often goes overlooked in discussions of workplace efficiency, yet noise is among the top complaints in office environments. Properly designed acoustic solutions can mitigate noise pollution, leading to decreased stress levels and increased concentration. Materials and office layouts that absorb or block sound contribute not only to employee wellness, but also to a culture of respect and attentiveness within the workplace.

Color psychology is another instrument at the disposal of those who design for well-being. Thoughtful use of color can energize, calm, or focus the mind, directly influencing productivity and workplace satisfaction. Integration of colors that reflect a company's brand identity not only reinforces organizational identity but can also play a covert role in anchoring the business's ethical commitment to a sustainable and healthful office environment.

The ergonomics of office furniture is a study in efficiency and wellness. Chairs, desks, and workstations designed to reduce physical strain can lead to fewer workplace injuries and less absenteeism. Introducing adjustable standing desks or incentivizing the use of ergonomic tools can demonstrate a company's dedication to employee health and reinforce a culture of caring.

Reevaluation of building materials and processes has brought forth an emphasis on sustainable sourcing and low environmental impact. Materials that are durable, recyclable, and have low embodied energy support the life cycle efficiency of a workspace and contribute to a healthier environment both indoors and out.

Light, both natural and artificial, plays a pivotal role in workplace efficiency. Maximizing natural light can reduce reliance on artificial lighting and positively affect circadian rhythms, while LED lighting offers energy savings and reduced heat emissions. Strategically placing artificial lighting to complement natural light reduces energy consumption and enhances the quality of the work environment.

Accessibility and inclusivity must be integrated into the design for efficiency and well-being. A workplace that can be navigated and enjoyed by people of all abilities not only fulfills ethical responsibilities, but also broadens the spectrum of potential employee talent, thus, enriching the workplace community and the quality of collective contribution.

Transportation to and from the workplace also constitutes an essential component of a sustainable design strategy. Companies that provide secure bicycle storage, charging stations for electric vehicles, or incentives for using public transport are aligning their commitment to the environment with their daily operations, thereby reducing their overall carbon footprint.

The physical and psychological dimensions of workplace design must be addressed holistically for companies to achieve sustainability in the truest sense. Designing for efficiency and well-being is not just about cost savings; it's about investing in the human capital of a business, and, thus, securing a more vibrant and resilient future for the organization and the planet. This holistic approach shows the profound interconnectedness between individual wellness and the environment, shining a light on pathways for businesses to contribute constructively to the health of both.

When workplaces become reflections of a company's ethical commitments to sustainability, employee engagement in green policies and practices is naturally fostered. The well-designed green workplace, thus, becomes a living testament to a company's steadfast dedication to sustainability, its employees, and the wider world, setting a standard for ecological and social responsibility in the business landscape.

In conclusion, designing for efficiency and well-being is an intentional act of corporate citizenship. It is a declaration of a business's ethos, a tangible expression of the values held by a company, and a cornerstone in the transformative shift toward a sustainable future. As these work environments become the norm, they will serve not only as hubs of innovation and productivity, but also sanctuaries that nourish the soul and respect the environment.

Promoting Green Policies and Practices Among Employees

In cultivating a green workplace, the collective engagement of employees is vital. Employers bear the responsibility of not only crafting sustainable business strategies, but also encouraging those within the organizational fold to take up the mantle of eco-conscious behavior. A harmonious and thriving company culture is one that champions sustainability at its core.

Establishing an effective communication strategy is fundamental in promoting green policies among employees. Clear, regular, and motivational messaging can inspire positive environmental changes within work practices. It's crucial for employees to comprehend the importance of individual actions in achieving broader environmental goals and how their daily habits contribute to the company's green vision.

Incentive programs can be a powerful tool to motivate and reward employees for adopting green practices. Offering recognition or rewards for eco-friendly behavior encourages participation and adds an element of competitiveness and fun to the workplace, propelling sustainable actions forward.

Leadership plays a critical role in setting an environmental example. Leaders who embody green practices in their own work and decision-making processes send a powerful message that sustainability is a key priority. When management leads by example, employees are more likely to follow suit and integrate eco-friendly practices into their daily routines.

Education and training are also pillars of promoting green policies among employees. Providing opportunities to learn about environmental issues, sustainability practices, and the impact of their actions empowers employees to make informed decisions and take meaningful steps toward reducing their carbon footprint.

To make sustainability a fluent part of the company's DNA, green teams or sustainability committees should be formed. These groups consist of volunteer employees who are passionate about environmental issues and who work together to come up with innovative ideas to make the office more sustainable.

Companies also need to integrate sustainability into performance metrics. When employee evaluations include sustainability criteria, it underscores the value placed on eco-friendly behavior and integrates it into the core expectations of every team member's role within the company.

Adapting the workspace to encourage sustainable choices is another effective strategy. By making recycling bins accessible, reducing paper usage by transitioning to digital workflows, and optimizing natural light to reduce energy consumption, employees are nudged toward greener practices simply by adjusting their environment.

Transitioning to sustainable office supplies is another tangible approach to promoting greener practices. Encouraging the use of recycled materials, providing reusable utensils and dishware for office kitchens, and selecting electronic devices with energy-saving features further embeds sustainability into everyday work life.

Furthermore, encouraging sustainable transport, such as bike-to-work schemes or incentives for carpooling, helps reduce the company's carbon footprint. Such strategies benefit the environment, support employee health, and promote community building.

Telecommuting options can also reduce the need for transport and the accompanying emissions. Embracing flexible work schedules and remote work when possible not only promotes well-being and work–life balance, but also serves environmental interests.

Corporate sustainability initiatives should also engage with broader community efforts. Encouraging volunteerism and participation in local environmental projects amplifies the message that the company and its employees are dedicated to a sustainable future beyond the confines of the office.

Collaborating with other organizations to create forums or workshops focused on sustainable practices promotes a culture of continuous learning and community engagement, further cementing the importance of environmental stewardship amongst employees.

It is paramount that all these efforts are rooted in a larger narrative that aligns with the employees' values and the company's mission. This creates a sense of shared purpose, where each employee understands how their contributions fit into the larger picture of environmental sustainability and corporate responsibility.

In summary, promoting green policies and practices among employees is a multifaceted endeavor. Through communication, incentives, leadership, education, workspace adjustments, performance metrics, sustainable transport, and community engagement, companies can foster an environment where sustainability becomes second nature to their workforce. Creating such a culture not only benefits the planet, but also nurtures a healthier, more dynamic, and committed workforce.

The Benefits of a Green Office Culture

At the heart of every forward-thinking organization lies an understanding of the interconnectedness between the well-being of the environment and that of its people. As we delve into the benefits of a green office culture, it is essential to recognize such a transformation extends beyond mere environment-friendly practices; it nurtures an ethos that resonates with all stakeholders, generates economic value, and, above all, honors our planet.

A workplace imbued with green principles steadfastly contributes to employee health. The implementation of natural lighting, ergonomic furniture, and toxin-free building materials carves a workspace that is not only physically lenient, but also mentally soothing. These optimizations are conducive to a significant decline in sickness-related absenteeism and a corresponding surge in productivity.

Moreover, a green office culture is influential in attracting and retaining talent. With an increasing number of job seekers placing a premium on sustainability, organizations that show a genuine commitment to environmentally friendly practices become employers of choice. This cultural alignment is crucial in fostering a workforce that is both talented and ethically engaged.

Embracing renewable energy and resource conservation results in tangible cost reductions. Whether it be through decreased utility bills from LED lighting and advanced HVAC systems, or the longevity granted by sustainable materials, the financial benefits over time are undeniable. Furthermore, these savings can be redirected to catalyze innovation or enhance employee benefits, compounding the organization's success.

Green office cultures are breeding grounds for innovation. When an organization actively promotes environmental responsiveness, it invites employees to think creatively about reducing waste and optimizing resources. This cultivates a mindset of continuous improvement and differentiates the company in a competitive marketplace.

Businesses that adopt green cultures often enjoy enhanced brand reputation and customer loyalty. As consumers become more environmentally conscious, they seek to align with companies that reflect their values. This conscientious preference can result in a stronger customer base and increased revenue opportunities as sustainability becomes part of the brand's unique selling proposition.

Building a green office culture aids in regulatory compliance and reduces the risk of falling behind ever-evolving environmental legislation. Companies proactive in sustainability can navigate the regulatory landscape with finesse, avoiding potential fines and staying ahead of competitors who lag in adopting green measures.

Moreover, well-implemented green office strategies contribute to mitigating climate change by reducing the organization's carbon footprint. This reduction in greenhouse gas emissions is a direct contribution to global efforts in combating adverse effects on the climate and exemplifies corporate responsibility on a planetary scale.

Enhanced employee engagement is yet another benefit of a green office culture. When employees perceive their organization's commitment to societal and environmental goals, it enhances their sense of purpose and pride. This alignment of personal and corporate values bolsters engagement, enriching productivity and fostering a cohesive work environment.

From a risk management perspective, green practices in office culture can be instrumental in protecting against the financial and reputational damage associated with resource scarcity and environmental disasters. Sustainable practices safeguard against these vulnerabilities, ensuring operational continuity in the face of ecological uncertainties.

Green office culture also serves the vital purpose of fostering community relations. Organizations actively participating in local environmental initiatives gain respect and good standing in the community. This grassroots relationship is foundational for robust partnerships and enhancing the social license to operate.

The green office also acts as an educational hub, where employees learn about sustainability and carry these teachings into their communities and homes. This ripple effect amplifies the impact of a single organization's green policies, contributing to a wider cultural shift toward environmental stewardship.

Financial incentives, in the form of tax breaks or subsidies for green buildings and practices, often accompany eco-friendly initiatives. Leveraging these incentives can provide an additional financial boost to organizations that are committed to sustainable practices, easing the transition and investment in green infrastructure.

Lastly, participative management plays a crucial role in a successful green transition. When employees are involved in the decision-making processes regarding green initiatives, they become ambassadors for the organization's sustainability efforts, inherently strengthening commitment and effectiveness.

In summation, the incorporation of a green office culture is a multifaceted approach that cultivates a workplace uniquely positioned to meet the challenges of the twenty-first century. It is a definitive step toward nurturing a resilient organization—one that thrives economically, socially, and ecologically. As we pursue the path of sustainability, the green office stands not merely as an option but as an essential embodiment of visionary and ethical business practice.

Chapter 19:
Leadership for a Sustainable Future

nherent in the vision of a sustainable future is a constellation of leadership qualities that epitomize both foresight and responsibility. As we pivot from the green office culture described in the previous chapter, it becomes clear that leadership is not merely a position but a dynamic process of inspiring and actualizing collective action toward ecological and social stewardship.

Within this realm, the demands placed upon executives and boards are tantamount to a reformation of ethical practices that extend beyond the boardroom and into the very fabric of society. The cultivation of leaders at every organizational level who are adept in ethical reasoning, empathetic engagement, and integrative thinking becomes a cornerstone for embedding a culture of responsibility. Such leaders are essential for engaging a multiplicity of stakeholders—employees, consumers, communities, and even the natural environment—in genuine sustainability efforts. The onus falls not only on installing capable figures at the helm but on nurturing an ethos where each member understands their role in charting the course toward long-term success.

This chapter is anchored in the premise that a paradigm shift is underfoot; one that aligns the compass of leadership with a map drawn not in the pursuit of mere profit but in the quest for a thriving planet. The lessons drawn from case examples here will illuminate the paths leaders are charting as they bravely champion transformative change against the tides of short-termism and societal inertia.

The Role of Executives and Boards in Ethical Reformation

The fulcrum points of any corporation are its leaders—the executives and their governing boards. It is here the values and ethical posture of an organization are steered. For a company aspiring to partake in the global sustainability movement, the role of its leadership cannot be overstated. These individuals set the course not just for fiscal success, but also for the moral compass of the enterprise, an imperative in today's world where stakeholders are intensely scrutinizing the ethical makeup of business actions.

In terms of ethical reformation, executives and board members hold a unique position. They must navigate the complex terrain of shareholder interests, consumer expectations, and environmental stewardship. It is their strategic vision that shapes how a company interacts with the planet and its inhabitants. They possess the power to integrate ecological considerations into financial decisions, thereby embarking on a path that fosters a sustainable and equitable future for both the company and society at large.

Leadership commitment is a cornerstone of effective sustainability strategies. Whether it is in policymaking, goal setting, or embedding ethical practices into the corporate culture, leadership's demonstrable commitment invites trust and engagement from all levels of the organization. Emerging from the moral shadows requires leadership to break free of the "business as usual" model, boldly championing initiatives that prioritize long-term ecological health over short-term gains.

Education plays a pivotal role in this transformation. Executives and board members themselves must be educated on the latest developments in sustainability, including environmental impact assessments, circular economy principles, and ethics in corporate governance. Fostering partnerships with academic institutions and thought leaders in sustainability can provide the essential knowledge and innovative insights needed to guide ethical reformation.

Transparency is another critical factor in the ethical transformation of businesses. Executives and board members must ensure sustainability efforts are not just touted in company reports but are manifest in company operations and results. This transparency can be realized through robust reporting mechanisms and embracing tools such as blockchain and artificial intelligence that allow for verifiable traceability in supply chains.

Embedding ethics into corporate governance requires a comprehensive approach. The board should actively review, and, when needed, revamp, ethical guidelines, ensuring they are aligned with the latest sustainability standards. Executive compensation and incentives must also be tied to sustainability performance, creating a tangible connection between reaching environmental targets and tangible rewards.

Commitment to diversity and inclusivity within the board itself is also fundamental. A multifaceted board brings a breadth of perspectives and can champion sustainability with understanding of different cultures, regions, and stakeholders. This diversity not only strengthens decision-making, but also aligns with societal expectations of corporate responsibility.

Stakeholder engagement is key for leaders to align their objectives with broader societal and environmental goals. This means listening to customers, employees, suppliers, NGOs, and community voices. Effective leaders leverage these insights to make ethical decisions that resonate with a wider audience and lead to sustainable outcomes.

Risk management in this reformed ethical landscape transcends financial risks to include reputational and ecological risks. Executives and boards should aim to preemptively address these risks through proactive sustainability strategies and by embracing a precautionary approach to the environmental and social impacts of their business activities.

Innovation must be encouraged and promoted at the board level. Leaders must recognize sustainable practices not only mitigate risks, but also present opportunities for new business models and revenue streams that are in harmony with ecological and social imperatives.

For a sustainable future, it's essential that executives and board members serve not just as decision-makers, but as thought leaders and ethical champions. They must be visible in their commitments, actively participating in discussions, and contributing to public discourses on sustainability. This presence endorses the company's ethical stance and encourages other businesses to follow suit.

Leadership development and succession planning should not be overlooked. A sustainable company cultivates future leaders with a strong sense of environmental and social ethics. Building a pipeline of ethically minded leaders ensures the company's commitment to sustainability endures beyond the tenure of its current executives and board members.

Finally, the evaluation of business performance should be reimagined. Executives and boards are accustomed to assessing financial performance, but it's just as important to evaluate how a business performs on its ethical and sustainability endeavors. It's these metrics that will narrate the company's true commitment to creating a sustainable future.

It is these leaders who are positioned to infuse ethical considerations into the DNA of their organizations, instigating the evolutionary change needed for a sustainable future. The path forward isn't one of ease but of determination, courage, and unwavering commitment to an ideal that benefits not just the bottom line, but the world as a whole. This role of executives and boards in ethical reformation is a testament to their capacity to shape an enterprise's legacy into one that is proactively written in the annals of ecological and social stewardship.

Developing Ethical Leaders at All Levels

Within the overarching goal of steering businesses toward a sustainable future lies the crucial task of nurturing ethical leadership throughout all tiers of an organization. No longer can we confine leadership to the gilded halls of executive suites; instead, we must instill a sense of moral stewardship at every level, forging a company-wide ethos that champions ethical conduct as much as it does success in business.

Leadership for a sustainable future requires an inclusive approach to decision-making, one that empowers individuals across all departments and roles to actively contribute to the organization's ethical momentum. In this way, ethical leadership becomes a shared responsibility that is embedded in the fundamental operations of the company, rather than a directive imposed from above.

To develop these leaders, an authentic commitment to ethical practices must be established, and it starts at the recruitment phase. Hiring processes should emphasize not only skills and experience, but also an alignment with the company's core values and sustainability ethos. Such criteria ensure the organization enriches its ranks with individuals predisposed to ethical thinking.

Once within the organization, continuous and comprehensive training in sustainability and ethics is essential. These programs must go beyond mere compliance; they should engage, challenge, and inspire employees, providing them with the tools to navigate complex moral landscapes and the encouragement to apply these lessons to their daily work.

Leadership development cannot exist in a vacuum—it must be integrated with the wider strategy and goals of the business. As such, including ethical considerations in objective setting, appraisals, and performance reviews sends a clear message that these factors are vital to the company's definition of success.

Creating spaces for dialogue and reflection is also vital. Forums, workshops, and team meetings that encourage open and honest conversations about ethical dilemmas can help employees develop the critical thinking and empathy needed to navigate these challenges. Such spaces cultivate a culture of trust where ethical issues can be raised without fear of retribution.

Mentoring is another potent tool for cultivating leadership. Pairing emerging leaders with experienced mentors who embody the organization's ethical standards can provide guidance, example, and reassurance. Through these relationships, values are transmitted and mentorship becomes a conduit for ethical leadership principles.

Recognition and rewards play a significant role in reinforcing ethical behaviors. A system that celebrates those who exemplify sustainable and responsible practices motivates others to emulate these traits. It is essential, however, that the recognition be meaningful and aligned with the organization's ethical framework to avoid the pitfalls of performative gestures.

Leadership isn't confined to humans in management positions; it also manifests in the systems we create. Technology and data analytics can support ethical decision-making by providing insights that may otherwise be missed and holding leaders accountable through transparent and traceable metrics.

While the development of individual leaders is critical, so too is the development of teams. An ethically conscientious team can elevate an entire organization. Team-building exercises that focus on sustainability challenges and ethical scenarios can help forge units that are collectively attuned to ethical imperatives.

An organization's adaptability to change is indicative of its ethical maturity. Ethical leaders at all levels must be equipped to foresee and navigate the moral implications of both incremental advancements and disruptive innovations within their industry.

Global perspectives must also be integrated into leadership development programs. Operating in a globalized economy means understanding and respecting cultural nuances in ethical considerations, and leaders should be prepared to engage respectfully with diverse norms and practices.

Lastly, businesses must look beyond their walls and collaborate with NGOs, universities, and other organizations to enrich their understanding of leadership in the context of sustainability. These partnerships can provide fresh insights, challenge the status quo, and cultivate a broader network of ethically aligned leaders.

To conclude, the development of ethical leaders at all levels forms the backbone of a business's journey toward sustainability. From entry-level employees to CEOs, a cohesive ethical vision allows for a unified push toward a sustainable future. Investment in the people who embody the values of the organization is an investment in the long-term health and success of not just the company, but also the wider community and world it serves.

Engaging Stakeholders in Sustainability Efforts

In the quest for a sustainable future, the calls from nature are urgent and the voices of stakeholders are paramount. Leaders who seek to redefine the ethical landscape of business must move beyond mere compliance and risk management to a place where engagement with stakeholders is a dynamic and vital force in shaping sustainability efforts.

It begins with understanding the fabric of our interconnections, where even the smallest thread can hold a critical weight. Stakeholders, from investors to community members and from employees to customers, are not just external entities; they are part of the ecosystem businesses inhabit. To engage them is to weave a tapestry of shared vision and collective action.

Transparency is our herald through this journey, laying the groundwork for meaningful dialogue. Sharing initiatives, challenges, and progress with candor assures stakeholders that their input is valued and the business is accountable. It's not enough to distribute annual reports or sporadic updates; continuous communication channels need to be established and maintained.

Participation is the next stride, inviting stakeholders to not only observe but take part in sustainability strategies. Whether through focus groups, surveys, or stakeholder panels, their insights can unveil previously unconsidered aspects of a business's operations and impact. Inclusivity in these participatory practices strengthens their effectiveness, ensuring a diversity of perspectives and expertise.

Empowerment becomes possible when stakeholders are equipped with the right tools and knowledge to contribute meaningfully. This may involve educational workshops, or access to resources, allowing them to understand sustainability in the context of the business and the wider world. An informed stakeholder is a powerful ally.

Collaboration is a natural progression from empowerment. Here, businesses and stakeholders co-create solutions. Cross-sector partnerships, co-investments in community projects, and joint research initiatives are just a few avenues where synergies can be fostered for sustainable outcomes.

Innovation emerges from the confluence of different perspectives. By tapping into the collective intelligence of stakeholders, businesses can unlock innovative approaches to sustainability challenges. The sustainability journey is one of exploration and adaptation, and stakeholders often hold the keys to paths less traveled.

Accountability measures, such as stakeholder advisory boards, give substance to the dialogue, translating engagement into responsible governance. These mechanisms can help ensure sustainability is not sidelined in pursuit of short-term profits but is integrated into the core strategic decisions.

Recognition of stakeholders' contributions reinforces their continued engagement. Celebrating the successes and acknowledging the efforts of those involved creates a sense of ownership and pride in the shared journey toward sustainability.

Feedback loops are essential; it's about listening and adapting. Stakeholders' assessments of sustainability practices provide critical inputs for ongoing improvement. A business should be agile in its response, evolving its strategies as needed.

Metrics and indicators should be co-developed with stakeholders to measure progress in a way that resonates with their expectations and values. This collaborative approach to performance measurement ensures relevance and credibility.

Conflict resolution mechanisms are an acknowledgment that not all paths will be smooth. Constructive engagement with stakeholders also means addressing disagreements and finding shared solutions that align with sustainability principles.

Education for stakeholders about the complex systems in which businesses operate illuminates the interconnectedness of economic, social, and environmental spheres. This holistic understanding is key to fostering engagement that is deep and continuous, rather than superficial and sporadic.

By fostering a culture of responsibility that permeates every layer of the organization, businesses ensure stakeholders see them as partners in a common cause, not adversaries or mere instruments of profit.

Visionary leadership is crucial for ensuring stakeholder engagement is not a token gesture but a transformative force. Leaders must embody the values of sustainability and instill them across the organization and its wider network.

Finally, sustaining engagement over time requires perseverance and commitment. Stakeholder relationships are not static; they evolve as the business and its environment change. Continually striving for meaningful engagement, therefore, is key to maintaining momentum in sustainability efforts.

In conclusion, as businesses chart their courses toward sustainability, stakeholders are not merely passengers but co-navigators. Their engagement is crucial for not only illuminating the route, but also giving it purpose and ensuring it is followed with integrity. It's through this collective journey that the aspirations of a sustainable future can be realized, one step, one voice, and one action at a time.

Creating a Culture of Responsibility for Long-Term Success

In the previous sections, we've explored the myriad ways in which leadership and business practices can contribute to a sustainable future. Now, we delve into the critical process of creating a culture of responsibility within organizations; this is the bedrock upon which long-term success is built in the context of sustainability. A culture of responsibility ensures every action and every decision are taken with consideration for both the immediate stakeholders and the broader impacts on global ecosystems and societies.

Developing such a culture begins at the very core of an organization's ethos. It demands conscious leadership—leadership that does not merely seek profit, but also considers the organization's footprint in the world. Leaders must embody the values they wish to see throughout their organization. They must demonstrate a commitment to ethical practices, environmental stewardship, and social responsibility in every decision they make.

Creating a culture where every employee feels responsible and empowered to make sustainable choices requires consistent and clear communication of the organization's values and goals. This involves not only crafting a strong vision, but also ensuring this vision is communicated effectively and resonates with all members of the organization. A shared language around sustainability helps solidify this collective responsibility.

Education and training are indispensable in fostering a culture of responsibility. Organizations must provide regular sustainability education, enabling employees to understand the importance of their roles in achieving sustainability goals. Alongside formal training, encouraging informal learning and sharing of best practices among employees can generate a more dynamic and committed workforce.

Accountability mechanisms are another critical factor. This means establishing clear metrics and Key Performance Indicators (KPIs) against which individuals and teams can measure their contributions to sustainability objectives. Incentivizing responsible behavior through recognition, rewards, and career advancement can reinforce positive actions.

An organization's culture is considerably influenced by the systems and structures within which its members operate. Therefore, embedding sustainability into every process and system—from procurement to performance management—can ensure responsibility isn't an afterthought but a fundamental criterion in every operation.

Engagement with stakeholders—both internal and external—can significantly enhance a culture of responsibility. By actively listening and responding to the concerns of employees, customers, suppliers, and the broader community, organizations can show they take their social and environmental impact seriously, further embedding this within the culture.

The integration of corporate social responsibility (CSR) initiatives into core business functions can act as a constant reminder of the organization's commitment to sustainability. Whether this is through volunteering programs, environmental audits, or partnerships with non-profits, such activities can cement a sense of purpose and responsibility among employees.

Leaders must also be ready to adapt and evolve the culture as new sustainability challenges emerge. This means staying informed about the latest developments in sustainability science and ethical business practices as well as being willing to pivot strategies and initiatives in response to new evidence and changing societal expectations.

In addition to fostering internal culture, organizations that strive for long-term success must also influence the broader business community. By sharing their journeys toward sustainability, including both their successes and challenges, they contribute to a global culture of responsibility and encourage other businesses to embark on similar paths.

Finally, it is vital for organizations to reflect on and learn from both successes and failures in their sustainability efforts. Continuous improvement, driven by reflective practice, ensures a culture of responsibility that is not static but grows more robust over time.

While the path to creating such a culture is neither simple nor easy, the rewards are significant. Companies that have embraced a culture of responsibility often find it leads to enhanced reputation, improved stakeholder relations, and, ultimately, better financial performance—all while contributing to the overall well-being of people and the planet.

In conclusion, a culture of responsibility is the keystone of sustainability in business. It is the embodiment of the ethical commitment that must underpin every level of operation if we are to work toward a sustainable future. By nurturing this culture, businesses can not only thrive, but also serve as stewards of a healthier, more just, and sustainable world for generations to come.

Case Examples: Leaders Championing Change

In our exploration of leadership for a sustainable future, it's essential to observe how leaders actualize their commitments to sustainability. This discourse unfolds real-world examples where heads of organizations catalyzed shifts toward eco-conscious and socially responsible business practices.

Consider the initiative by Yvon Chouinard of Patagonia, who pioneered the adoption of organic cotton in manufacturing, thereby reducing environmental harm. His leadership exemplifies how a dedication to product responsibility can permeate an entire industry, eliciting change that echoes beyond the boundaries of one company.

Likewise, Paul Polman, during his tenure as CEO of Unilever, reimagined corporate success. By integrating the Sustainable Living Plan into the company's operations, he sought not just profitability, but also positive impacts on people and the planet. Polman championed the notion that sustainability and financial performance aren't mutually exclusive but rather mutually reinforcing.

An exemplary figure in the energy sector is Ørsted's Henrik Poulsen, who transformed the organization from a fossil-fuel-centric utility into a leader in renewable energy. This pivot to renewables underlines the potential for sustainable leadership within traditionally high-impact industries.

In technology, Google's Sundar Pichai has put forth an ambitious goal for the company to operate on carbon-free energy 24/7 by 2030. Google's commitment illustrates how entities with significant digital footprints can pioneer the frontiers of sustainable energy consumption.

On the financial front, Jess Staley, ex-CEO of Barclays, advocated for green bonds and sustainable finance initiatives, signaling to the market the viability and necessity of environmentally friendly investment products. Staley's approach sought to align the bank's strategies with ethical goals, emphasizing sustainability's role in modern finance.

Indra Nooyi, formerly at the helm of PepsiCo, is renowned for instilling a sense of purpose throughout the company's global operations. By advancing the "Performance with Purpose" agenda, she demonstrated how processing and consumer goods corporations could leap toward health-conscious and environmentally considerate portfolios.

Looking toward retail, Rose Marcario, who served as CEO of Patagonia, showcases fearless leadership. Not only did she implement groundbreaking eco-friendly policies, but Patagonia also sued the U.S. government to protect public lands—a potent example of corporate advocacy for environmental justice.

In the realm of social enterprise, Jacqueline Novogratz's work with Acumen demarcates a compelling narrative where leaders invest in services and products that empower low-income communities, turning philanthropy into actionable, sustainable impact.

Automotive giant Tesla, under Elon Musk, continues driving the shift to electric vehicles (EVs), reinventing transportation's impact on the environment. Musk's audacious targets for EV production and the expansion of renewable energy ventures model how visionaries can steer incumbent sectors toward sustainability.

Amidst the corporate sphere, NGOs play an instrumental role. Leaders such as Hilde Schwab of the World Economic Forum have convened global stakeholders to commit to collective actions for sustainability; integrating vigorous dialogue and collaboration into global corporate practices.

On the supply chain side, Stella McCartney stands out as a fashion industry leader in advocating for sustainable materials and manufacturing processes. Her brand's refusal to use leather or fur and investment in novel eco-textiles demonstrate how a luxury brand can lead industry change.

In the consumer goods sector, IKEA's Jesper Brodin illustrates leadership through the company's commitment to becoming "climate positive" through reducing the emission of greenhouse gasses by more than the IKEA value chain emits them, setting an aggressive timeline to achieve this goal by 2030.

Despite challenges intrinsic to aviation, JetBlue's Robin Hayes champions eco-conscious air travel. The airline's pledge to offset carbon emissions from all domestic flights presents a template for sustainability within an industry often criticized for its environmental footprint.

Lastly, Microsoft's Satya Nadella has pledged to be carbon negative by 2030 and, by 2050, to remove all the carbon the company has emitted since its founding. Nadella's plans underscore the capabilities of large corporations to make substantial contributions to combating climate change.

These leaders have illuminated diverse paths to sustainable transformation. By leaning into innovation, stakeholder engagement, and ambitious visioning, they demonstrate how resilience, adaptability, and fervent commitment can steer large-scale positive change, embedding sustainability deep into the corporate DNA.

Chapter 20:
Entrepreneurial Solutions to
Environmental Challenges

As we've explored the multifaceted nature of sustainability in business, from supply chain ethics to the influence of technology, we now turn to the pioneering spirit inherent in entrepreneurial ventures that address environmental challenges.

Entrepreneurs worldwide are demonstrating it's possible—and profitable—to run businesses that contribute to the health of our planet. These trailblazers are not only employing resourceful solutions that heal and preserve the environment, but also reshaping perspectives on how businesses can succeed while nurturing the planet. They've recognized the urgency of our ecological crisis and are responding with innovations that span from green technology to sustainable product design, all while maintaining an ethical compass that directs toward a just society.

With vigor and creativity, these eco-entrepreneurs prove environmental considerations are not at odds with economic success. Instead, they spotlight a synergy traditional business models often overlook. Their accomplishments guide a new generation of businesses hungry for change, displaying convincingly that through tenacity and ingenuity, it is possible to alleviate our ecological woes without sacrificing the entrepreneurial dream. In doing so, they inspire hopeful pathways forward, exemplifying how the intersection of commerce and sustainability can bloom into impactful solutions that reverberate beyond the immediate scope of business and into the broader narrative of human progress.

Social Entrepreneurship and Its Impact

At the heart of entrepreneurial innovation for environmental challenges lies the concept of social entrepreneurship—a model where the primary objective is to apply business strategies to achieve significant social or environmental change. This movement—pioneered by trailblazers seeking to create enterprises that can sustainably manage our planet's resources while addressing the pressing needs of society—has surged in recent years. The thrust of this practice is the belief that profit and purpose can—and should—coexist harmoniously.

What differentiates social entrepreneurs from their traditional counterparts is their unwavering commitment to cause-centric business models. Social entrepreneurs forge ventures aimed at combating issues first, with profits—though essential for sustainability—being a secondary motivation. They seek to measure their success principally through their impact on society and the environment, employing a blend of strategic malleability and rigorous resourcefulness.

The impact social entrepreneurship has on environmental challenges cannot be understated. By focusing on innovating solutions that directly address ecological deterioration, social enterprises are not merely profiting from a niche market; they are actively contributing to the restoration and preservation of ecosystems. These enterprises, for example, may develop new methods of recycling, advocate for sustainable agriculture, or create products that slash energy consumption.

Moreover, the influence of such enterprises stretches beyond environmental rejuvenation. The ripple effect of their pursuit of social good trickles down through various domains. They can empower local communities by creating jobs, enhancing education, ensuring food and water security, and improving health outcomes—all of which are interlinked facets of environmental sustainability.

The infusion of social entrepreneurship into the mainstream economy has acted as a catalyst for larger corporations to adopt more sustainable practices. The rising tide of ethical consumer demands has incentivized bigger players to align their operations with principles of sustainability and social responsibility in response to the benchmarks set by these socially driven ventures.

Social entrepreneurs are also found at the vanguard of policy changes, advocating for regulations that incentivize sustainable practices and discourage environmentally harmful behavior. Their advocacy has the potential of shifting the policy landscape, leading to widespread adoption of improved standards for environmental protection and social progress.

An obstacle commonly encountered by social enterprises is the challenge of capital acquisition. Traditional funding streams may be reticent to invest in businesses that prioritize social impact over financial returns. However, the advent of impact investing—a strategy focusing on generating positive, measurable social and environmental impact alongside a financial return—has begun to create pathways for the necessary influx of capital into these purpose-driven businesses.

Yet, social entrepreneurship isn't without its critics. Skeptics question the scalability of such ventures, as many operate locally or within niche markets. This criticism is being answered through strategic collaborations, innovative scaling approaches, and the blending of traditional business acumen with social innovation, which can fortify the reach and effectiveness of social enterprises.

Education plays a pivotal role in fostering and nurturing future social entrepreneurs. Educational programs and workshops that emphasize ethics in business, sustainability, and social change are essential for equipping aspiring entrepreneurs with the skills and knowledge they need to thrive within this arena.

Also of significance is the impact of social entrepreneurship on corporate culture. As social enterprises demonstrate it is possible to do well by doing good, more traditionally structured companies are adopting similar values. This shift not only helps in retaining and attracting talent who seek purpose in their work, but also cultivates an environment where innovative, ethical problem-solving thrives.

Furthermore, social entrepreneurship serves as a barometer for societal values, reflecting a growing expectation that businesses contribute positively to the world. The social enterprise movement gives form to the notion that commerce does not have to be a zero-sum game and the synergistic melding of profit and purpose may hold the key to addressing many of the world's challenges.

As the urgency for actionable solutions to environmental degradation escalates, social entrepreneurship stands as a beacon of practical hope. Social entrepreneurs provide a prism through which we can view the possibility of an economic framework that fosters ecological balance, social equity, and long-term profitability.

In conclusion, social entrepreneurship offers a pragmatic blueprint for businesses to directly confront environmental issues while fostering social welfare. Its growing prominence portends the evolution of an economy that not only tolerates—but insists upon—a relationship between industry and the environment built on reciprocity and mutual enhancement.

Despite challenges ranging from funding to scale, social enterprises continue to push boundaries, inspire traditional businesses, and promote a world where environmental solutions and economic vigor are not mutually exclusive but rather inherently bound—an essential mindset for any business striving to exist in harmony with our planet's ecosystems. Such a revolution in thought and practice is more than a possibility—it is an unfolding reality that behooves us all to foster and support.

Scaling Sustainable Innovations

The metamorphosis of our world hinges on the successful scaling of sustainable innovations. Businesses are increasingly stepping into the limelight, recognizing that integrating ecological and social ethics is not only beneficial for the environment, but also critical for long-term profitability and societal acceptance. It is within the entrepreneurial crucible that such innovations are fired, refined, and brought to scale.

Scaling is a nuanced art, demanding more than just an impeccable business plan or an innovative product. It involves amplifying the impact of sustainable innovations without diluting their core environmental and social values. When an innovation scales, it travels beyond its incubation zone, evolving through iterations, adapting to different markets, and underpinning transformations across the economic landscape. The challenge for entrepreneurs lies in achieving scale while maintaining the integrity of their environmental mission.

Maintaining fidelity to sustainable values while scaling requires a robust framework. Institutions are an integral part of this, providing not just capital, but also guidance, mentorship, and networks. The active engagement of stakeholders—customers, investors, and employees—is also critical. Companies must communicate transparently and build trust that their sustainable values remain non-negotiable, even in the face of rapid expansion.

Succeeding at scale calls for a strategic marriage between innovative thinking and sound business practices. Companies such as Tesla and Patagonia have demonstrated it is possible to disrupt markets with sustainable products, although each pathway to scale is unique. For some, it involves leveraging technology or tapping into sharing economy principles. For others, it is about reinventing supply chains to mirror circular economy models, ensuring resources are used efficiently and waste is minimized.

Businesses aiming to scale sustainable innovations need to navigate the balance between growth and sustainability. They must consider the life cycle impacts of their products, engage in continuous improvement, and reassess how success is measured—shifting focus from short-term profits to long-term sustainability performance. Expanding sustainable business practices necessitates constant learning, evolution, and a willingness to pivot strategies in response to environmental feedback.

Access to finance is often cited as a critical factor in the ability of sustainable innovations to scale. Traditional funding mechanisms are being augmented or replaced with impact investing, green bonds, and crowdfunding platforms, which specifically target ventures designed with ethical and sustainable intent. These financial instruments not only provide the necessary capital, but also validate the market acceptance of sustainable principles.

On the journey to scale, regulation plays a dual role. While it sets standards that protect the environment and promote fair practices, it can either impede or facilitate the growth of sustainable businesses. To this end, the interplay between governance structures and business innovation becomes pertinent. Progressive policies and incentives can help level the playing field and make scaling easier for sustainable solutions.

An ecosystem approach to scaling is vital. It positions businesses within a collaborative network, connecting them with research institutions, NGOs, and government agencies. This can accelerate the diffusion of sustainable innovations, as cross-sector partnerships can provide support on multiple fronts—from technical expertise to market access.

Consumer awareness and demands for greater sustainability act as powerful catalysts for scaling. As societal norms shift toward valuing sustainability and transparency, businesses are propelled to adapt and scale their ethical practices to meet these expectations. Consumer choices play a significant role in driving market changes and elevating sustainable products and services.

Talent is the lifeblood of any enterprise seeking to scale. Attracting and retaining individuals who are committed to sustainability can create a strong organizational culture that supports ethical decision-making and innovative thinking. Companies such as Google and Interface have shown how cultivating a culture that rewards sustainable thinking can unleash employee creativity and drive business success at scale.

Technology, while not a panacea, is a critical enabler in scaling sustainable innovations. The strategic use of digital tools such as blockchain and artificial intelligence can increase efficiency, transparency, and the ability to track the social and environmental impact of products across the supply chain. As digital connectivity grows, it opens new horizons for scaling innovations globally, thereby multiplying their positive impact.

Ultimately, the path of scaling sustainable innovations involves navigating a complex and dynamic system in which entrepreneurs must be visionary yet pragmatic, ambitious yet grounded. It demands a steadfast commitment to values, agility in execution, and a clear understanding of the evolving environmental, social, and economic context.

As this section has shown, scaling sustainable innovations is not simply a matter of increasing production volumes or market shares—it's about embedding sustainability into the DNA of businesses and allowing it to guide growth and development. With every scaling success, the narrative of sustainability becomes more deeply ingrained in global economic paradigms, bringing us closer to a future that is both thriving and sustainable.

Nurturing the Eco-Entrepreneurial Spirit

In the journey toward a greener future, cultivating the eco-entrepreneurial spirit is paramount. Entrepreneurs have always been the vanguard of innovation but, when paired with environmental consciousness, their potential to effect change multiplies. To truly transform the industrial landscape, we must encourage and support those who see beyond the confines of profit margins and envision a world where business aligns harmoniously with ecological well-being.

The notion of entrepreneurship is historically intertwined with risk-taking and economic growth, often at the expense of the environment. However, the eco-entrepreneur stands apart by approaching this risk with a different metric for success: the health of our planet. They balance ambition with humility, recognizing economic activity cannot operate in isolation from the ecosystems that support life.

Eco-entrepreneurship requires a distinct mindset, one that sees opportunity where others perceive constraints. It is a call to align business models with sustainability principles, ensuring every venture not only minimizes environmental impact but actively contributes to ecological restoration. This entrepreneurial philosophy isn't merely a niche or a trend; it's the bedrock of a sustainable future in which business serves as a steward of the Earth, not its adversary.

To nurture such a spirit, education plays a pivotal role. Academic institutions and business schools must embed sustainability into their curricula, inculcating an understanding that profitability cannot be severed from environmental responsibility. Graduates stepping into the business world must be equipped with the knowledge and skills to innovate sustainably. By doing so, we shape a new generation of leaders primed to revolutionize industries with green principles at their core.

Capital, both financial and social, is also a critical catalyst. Eco-entrepreneurs often face substantial barriers in accessing the funds needed to bring their sustainable visions to life. Environmental start-ups, more so than their conventional counterparts, require investors who are patient and value-driven, and who understand the extended timeframes needed for sustainable innovations to flourish. The rise of impact investing and green bonds signals a promising shift, where money flows to initiatives with positive environmental outcomes.

Furthermore, network building is essential in fostering the eco-entrepreneurial spirit. The challenges of sustainable business are too complex to be tackled in silos. By cultivating partnerships among entrepreneurs, NGOs, governments, and academia, we can create a supportive ecosystem that shares knowledge, collaborates on solutions, and accelerates progress. These networks serve as a cradle for innovation and a springboard for scaling sustainable solutions.

Policy plays a foundational role as well. Governments can nurture eco-entrepreneurship by establishing regulations and incentives that encourage sustainable practices while disincentivizing environmental harm. Such policies not only level the playing field, but also send a clear signal that sustainability is not a mere option but a priority for business operations.

Mentorship is another cornerstone in nurturing the eco-entrepreneurial spirit. Seasoned sustainability professionals and successful green entrepreneurs must impart their wisdom and experience to up-and-coming innovators. This guidance is invaluable as emerging entrepreneurs navigate the complex terrain that merges ethical concerns with business acumen.

Recognizing and celebrating success stories is just as important as providing financial and educational support. When eco-entrepreneurs achieve breakthroughs, these must be widely publicized to serve as both inspiration and evidence that sustainable businesses can thrive. Their accomplishments help dispel the myth that environmental consideration is a constraint on business success.

Diversity must also be part of the equation. By welcoming perspectives from different cultures, genders, and socioeconomic backgrounds, we enrich the pool of eco-entrepreneurial ideas. A diverse array of thinkers challenges conventional wisdom and fosters innovative solutions that may otherwise go unrealized.

Adopting long-term thinking is vital for nurturing an eco-entrepreneurial spirit. Sustainable ventures often don't yield immediate returns; their benefits unfold over years—or even decades. Entrepreneurs and investors alike must embrace this temporal shift, valuing the enduring legacy of environmental stewardship over the fleeting allure of quick profits.

Technology, as well, is a powerful enabler for eco-entrepreneurs, offering tools and platforms that can amplify their impact. From leveraging big data for environmental analytics to utilizing renewable energy sources, technology can propel their initiatives to new heights. However, it is crucial that tech adoption is considered through a green lens, ensuring even our technological solutions contribute positively to the planet.

Lastly, we must advocate for cultural change that elevates the eco-entrepreneurial spirit from a niche interest to a societal norm. Awareness campaigns, media representation, and public discourse play fundamental roles in shifting perceptions, illustrating green business is smart business. As society begins to value environmentally conscious entrepreneurship, the commercial landscape will transform to reflect these priorities.

The journey to nurture the eco-entrepreneurial spirit is a multifaceted endeavor that touches upon education, finance, policy, mentorship, diversity, long-term thinking, technology, and cultural change. Each of these elements serves as a thread in the larger patchwork of creating a sustainable business environment that can carry us into a resilient future.

In conclusion, nurturing the eco-entrepreneurial spirit is not just about generating new businesses; it's about redefining the very notion of success in the business world. It's a crusade for ecological harmonization where every venture enriches our planet, fostering a world where tomorrow's children will inherit an Earth more vibrant and more abundant than the one we know today.

Chapter 21:
The Rise of Conscious Capitalism

As we transition from the grassroots brilliance of eco-entrepreneurship, this chapter seeks to illuminate a transformed business ethos that vitally recognizes the interconnectedness of economic success and social responsibility. "The Rise of Conscious Capitalism" encapsulates an emergent paradigm that not only values profit, but also purpose, people, and the planet. It is an ethos that stands on the revelations of the third book in the *Our Changing World* series, *A Planet in Balance*, embodying an acute awareness that business practices must be reframed in an ethical and sociocultural context to navigate the sustainability landscape effectively.

This chapter presents the essential characteristics of conscious capitalism, where businesses are seen as integral citizens of the world and their strategies as interwoven with the pursuit of environmental justice, social equity, and human rights. Here lies a blueprint for a future in which businesses serve the larger good, operating as custodians of societal and ecological well-being.

Embracing conscious capitalism means transcending traditional metrics of success, investing in community resilience, and transforming supply chains, thereby cultivating a legacy that harmonizes the aspirations of a more sustainable and equitable future. This chapter sets forth the guiding principles for companies aspiring to be vanguards of a new, ethical horizon in commerce, exploring the symbiotic relationship between economic vitality and global stewardship.

Defining and Embracing Conscious Capitalism

As we delve into the heart of conscious capitalism, it's essential to define this transformative approach to business and underscore the practices that can galvanize an ethical reformation within the corporate realm. Conscious capitalism isn't just a fleeting trend or a superficial patina of good deeds overlaying traditional profit-driven practices. It's a philosophical underpinning and a strategic framework that proposes a vision of business as a force for good with the power to create a flurry of positive impacts that reach far beyond the balance sheet.

Rooted in a thoughtful deliberation about the purpose of enterprise, conscious capitalism challenges leaders and organizations to redefine their missions. An enterprise, according to this paradigm, exists not solely to enrich shareholders but to serve a broader spectrum of stakeholders, including its employees, customers, suppliers, community, and the environment. The bedrock of this concept underscores a harmonious balance between humanism and economic viability.

In a conscious capitalist model, governance and executive decisions spring from a deep well of ethical contemplation. Here, companies find their economic and moral objectives aren't at loggerheads; in fact, they are improbably yet inextricably linked. These companies build strategies that are as sustainable as they are profitable, recognizing genuine care for people and planet is not only ethically commendable, but also economically sound.

To fully embrace conscious capitalism, businesses must weave this ethic into the very fabric of their corporate cultures. This means creating work environments that are not just conducive to productivity, but also nurture the collaborative spirit, respect, and psychological safety that underpin any thriving human collective. It's about leading by example, where the values promulgated at the highest levels are lived out in day-to-day interactions.

Leadership in a conscious enterprise takes on a new dimension. It becomes servant leadership, with executives viewing their role as stewards of their employees' well-being and champions of the company's positive impact. Serving a dual role as visionary and implementer, these leaders strive to align their company's purpose with the pursuit of what's good for the broader world.

At the core of conscious capitalism is also a keenness for long-term planning. Short-term gains are not pursued at the cost of sustainable profits and societal welfare. As such, conscious businesses adopt practices that may require an initial investment or seem less profitable in the immediate sense but promise enduring benefits to a wider community and future generations.

Another cornerstone is transparency, which goes hand in hand with accountability. Practitioners of conscious capitalism aren't afraid to pull back the curtain, for they understand trust is built on forthrightness about operations, successes, and even failures. This openness is not only about reporting profits and losses; it's about disclosing the company's social and environmental impact with just as much candor.

The concept extends to fostering genuine relationships with suppliers and customers, moving away from arm's length transactions to partnerships based on mutual respect and shared values. Likewise, conscious companies are actively involved with the communities they inhabit, contributing to local economies not merely as employers but as invested citizens.

Moreover, the philosophical underpinnings of conscious capitalism demand businesses consider the ecological footprint of every decision made. This encompasses everything from sourcing raw materials sustainably to minimizing waste through innovative strategies. A sincere commitment to environmental stewardship is not only a moral imperative but a competitive differentiator.

Employee engagement and development are integral components of this model. These enterprises recognize their employees are not cogs in a machine but human beings with aspirations, potential, and a need for meaning in their work. By providing opportunities for growth and recognizing each individual's contribution, conscious companies foster a more motivated, productive, and satisfied workforce.

In the realm of product and service delivery, conscious capitalism espouses creating genuine value rather than engaging in predatory or manipulative tactics. Companies aim to contribute positively to their customers' lives, garnering loyalty not through gimmicks but by enriching experiences and offering solutions that truly resonate with consumer needs.

Finally, conscious capitalism embodies a recognition that every enterprise is part of a more extensive system. It maintains businesses should be not just good corporate citizens but active players in shaping a more ethical, sustainable, and equitable future. The interplay of these principles leads to robust ecosystems where businesses, people, and the planet can flourish.

It's crucial to acknowledge adopting conscious capitalism isn't just about making charities of enterprises. It's a strategic maneuver that significantly contributes to a company's bottom line. Studies have shown companies adhering to conscious practices often perform well financially, indicating that ethical conduct and economic success are not only compatible but can be coalescent.

In essence, defining and embracing conscious capitalism is akin to mapping the DNA of businesses that aspire to be not only the best in the world, but also the best for the world. In the subsequent sections of this book, we will delve deeper into the models, strategies, and case studies that illuminate how this approach is brought to life in diverse industries and contexts. For now, it suffices to say conscious capitalism isn't merely a business strategy; it's a movement swelling in ranks—a beacon of hope for those who believe in an economy that serves humanity in its fullest expression.

Doughnut Economics and its Relation to Conscious Capitalism

The prevailing perception of capitalism is often one of relentless pursuit of profit at the expense of social and environmental welfare. Yet, amidst the looming threats of climate change, resource depletion, and societal inequities, an alternative has arisen that aligns more closely with the principles of sustainability—conscious capitalism. To comprehend the potential of this emergent economic philosophy, it is essential to consider its relationship to a novel, transformative economic model: doughnut economics.

Conceived by Oxford economist Kate Raworth, doughnut economics presents a comprehensive framework to meet the needs of all within the means of the planet. It visualizes the economy as a doughnut, with an inner ring representing the social foundation below which nobody should fall and an outer ring signifying the ecological ceiling humanity must not exceed. This model underscores the interdependency of human well-being and ecological health, positing both as foundational objectives of a reformed economic system.

Conscious capitalism, meanwhile, promotes a business paradigm that transcends profit maximization to incorporate broader societal benefits. It champions purpose-driven businesses that serve the interests of all stakeholders—customers, employees, investors, communities, and the environment. The synergy between these two concepts lies in their mutual advocacy for an inclusive, sustainable approach that respects both human and planetary boundaries.

Operating within the "safe and just space" doughnut economics advocates, businesses practicing conscious capitalism can create value in a way that protects natural resources and improves societal well-being. They recognize their long-term success is contingent upon the health of the ecosystems and communities in which they operate. Hence, they strive to minimize environmental impact and contribute positively to society, reflecting a shift in corporate identities and value systems.

This approach counters traditional economic theories that have largely ignored ecological limits and social foundations, often leading to unsustainable business practices. The integration of doughnut economics with conscious capitalism offers a compelling narrative wherein economic activities are confined within ecological limits while elevating humanity's collective welfare.

Conscious capitalism relies on four tenets: higher purpose, stakeholder integration, conscious leadership, and conscious culture. These tenets are intrinsically aligned with the inner workings of doughnut economics. Higher purpose resonates with the model's core imperative to ensure economic activities contribute to societal advancement without ecological degradation. Stakeholder integration reflects the consideration of broader impacts on society and the environment in business operations, effectively addressing the inner and outer rings of the doughnut.

Conscious leadership, a pillar of conscious capitalism, is about leaders who understand and are committed to their organization's role in the wider economic ecosystem. Similarly, doughnut economics calls for decision-makers who can navigate complex systems and govern toward sustainability. Manifestations of conscious leadership often involve strategic decisions centered on environmental regeneration and social value creation.

Conscious culture, the fourth tenet, pertains to the cultivation of organizational norms and values that foster sustainability and equity. Doughnut economics embraces this cultural ethos, advocating for transformative shifts that redefine progress and eschew exploitation or inequality within economic systems.

However, the relationship between doughnut economics and conscious capitalism isn't without its challenges. The pursuit of environmental and social goals may potentially conflict with profit motives, particularly in the short term. Conscious capitalism asserts businesses are ethically obligated to overcome these challenges and doing so is ultimately to their own advantage.

Moreover, the adoption of doughnut economics necessitates systemic changes in how economic success is measured—shifting from gross domestic product growth to holistic assessments that factor in ecological integrity and human flourishing. This transformation is closely mirrored by conscious capitalism's contention that financial metrics should be accompanied by social and environmental indicators to judge a company's true performance.

Ultimately, the marriage between doughnut economics and conscious capitalism can redefine success in business, encouraging firms to become stewards of the environment and society. This alliance not only calls for corporate responsibility, but also presents viable pathways for achieving a sustainable economy that works for both people and the planet.

Indeed, companies worldwide are increasingly embracing this integrated perspective, recognizing economic activities have to be redesigned to ensure equity, longevity, and respect for natural systems. Such organizations serve as leading examples of how the principles of conscious capitalism, underpinned by doughnut economics, can be operationalized to catalyze positive change.

In summary, the convergence of doughnut economics and conscious capitalism marks a significant stride toward an economic system that is inclusive, regenerative, and resilient. This necessary evolution addresses the dual challenge of social and environmental sustainability head-on, offering hope for a balanced future.

Case Studies of Companies Leading the Conscious Capitalism Movement

In recent years, the concept of conscious capitalism has not only gained traction but become a guiding principle for businesses that want to thrive in a world increasingly conscious of its social and environmental footprint. Through their distinct practices, these businesses reveal profitability and a positive impact can go hand in hand. Let's explore a few case studies of companies that are championing the conscious capitalism movement, setting a precedence for sustainable and ethical business models.

One exemplary beacon in the landscape of conscious capitalism is Patagonia. Known for its environmental activism, Patagonia has embedded sustainability into the core of its business operations. It's more than a trend for this outdoor clothing company; it's a commitment as strong as the materials in their gear. Patagonia assures rigorous standards for the sourcing of materials and actively invests in grassroots movements fighting for environmental preservation. Their Worn Wear initiative encourages reuse and repair of garments instead of discarding them, emphasizing longevity over the disposable nature of consumer goods.

Similarly, Interface, a modular flooring company, has risen as a pioneer in the shift toward ecological responsibility. Under the late visionary CEO Ray Anderson, the company completely rethought its production process, setting a target to have no negative environmental impact by 2020. Its success lies in not only reducing waste and emissions, but also in innovating new products and redesigning processes to be restorative to the planet. Interface showcases the feasibility of radical transformation within an industry often criticized for its ecological footprint.

Another example is Whole Foods Market, which has made broad strides in ethical sourcing and promoting organic and local produce. Their commitment to GMO transparency and support of animal welfare reflects a responsible approach to every facet of their supply chain. Whole Foods demonstrates a supermarket can be both a profitable business and a force for good in food ethics and community health.

Danone, the French multinational, stands out for embracing the concept of a dual economic and social value. With initiatives such as the Danone Ecosystem Fund, the company contributes to the resilience of the communities in which it operates, strengthening both local economies and the company's supply chains. By aligning its missions with the Sustainable Development Goals (SDGs), Danone proves corporations can take on a contributory role in solving global challenges.

TOMS Shoes has mastered a retail business model with humanitarianism at its heart. Their One for One program, donating a pair of shoes for every pair sold, has garnered both criticism and praise. However, this initiative has expanded to other domains such as vision care and clean water access, proving a scalable method of delivering on corporate social responsibility promises.

Another inspiring entity in the conscious capitalism realm is Etsy, an e-commerce company focused on handmade or vintage items and craft supplies. Committed to creating a more fulfilling and lasting world, Etsy has been a certified B Corporation since 2012. The company's mission goes beyond the products it sells; it invests in renewable energy projects to offset the ecological impacts of shipping and emphasizes a strong in-house culture of diversity and inclusion.

Seventh Generation, a company producing eco-friendly cleaning products, has always put transparency and advocacy at the forefront of its business. Their ingredient disclosure and dedication to sustainable packaging have set new standards in an industry slow to change. It's not just about cleaning; it's about caring for future generations by being mindful of the products and chemicals we release into our environment.

Ben & Jerry's is not just known for delectable ice cream flavors, but also for its social consciousness. The Vermont-based company has tackled issues ranging from climate change to marriage equality head-on, using their brand as a platform to promote change. They incorporate sustainability into their value chain, supporting fair trade practices, and sourcing from farmers with environmentally friendly practices.

These case studies exemplify businesses that understand their broader role in society and align their operations and objectives with ecological and social imperatives. They show the surmounting challenges of our time don't just demand shifts in policy or consumer habits; they require an evolution in the orientation of businesses. The conscious capitalism model these companies embody extends beyond philanthropy—it is about integrating purpose into profit, ensuring every business decision made is done with mindfulness toward the planet and its inhabitants.

Conscious capitalism is an acknowledgment of interdependence; the understanding that the success of a business is tied to the well-being of all its stakeholders, from employees and customers to communities and the environment. These companies have turned this acknowledgment into action, displaying commercial endeavors and environmental and social stewardship are not mutually exclusive.

As these companies illustrate, the journey toward conscious capitalism often involves innovation, a daring to reimagine what is possible, and the courage to lead change even when the path is uncharted. It's a journey of continuous improvement, with the understanding that the solutions which seem radical today may well become the benchmarks of tomorrow.

Reflecting on these case studies imparts a critical lesson: in an economy where many claim business is business and nothing more, there lies untapped potential for companies to act as engines of positive change. By doing so, they not only nourish the environment and communities they touch, but also secure their place as future-ready and resilient entities in the market.

Therefore, the vision for future-oriented businesses should not only be about mitigating harm, but also creating an abundance of good— revitalizing ecosystems, building social equity, and fostering well-being. This is the essence of conscious capitalism, and companies that embrace this tenet are the trailblazers, effectively showing us profitability with a conscience is not an abstract ideal but a road that is being paved in real time.

The Future Outlook for Conscious Corporate Behavior

The notion of conscious capitalism has become increasingly popular among businesses striving to blend financial success with positive societal impact. Its promising trajectory plots a course toward a period when a company's worth is gauged not solely by profit margins, but also by its benevolence to the planet and humanity. With strides already taken in embracing this paradigm, the outlook invites cautious optimism for the entrenchment of conscious corporate conduct in the years to come.

The concept of conscious capitalism is predicated upon its four pillars: higher purpose, stakeholder orientation, conscious leadership, and conscious culture. Businesses steadily awakening to the importance of these tenets are setting the stage for a transformation in how they operate. The trajectory foresees an increasing number of companies integrating Environmental, Social, and Governance (ESG) factors into their core strategies, thus, not only generating profit but enriching the wider ecosystem in which they exist.

Looking to the future, stakeholder orientation is expected to evolve. No longer will success be seen as a zero-sum game; rather, corporations will seek win-win scenarios that benefit customers, employees, suppliers, society at large, and the environment. This holistic approach underscores the interdependence between a company and its wider community and necessitates a broader understanding of value creation.

Conscious leadership will become more than a mere buzzword. The leaders of tomorrow are envisaged to be empathetic, inspiring, and guided by a sense of purpose that transcends personal gain. These forward-thinking individuals will champion sustainability and ethics, becoming role models for both their peers and future generations.

Moreover, a conscious culture that fosters inclusivity, moral integrity, and mutual respect will solidify within organizations. As employees align with the organization's purpose and values, they become more engaged and productive, which in turn drives the company's sustainable success.

Anticipated developments in technology will play a pivotal role in championing this conscious behavior. Emerging tools and platforms will offer companies unprecedented abilities to track their supply chain sustainability, analyze big data for better decision-making, and engage with stakeholders through transparent communications. Technology's potential to bolster conscious capitalism is boundless.

Soon, the narrative around business responsibility is expected to shift from why it should be adopted to how best it can be implemented. Practical methodologies and frameworks will be crucial in helping businesses transition their operations to align with conscious capitalism principles. This action-oriented focus will help consolidate conscious behavior in corporate strategies and everyday practices.

The regulatory environment is also likely to evolve in support of this movement. Governments and international bodies may introduce more stringent policies, demanding greater corporate accountability in sustainability and social welfare matters. Such regulatory changes are likely to complement the intrinsic motivation driving businesses toward ethical conduct.

Education, too, will be transformative, with business schools and professional development courses incorporating sustainability and ethics into core curricula. This will instill conscious capitalism's values into the leaders of tomorrow, thus, perpetuating the cycle of ethical corporate behavior.

Consumer dynamics must not be overlooked in this future outlook. As consumers become increasingly aware and demanding of corporate responsibility, companies that fail to adopt conscious behaviors risk obsolescence. In this way, market forces will serve as a corrective, promoting businesses that act in the interest of all stakeholders.

Furthermore, the investment community is anticipated to further recognize the long-term value of conscious corporate behavior. Sustainable and responsible investing is expected to surge, steering capital toward those that align profit with purpose. Investors' increasing scrutiny of ESG criteria will channel financial resources toward driving systemic change.

Additionally, as the impact of climate change becomes more pronounced and urgent, conscious corporate behavior will necessitate embracing innovative solutions to mitigate environmental harm. The stewardship of natural resources will become an imperative integrated into the DNA of future-conscious corporations.

Lastly, collaboration will be central to the future of conscious corporate behavior. Companies will increasingly partner with NGOs, civil society, and governments, recognizing the most-pressing challenges cannot be tackled in silos. This collaborative approach will magnify the impact of ethical business practices and spawn more comprehensive solutions to societal and environmental issues.

Yet, there will be challenges. The journey toward fully conscious capitalism will involve navigating complex trade-offs, overcoming entrenched short-termism in business, and constantly adapting to a changing world. Nevertheless, those companies that wholeheartedly embrace this journey will be well. positioned to thrive.

While the horizon is promising, the transformation to conscious corporate behavior is not guaranteed. It will require the sustained commitment of all sectors—business, government, academia, and civil society. With this collective effort, however, the prospects for a more sustainable and equitable world emerge not as a distant hope but as an attainable reality.

Chapter 22:
Circular Economy:
Redefining Growth and Consumption

n the march toward a more sustainable future, this chapter delves into the transformative concept of the circular economy, a model where growth and consumption no longer mean increased resource extraction and waste, but rather a continuous loop of use and reuse.

Circular economy transcends the traditional "take-make-waste" paradigm by reimagining product life cycles such that materials are maintained in use at their highest utility and value at all times. Central to this is Dr. Walter Stahel's pioneering vision that not only mitigates waste, but also promotes an innovative way for businesses to unlock efficiencies and drive economic growth through longevity, renewability, and resource efficiency.

This chapter unpacks the principles underlining this revolutionary economic system and how businesses can effectively apply it, shifting the narrative from producing more with less to circulating more with what we already have. By embracing such principles, companies can not only reduce their environmental footprint, but also create new value propositions for customers and stakeholders alike, propelling society toward a regenerative and resilient future.

Principles of the Circular Economy

The circular economy offers hope, illuminating a path toward sustainability that departs from the traditional, linear model of "take-make-waste." It is a model that calls for an inclusive approach, understanding growth and consumption can be redefined to support not only economic prosperity, but also environmental preservation and social equity. As such, circular principles seek to create a regenerative system, minimizing waste and making the most of resources.

At the heart of the circular economy is the principle of designing out waste and pollution. Instead of viewing waste as an inevitable result, this principle calls for it to be designed out of products and processes from the very beginning. An entire life cycle approach, considering the end-of-life phase during the design stage, can dramatically reduce the environmental footprint of goods and services.

Another fundamental principle is to keep products and materials in use. Unlike disposable goods that populate the linear economy, the circular approach values durability, repairability, and longevity. By encouraging multiple life cycles through refurbishing, remanufacturing, and repurposing, we sustain the value of materials and reduce the need for additional resource extraction.

An equally important principle is the regeneration of natural systems. The circular economy recognizes the need to replenish and enhance the ecosystems that provide vital resources. It promotes practices such as regenerative agriculture and the use of renewable energy, ensuring business operations can replenish rather than deplete the Earth's resources.

Within these broad strokes lies a diverse array of strategies. Product-as-a-Service (PaaS) models exemplify a shift away from ownership toward access and functionality, ensuring the optimization of product use and extension of their lifespans while enabling companies to retain control over their product's end-of-life fate.

Material innovation plays a significant role in the transition to circularity. The development and use of biodegradable materials, biomimicry solutions, and non-toxic substitutes all align with the ethos of the circular economy—these materials can safely re-enter the biosphere, causing minimal environmental disruption.

Modularity and adaptability are also essential design aspects of the circular economy. By creating products that can be easily upgraded or modified, we extend their usefulness and adapt to changing consumer needs without complete disposals—a stark contrast to planned obsolescence.

A principle that is often overlooked but holds considerable weight in the circular economy is the use of digital technology to enable circularity. Technologies such as blockchain and Internet of Things (IoT) enhance the traceability of products, optimize resource flows, and manage the complexities of reverse logistics in product life cycles.

Closing the loop through circular supply chains is another principle that challenges the status quo. It requires collaboration across all stages of the supply chain to ensure materials are looped back into the production process after their initial use has ended.

The principle of systems thinking underlines the necessity of understanding the interconnections and interdependencies in economic, environmental, and social systems. This holistic approach enables stakeholders to identify leverage points for circular interventions and to comprehend the broader impacts of their actions.

Embedded within the circular economy is the acknowledgment of the intrinsic value of biodiversity. By conserving and restoring natural habitats and biological diversity, businesses safeguard the resilience and productivity of the systems on which they and society rely.

Engaging stakeholders represents a principle that cannot be understated. In the circular economy, stakeholders' active participation and collaboration are critical in driving systemic change. This encompasses consumers, who are often encouraged to take on more active roles through models such as sharing platforms.

Educating and empowering are principles that go hand in hand. The circular economy requires a shift in mindset, and education is vital in fostering this transition. Equipping current and future generations with the knowledge and skills to think and act circularly is fundamental for sustainable progress.

Finally, circular economy principles emphasize the importance of innovation not just of technologically, but also in business models, policy frameworks, and societal behavior. Innovation in business models, for instance, demands rethinking value creation and delivery, often involving cross-sectoral partnerships and collaborative value chains.

Circular economy principles, therefore, offer a blueprint for businesses to reconceptualize growth and consumption. By embedding these principles into their DNA, companies can lead the charge in the transition toward a more sustainable future—an era in which economic vitality thrives in harmony with planetary boundaries and social well-being.

Implementing Circular Strategies in Business Practice

The quest for a more sustainable future beckons us toward the circular economy—a transformative approach redefining growth and consumption by valuing resources, minimizing waste, and regenerating natural systems. To move from theory to practice, businesses must adopt circular strategies that disrupt traditional linear models of "take-make-dispose." Implementing circular strategies is not merely an environmental imperative; it is a conduit for innovation, resilience, and competitive advantage.

At the heart of circular business practices lies the design stage, where products are conceived with their entire life cycle in mind. The objective is to design for longevity, reparability, and recyclability. Companies such as Fairphone, for instance, have embraced modular designs, allowing customers to replace individual components rather than discarding the entire device. Such strategies extend the usable life of products and diminish the demand for raw materials.

A circular business model also encourages adopting new materials that are sustainable and reduce the ecological footprint. Biodegradable materials or those that come from renewable sources can replace traditional plastics and non-renewable resources. Interface Inc., a manufacturer of modular carpets, has pioneered the use of recycled nylon, significantly reducing its dependence on virgin petrochemicals.

However, it's not enough to change materials and designs; businesses must also transform their production processes. By adopting lean manufacturing techniques, companies can reduce waste and increase efficiency. The utilization of waste as a resource—turning scrap materials into new inputs—is a hallmark of a circular approach.

Equally essential is the innovation in business models that support circularity. From product-as-a-service models to take-back schemes, companies are finding new ways to maintain ownership of the resources they use. Philips' "lighting as a service" model, where customers pay for the light rather than lightbulbs, exemplifies this shift. As businesses retain product ownership, they have greater incentive to create durable products and to reclaim and reuse them at end-of-life.

An integral component of circular strategies is building robust reverse logistics capabilities. This enables the return of products post-use for refurbishment or recycling. Reverse logistics not only recovers value from used products, but also fosters customer engagement and loyalty.

As businesses revise their supply chains to become more circular, they have to consider the role of suppliers. Partnering with suppliers who also commit to circular principles forms a supply chain that is cohesive in its sustainability goals. Apple's partnership with suppliers to produce aluminum through a carbon-free smelting process is a case in point.

Transparency and consumer engagement are pivotal to circular economy success. Businesses must educate consumers about the longevity and end-of-life options for their products. When consumers understand the value of circularity, they become active participants in the circular process, valuing durability over disposability.

For circular strategies to have a systemic impact, collaboration across industries and with public entities is essential. The Ellen MacArthur Foundation's Circular Fibres Initiative, bringing together apparel industry stakeholders to build a circular textiles economy, is an example of such collaborative efforts.

Implementing circular strategies also necessitates rethinking performance metrics. Companies must move beyond measuring success solely through sales volume and profit margins. As an alternative, they can include metrics that reflect material circularity, energy reductions, and waste diversion rates to incentivize circular performance.

Digital technologies play a crucial role in advancing circular strategies. The deployment of the Internet of Things (IoT) can track products throughout their life cycle, providing valuable data for optimizing usage and planning for end-of-life recovery. Blockchains can ensure the transparency and traceability of materials, crucial for circular ecosystems in which material origins and environmental impacts must be clear.

Nevertheless, implementing circular strategies is fraught with challenges. It invites upheaval to ingrained business practices and requires initial investments that can be daunting for companies, especially small to medium enterprises (SMEs). However, innovative financing models and government incentives can play a significant role in facilitating this transition.

Ultimately, realigning business practices to fit within a circular economy framework is not just a means to an environmental end. It's a strategic move to position a company as resilient and forward-thinking in a world where resources are finite and customer values are evolving. Those who lead in circular innovation will not only safeguard the planet, but also pave the path for business success in a circular future.

As companies embark on this journey, they join a growing chorus of businesses that contribute to a thriving, biodiverse planet and a sustainable economy. With each circular stride, they do not just commit to their own longevity, they also contribute to the creation of a world where growth and consumption exist in harmony with the Earth's ecological balance.

Indeed, the shift to a circular economy is more than a collection of good deeds—it is an act of vision and leadership. Those who recognize the value latent in our refuse and scrap heaps and see wealth in durability and reuse are the true architects of tomorrow's economy. For a business to thrive in perpetuity, it must invite nature into its ledger books, counting each tree, stream, and mineral as partners in prosperity.

Success Stories: Circular Economy in Action

The discourse surrounding a circular economy is often dense with theory and abstraction, leaving some to wonder how these concepts are applied in the real world. This section illuminates the principles of a circular economy through a showcase of real-life success stories, detailing how specific businesses have embraced this sustainable paradigm to redefine growth and consumption.

In the journey toward circularity, global giants such as Philips have become frontrunners. Their "pay-per-lux" model revolutionizes how we consume light by selling the service of lighting instead of physical light bulbs. Philips retains ownership of the fixtures, is responsible for their maintenance, and, at the end of their life cycle, repurposes the materials. This strategic shift not only reflects substantial energy savings, but also demonstrates the financial viability of service-based business models.

The fashion industry, one of the most scrutinized for its environmental impacts, also showcases circularity champions. Patagonia's Worn Wear program is an exemplary initiative. By encouraging consumers to repair, share, and recycle their gear, the company successfully extends the life cycle of their products. This commitment not only diverts waste from landfills, but also fosters brand loyalty and consumer trust in their commitment to sustainability.

In the technology sector, Fairphone emerges as a paradigm of ethical considerations intertwined with circular practices. This social enterprise has developed modular smartphones designed for longevity and made from ethically sourced materials, embodying the cradle-to-cradle philosophy. By doing so, they tackle the e-waste challenge while also advocating for fair labor conditions in the supply chain, exemplifying a holistic approach to circularity.

Renewable energy also finds its place within the circular economy through companies such as Vestas. The wind turbine manufacturer has committed to producing zero-waste turbines by 2040. Their approach involves designing for recyclability, repowering existing turbines, and exploring new solutions for blade disposal. Vestas has initiated a genuine shift in an industry where large-scale infrastructure often goes overlooked in circular conversations.

On a smaller scale, start-ups such as Ecovative Design harness the power of mycelium to create compostable packaging materials, offering a compelling alternative to polystyrene. These materials can not only be grown to fit specific shapes and sizes, making them highly versatile, they also decompose naturally, thus, fully embracing the principles of a bio-based circular economy.

Agriculture, a sector foundational to human society, is being transformed by circular economy principles through organizations such as AeroFarms. This company pioneers commercial-scale vertical farming that uses aeroponics, reducing water usage by 95% compared to traditional farming and recycling nutrients through closed-loop systems.

In the automotive industry, BMW Group's strategy to design vehicles with disassembly in mind fosters circular principles. With initiatives such as using recycled plastics and remanufacturing car parts, BMW not only conserves resources, but also substantially reduces the environmental impact of vehicle production and waste.

The construction sector also illustrates circularity in action. The Delft University of Technology's Circular Pavilion is an impressive feat, constructed entirely from reusable materials. From glass to structural components, every element is designed to be dismantled and repurposed, effectively turning the building into a material bank for future constructions.

A notable circular approach in the realm of home appliances is pioneered by Bosch with its use of green technology and commitment to a closed material cycle. Bosch designs products for energy efficiency and recyclability, provides repair services to extend product life, and recovers and uses recycled materials wherever possible.

Similarly, IKEA's venture into a circular business model is materializing through initiatives such as offering furniture leasing and taking back used products for refurbishing or recycling. The conglomerate is shifting away from merely being purveyors of flat-pack furniture to becoming leaders in circularity.

In the realm of waste management, TerraCycle has become an iconic emblem of circular solutions. This firm specializes in recycling the "non-recyclable," partnering with other companies and consumers to ensure the reuse and repurposing of complex materials, driving the idea of a zero-waste world forward.

Food and beverage entities are not left behind in this movement either. Toast Ale demonstrates an innovative circular approach to brewing, using unsold loaves and unused crusts from bakeries to craft beer. This not only reduces food waste, but also creates delightful products with a story that resonates with environmentally conscious consumers.

Through a myriad of industries, these stories embody the essence of the circular economy—retaining the economic value of products and materials while exercising stewardship over natural resources. Each narrative is a testament to the potential of circularity to shape industries and redefine growth in line with our planet's finite resources.

The circular economy is not a distant utopian vision but is happening now, brought to life by businesses committed to the path of sustainability. These enterprises serve as inspiration, proving economic success and environmental responsibility can coalesce into a model that promises prosperity for future generations.

We stand on the precipice of change—the current of circularity has set forth, challenging the status quo and illuminating a path toward sustainability that honors both our ecological and financial foundations. As these case studies demonstrate, there is both a moral imperative and a profitable reality in adopting circular economy frameworks.

Chapter 23:
Global Partnerships for Sustainable Development

I n pursuit of a sustainable future, we can't overlook the fortitude of international collaborations. This chapter examines the synergy achieved when diverse stakeholders—governments, NGOs, businesses, and communities—coalesce with a common intent to address pressing global challenges. Such partnerships, resolutely cross-border and cross-sector in nature, exemplify the essence of unified goal setting and resource sharing to harness the full spectrum of human ingenuity and technological advancement.

Corporations, seeing beyond immediate gains, are aligning their strategies with the Sustainable Development Goals (SDGs), thereby committing to a shared blueprint for peace and prosperity. Moreover, as they create coalitions with various entities, they contribute to a collective impact that transcends individual capabilities. This solidarity turns aspirations for a balanced ecosystem, a just economy, and inclusive societies into tangible outcomes.

We delve into this cooperativeness that powers the wheel of innovation, ensuring it rotates in favor of both people and the planet, and we explore the fabric of strategic alliances that anchor businesses as anchors in the global sustainability movement—accelerating us toward a more sustainable, equitable future.

Collaboration Across Borders and Sectors

As we venture deeper into the age of globalization, sustainable development increasingly requires multifaceted and transnational approaches. Collaboration across borders and sectors has emerged not merely as an inspiring ideal but as a practical necessity to address intertwined global challenges. The interconnected nature of economies, ecologies, and societies, means silos in thought and action are no longer viable. Sustainable solutions must be co-created, harnessing diversity of thought, expertise, and resources from a broad spectrum of actors.

Public-private partnerships (PPPs) serve as a testament to the power of cross-sector alliances. When governments join forces with businesses, the synergies can result in innovative solutions that neither could achieve alone. For instance, the blend of public regulation and oversight with corporate efficiency and capital can create sustainable infrastructure that serves public interests while maintaining profitability.

The private sector's extensive reach also provides a unique platform to foster international collaborations. Multinational corporations, with their global supply chains and markets, are uniquely positioned to disseminate best practices and facilitate technology transfer between regions, cultivating a more unified global response to sustainability challenges.

Non-governmental organizations (NGOs) hold a critical place in this collaborative framework. With their on-the-ground insights and action-oriented missions, NGOs can act as intermediaries, connecting disparate groups and ensuring local knowledge and needs are integrated into broader sustainability initiatives.

Academic and research institutions have a vital role to play in facilitating cross-border collaboration. Through their research, they can support evidence-based policy and innovation, as well as provide a neutral ground for stakeholders from different sectors to come together and engage in dialogue.

Building effective cross-border partnerships also entails navigating cultural diversity. Understanding and respecting cultural nuances is essential, not only to avoid misunderstandings but to enrich sustainability strategies with innovative perspectives derived from local knowledge and practices.

However, cross-sector and international collaborations come with inherent complexities. Differing goals, values, and expectations can lead to conflict or inertia if not managed carefully. A clear governance structure with defined roles and objectives is crucial to ensuring collaborative efforts are harmonious and goal oriented.

Technology has emerged as a force multiplier in cross-border collaborations. Digital platforms can facilitate communication and coordination among diverse partners distributed around the globe. Moreover, technology can enhance transparency and accountability— essential ingredients for trust in any collaborative venture.

Data sharing is another cornerstone of cross-sector collaboration. Shared access to valuable data can lead to better decision-making and more robust sustainability efforts. However, this requires sound data governance to ensure sensitive information is protected and data is used ethically and for the intended purpose.

Financing these partnerships is another critical consideration. Sustainable finance mechanisms, such as green bonds, can provide the capital necessary for large-scale sustainability projects that benefit multiple stakeholders and transcend national boundaries.

The UN's Sustainable Development Goals (SDGs) present a framework around which global partnerships can coalesce. The SDGs' broad and interconnected targets encourage sectors and nations to align their sustainability efforts toward common benchmarks, thereby streamlining collaborative processes and measuring progress collectively.

Success stories of cross-border collaborations serve as inspiration. Take, for example, multinational renewable energy projects that bring together finance, technology, and local communities, demonstrating how sustainable initiatives can generate economic, social, and environmental value simultaneously.

Moving forward, cross-border and cross-sector partnerships should continue to evolve. These collaborations must become more agile to be able to respond to the dynamic nature of global challenges. Shared visions, complemented by the ability to adapt quickly to changing circumstances, will be crucial for enduring success.

The urgency of our global sustainability challenges demands no less than a collaborative spirit that transcends borders, sectors, and ideologies. In harnessing the collective wisdom, resources, and innovation at our disposal, there lies hope for a sustainable and equitable future for all.

In conclusion, collaboration across borders and sectors isn't just beneficial; it's imperative for sustainable development. Fostering collaborative environments where trust, mutual respect, and shared goals drive collective action will pave the way toward a more robust and sustainable global community. The task ahead is complex, but through committed and coordinated efforts, businesses, governments, NGOs, academia, and citizens can build a collaborative ecosystem to support the planet's welfare and the common good.

Aligning Corporate Strategies with the Sustainable Development Goals

Global partnerships for sustainable development necessitate an unwavering commitment to the Sustainable Development Goals (SDGs), a set of benchmarks that guide the world toward prosperity for all on a healthy planet. Corporations, seen both as engines of innovation and bastions of resources, have a critical role in aligning their strategies with the SDGs to foster sustainability in a way that extends beyond philanthropy into the core of their business functions.

The SDGs, established by the United Nations in 2015, are a universal call to end poverty, protect the planet, and ensure all people enjoy peace and prosperity by 2030. These seventeen goals are integrated—they recognize actions in one area will affect outcomes in others and development must balance social, economic, and environmental sustainability. Corporations, when they internalize these goals, can catalyze a transformative shift that transcends any single entity's efforts.

Aligning corporate strategies with SDGs entails embedding sustainability at the heart of business models. It's not just about corporate social responsibility (CSR) as a separate arm or public image facade; it's about redefining the purpose of the corporation to serve broader societal needs while achieving economic returns. This often requires rethinking product lines, supply chains, and operation standards to reduce environmental impacts, promote social inclusion, and foster economic growth within planetary boundaries.

Leadership commitment is the cornerstone of aligning with SDGs. CEOs and executive teams need to champion the integration of the SDGs into their corporate strategies, setting a clear vision, measurable targets, and holding the company accountable. This visionary leadership opens the door to innovation—creating new markets and opportunities that are aligned with societal needs and driving long-term value for the company and its stakeholders.

Collaboration is another key facet. No single corporation can achieve the SDGs on its own. Effective partnerships with governments, civil society, and other businesses are essential. Such synergies multiply the impact a company can make on the SDGs, leveraging different strengths and compensating for individual weaknesses—enabling shared value creation in the truest sense of the phrase.

Moreover, aligning with SDGs mandates transparency and accountability. Companies need to report on their sustainability performance with as much rigor as their financial performance. This transparency enables stakeholders, including investors, to assess a company's true long-term value and its impact on society and the environment. Standardized reporting frameworks such as Global Reporting Initiative (GRI) provide guidance on communicating impact through the lens of the SDGs.

Research indicates that SDG-aligned businesses often find improved operational efficiencies, enhanced risk management, and increased attractiveness to investors and talent. The SDGs offer a lens through which business innovation can be directed toward areas of greatest global need—be it renewable energy, food security, health, education, or infrastructure development.

Consumers, too, are a driving force for SDG alignment. A burgeoning global constituency is demanding products and services that do not merely serve personal needs but advance global welfare. Companies acting on this awareness not only gain loyalty, but also tap into new consumer segments that value ethical practices and sustainability.

Education and continual learning are essential in this journey. Businesses need to ensure their employees at all levels understand the SDGs and how their daily work contributes to these global goals. This often involves training programs and workshops, as well as creating collaborations with educational institutions to stay abreast with sustainability knowledge and skills.

One of the significant challenges in aligning with the SDGs is the apparent conflict between short-term profitability and long-term sustainability. It's a myth that needs debunking. Evidence demonstrates businesses that think long-term outperform their peers in revenue, earnings, investment, and job growth. SDG alignment is not just good ethics—it's sound business strategy.

Innovative financial mechanisms such as green bonds, social impact investing, and Environmental, Social, and Governance (ESG) funds are vital. They provide the capital necessary for companies to invest in sustainable projects and technologies. These instruments enable corporations to align their financial strategies with ethical goals, attracting investors drawn to sustainability-oriented instruments.

Digital technologies play a pivotal role in aligning with SDGs by facilitating tasks such as tracking supply chain sustainability, predicting risks, and calculating impacts with greater precision. AI, blockchain, and IoT are just some of the technologies that are transforming how companies approach and report on sustainability.

In conclusion, aligning corporate strategies with the SDGs is not just a moral obligation but a strategic imperative. Businesses that heed this call are poised to lead in the new economy, secure in the knowledge they are contributing to a sustainable future for all. Far from being an impediment to success, sustainability is the most-significant pathway to it.

Building Coalitions for Collective Impact

In the quest for sustainable development, the creation of broad coalitions represents a pivotal turn in the roadmap of collective action. Businesses are increasingly recognizing the complex web of environmental and social challenges we face cannot be tackled in isolation—despite their power, resources, and innovative capacities. The necessity for coalitional frameworks that transcend sectoral boundaries and geographic confines is clearer than ever. Thus, the fabric of our global partnerships is compelled to evolve, not merely as a demonstration of ethical solidarity but as a pragmatic strategy for amplifying impact and effecting palpable change.

Coalitions bridge the gap between the intentions of individual entities and the expansive scope of global objectives such as the Sustainable Development Goals (SDGs). By unifying diverse actors—private sector businesses, government bodies, non-governmental organizations, academic institutions, and local communities—coalitions marshal a spectrum of expertise, resources, and influence. This convergence forms the bedrock for strategies that can leverage systemic transformation.

For businesses, engaging in coalitions does not merely complement their corporate responsibility agenda; it reinvigorates their strategic approach to sustainability. Through collective action, corporations can overcome the limitations of scale that often impede the implementation of sustainable practices. The synergistic potential of coalitions enables participating businesses to extend their reach, share risks, and access novel opportunities.

This collective approach responds to the multifaceted nature of sustainability challenges that demands interdisciplinary solutions. Coalitions provide the latitude to address issues in their interconnectedness, thus, preventing the siloed interventions that may fail to account for the complexity of ecosystems and human societies. A coalition-centric strategy recognizes actions in one domain can have far-reaching, unforeseen consequences in another. As a result, a holistic approach is not just wise but indispensable.

Indeed, coalition building requires a conscious navigation of differences and alignment of interests. Effective coalitions foster a culture of mutual respect, shared vision, and reciprocated value. The success of such alliances hinges on transparency, open communication, and trust among stakeholders—a trust that is earned through the demonstration of commitment and consistency in action.

The mechanics of these partnerships are nuanced and demand intentional design. Establishing common goals, metrics for progress, coordinated planning, and regularly scheduled evaluations are essential for maintaining momentum and ensuring accountability. The governance structures within coalitions must be crafted to encourage equitable participation and leverage the unique strengths of each member.

A critical strength of coalitions lies in collective advocacy, a powerful tool for policy influence. While individual businesses can lobby for legislative changes, a united voice of a well-structured coalition advocating for sustainability can significantly impact political will and policy development. This is particularly relevant in instances when the encouragement of green policies or the regulation of harmful practices requires a push from united and credible entities.

Data and knowledge sharing are other critical facets of coalitions. In a world where information is currency, coalitions can act as repositories and disseminators of best practices, innovative technologies, and sustainability solutions. Businesses that may struggle to undertake extensive research and development can benefit from the shared intelligence that coalitions can afford.

Equity is a principle that cannot be overstated in the context of coalition building. Global partnerships must be sensitive to the power dynamics at play and ensure local communities and minority representatives have voice and agency within the coalition. The goals of sustainability cannot be fully met without attention to the inclusivity of the marginalized, whose lives are often most-directly impacted by environmental and social issues.

Implementing sustainability through such collective efforts is a learning process for all involved. It requires a willingness to adapt, an openness to novel ideas, and a commitment to redefining traditional models of competition. In coalitions, businesses can experience a shift toward a paradigm of "co-opetition," where cooperating with potential competitors in certain domains can lead to greater shared value than operating in isolation.

Examples of successful coalitions are abundant and diverse. The Renewable Energy Buyers Alliance (REBA), a coalition committed to scaling corporate purchasing of renewable energy, demonstrates the potential of aligning interests across sectors to progress toward energy sustainability. Such examples serve as lighthouses, guiding the way for other businesses and coalitions seeking to make a significant mark on the sustainability landscape.

As businesses continue to navigate the landscape of sustainability, it is apparent that the future of corporate impact rests not only within the four walls of the firm, but also within the broader network of allies they can galvanize. Companies must, therefore, see coalition building not as an ancillary activity but as a core strategy of their sustainability ethos—an ethos that recognizes the transformative power of collective impact.

Adopting a coalition mindset allows businesses to step beyond the narrow confines of self-interest and participate in the co-creation of pathways to a sustainable future. It is a call to action—combined, coordinated, and exponential in its ability to set forth ripples of positive change. The task at hand is immense, but so is the potential when we unite for a common cause. To build a future that honors both humanity and Earth, we cannot stand apart; we must stand together.

Chapter 24:
Climate Change Mitigation:
The Business Response

n the continuing dialogue on sustainability and corporate responsibility, this chapter dives into the strategic responses businesses are implementing to address climate change—one of the most pressing challenges of our time. Corporations, once seen as mere contributors to environmental degradation, are now metamorphosing into stewards of the planet by proactively deploying innovative strategies to curtail their carbon footprint and elevate their role in climate change mitigation. They're leveraging emerging technologies, overhauling obsolete practices, and, more importantly, recalibrating their core values to promote environmental ethics.

This conscious shift isn't just about compliance or brand image; it's about survival, resilience, and aligning with a global movement toward a sustainable future. By investing in renewable energy solutions, scrutinizing their supply chains for eco-friendly alternatives, and redefining corporate governance with a verdant brush, businesses are not just adapting—they're leading the charge in the crusade against climate upheaval.

This voyage toward sustainability isn't an effortless endeavor; it requires tenacity and a pledge to continuous improvement. But the fruits it bears can enshrine a legacy of ecological and social responsibility. The crux of the matter? Businesses that integrate climate action into their strategies aren't just doing good—they're pioneering a transformative and collaborative narrative that resonates with investors, consumers, and communities alike, beckoning a shared vision of a thriving, equitable planet.

Corporate Strategies for Reducing Carbon Footprints

In a world grappling with the ramifications of climate change, the call for businesses to step up and implement strategies to reduce their carbon footprints has never been more urgent. Corporate strategies for reducing carbon footprints are not just about compliance; they are about taking responsibility for the future of our planet. The journey toward carbon neutrality requires innovation, commitment, and a substantial shift in the corporate mindset.

Firstly, an effective strategy starts with measuring and understanding emissions. Companies must identify and track their prime sources of greenhouse gas emissions, including both direct operational emissions and indirect emissions, such as those from the supply chain. This detailed inventory is the bedrock upon which reduction goals are set and progress is measured.

Energy efficiency is the cornerstone of reducing emissions. By optimizing energy use, companies can significantly decrease their carbon footprints. This involves retrofitting buildings with energy-efficient lighting, heating, and cooling systems, as well as considering design aspects that reduce the need for artificial lighting and temperature control. Investments in energy-efficient equipment and processes not only cut emissions but often result in substantial cost savings.

The transition to renewable energy sources is another critical component. Businesses are increasingly investing in renewable energy projects such as solar and wind power, either through direct installation on their premises or through the purchase of renewable energy certificates (RECs). This shift not only helps mitigate climate change, but also ensures energy security and price stability.

Aside from energy, another significant contributor to a company's carbon footprint is its supply chain. By choosing suppliers that are committed to sustainable practices and working with them to improve environmental performance, companies can exert influence far beyond their immediate operations. This may involve supporting producers in adopting renewable energy or fostering more efficient manufacturing processes.

Resource efficiency extends to the principles of the circular economy, wherein products are designed for durability, reuse, and recyclability, thus, reducing waste and conserving resources. Engaging in circular business models can radically decrease a company's carbon footprint while fostering innovation.

Carbon offsetting is used by some businesses to compensate for emissions they are currently unable to reduce directly. This involves investing in environmental projects that reduce carbon dioxide elsewhere, such as reforestation or clean energy initiatives. While offsetting is controversial, it can be part of a broader strategy if combined with genuine efforts to reduce actual emissions.

Travel and transportation often contribute significantly to a company's carbon emissions. By adopting a sustainable transport strategy, including the use of electric vehicles, encouraging telecommuting, video conferencing, and optimizing logistics to reduce the number of trips required, organizations can make a sizeable dent in their carbon output.

Employee engagement is also vital in achieving carbon footprint reduction. Corporations that promote a culture of sustainability through education and incentives encourage employees to act in environmentally responsible ways, both at work and in their personal lives. This cultural shift can manifest in simple actions, such as reducing single-use plastics or incentivizing public transport usage for commuting.

Another key strategy involves setting science-based targets, aligning corporate emissions reduction goals with climate science recommendations to limit global warming. These targets provide a clear roadmap for companies to contribute meaningfully to global climate goals and to signal their commitment to stakeholders.

Beyond individual corporate actions, there is a growing movement toward industry collaboration. Companies within the same sector are coming together to share best practices, invest in sector-specific research and development, and lobby for policies that support a transition to a low-carbon economy. Collective action amplifies the impact individual businesses can have on reducing emissions.

Innovation in product development and service delivery is also critical. By rethinking how products are made and services are rendered, companies can dramatically reduce their carbon footprints. This may involve the use of sustainable materials, investing in new technologies, or reimagining entire business models to be more environmentally friendly.

Communication and transparency play an important role in galvanizing action and building trust. By openly reporting on emissions, reduction initiatives, and progress toward set goals, companies can maintain accountability to stakeholders and the public. This transparency can bolster a company's reputation and inspire others to follow suit.

Financial instruments such as green bonds or sustainability-linked loans can be leveraged to finance projects that have positive environmental benefits, including emissions reduction measures. By tying financial performance to sustainability performance, these instruments ensure there is a material incentive tied to a company's carbon reduction efforts.

The decision to integrate carbon footprint reduction into business strategies is no longer just an environmental choice; it is becoming a financial and ethical imperative. Consumers, investors, and employees are increasingly aligning with companies that demonstrate environmental stewardship. As such, reducing carbon footprints is integral to the long-term sustainability and competitiveness of businesses.

Ultimately, the confluence of dedication, innovation, and ethical responsibility will define the corporate leaders of tomorrow. As they forge a path of sustainability, they will not only be reducing their carbon footprints, but also leading the charge in the global effort to ensure a thriving, healthier planet for generations to come.

Renewable Energy: Opportunities and Challenges for Businesses

As we delve into the realm of corporate responses to climate change, a pivotal topic emerges: renewable energy. This field represents progression for those vying for a more sustainable and equitable future. It's a landscape ripe with possibilities yet beset with hurdles that demand innovative solutions. In the following passages, the dual nature of renewable energy—its promises and its impediments—will be contemplated from a business perspective.

Firstly, it is imperative to acknowledge the colossal potential of renewable energy sources such as solar, wind, hydro, and geothermal. These resources offer businesses the means to dramatically lower their carbon footprints, aligning operational activities with the goals of environmental stewardship. By transitioning to renewables, corporations can decouple economic growth from environmental degradation, allowing them to adhere to an ethic that prioritizes planet and people alongside profit.

The financial viability of renewable energy, once a barrier, has improved significantly. This positive shift can be largely attributed to technological advancements and economies of scale. As production costs for wind turbines and solar panels decrease, the economic case for transitioning away from fossil fuels strengthens, enabling businesses to make investments that are prudent both ethically and financially.

Moreover, integrating renewable energy can bolster a company's public image, appeal to environmentally conscious consumers, and satisfy the growing chorus of stakeholders demanding corporate responsibility. Those that establish themselves as green leaders may enjoy enhanced brand loyalty and competitive advantages. Brand integrity rooted in actualized sustainable practice resonates deeply with a market increasingly skeptical of shallow commitments.

Despite these opportunities, businesses face significant challenges in harnessing renewable energy. Scaling up renewables to meet industrial demands often requires substantial upfront investment. Smaller firms, in particular, may find this initial cost daunting, although various financing models and government incentives offer some relief.

Intermittency and storage currently baffle even the most-committed businesses. The sun doesn't always shine, and the wind doesn't always blow, necessitating reliable energy storage systems or backup sources to ensure consistent power supply. Innovation in battery technology and grid management holds solutions, but we're still en route to their full realization and deployment.

The infrastructure to support a comprehensive shift to renewable energy is also lacking. A transition of this magnitude requires wide-reaching changes in energy grids, a challenge that intertwines with urban planning and affects the capabilities of many businesses to operate solely on renewable sources. Public and private sector colossi must collaborate to restructure our energy foundations in preparation for this sustainable shift.

Pertinently, the knowledge and skills needed to implement and maintain renewable energy solutions are not uniformly distributed. Businesses must invest in workforce training in order to cultivate expertise that will be essential in the upkeep of renewable energy systems. Connection with academic institutions and vocational training programs to prepare tomorrow's workforce is more crucial now than ever before.

Policy inconsistency also poses a challenge. In the tussle between old and new energy regimes, fluctuating government policies can create instability, making long-term investments in renewable energy riskier. Companies must navigate a political climate that may support fossil fuels one term and renewables the next, causing hesitancy in committing to either path.

Despite these impediments, the call to action for the use of renewable energy resonates powerfully. It is no longer a lofty ideal but a strategic imperative. Firms that recognize the inevitability of the global shift toward sustainability are positioned to thrive, while those that delay may face obsolescence or public censure.

Equally important is the connection between renewable energy initiatives and the broader imperative of social responsibility. Businesses taking the lead on renewables must ensure their endeavors do not replicate inequalities or create new forms of social or environmental injustice to forge a path forward that is genuinely inclusive and equitable.

Furthermore, participation in renewable energy projects can foster partnerships and collaboration, drawing together diverse stakeholders in pursuit of common goals. Through these partnerships, businesses can access novel financing methods, share risks, and benefit from shared expertise, driving innovation and mitigating the challenges of adopting sustainable practices.

It's clear renewable energy is more than an energy choice; it's an ethical one, as well as a symbol of commitment to future generations. Intrepid businesses that embark on this journey will not only pioneer new standards of corporate responsibility, but also partake in crafting a narrative of hope, daring to imagine a replenished world powered by forces that do not pilfer from the Earth, but dance in harmony with her rhythms.

In summation, the intersection of business and renewable energy is fraught with complexity yet vibrant with potential. Overcoming the hurdles requires courage, innovation, and a clear-eyed vision of the future we aspire to create. It's an undertaking that necessitates both unwavering resolve and the capacity to envisage a dramatically altered energy landscape and a world where commerce serves, sustains, and celebrates the planet it inherits.

As stewards of tomorrow's legacy, businesses wield extraordinary influence and bear a heavy responsibility. The collective decisions made in boardrooms and factories today are indelibly etching the contour lines of our shared future. It's a monumental task, one that should be carried with sincerity and an unyielding commitment to the values of sustainability, justice, and human dignity.

In essence, renewable energy is not just an opportunity or challenge; it's a testament to what can be achieved when business integrates ecological sensibility into the heart of its ethos. Our pursuit should not be merely for energy that sustains but for a flourishing kineticism that regenerates and renews, cheerleading humanity away from the precipice of ecological despair and toward a luminescent dawn.

With a confluence of ethical rigor, economic acuity, and technological savvy, the journey toward embracing renewable energy becomes not just plausible, but also paramount for businesses committed to the grander vision of a sustainable future. This section has sought to elucidate this intricate tapestry, tugging at the threads that may weave into a more resilient, equitable, and ecologically attuned commercial enterprise. It's a story still being written, not with ink, but with action, collaboration, and an unwavering belief in what can be achieved when we dare to reimagine the possible.

Adapting to Climate Risks: Business Continuity and Resilience

In the face of relentless climate change, it is no longer sufficient for corporations to simply reduce their greenhouse gas emissions. To ensure long-term prosperity, businesses must also adapt to the prevailing climate risks, fostering business continuity and resilience that stand against the crescendo of ecological disruptions. Adaptation strategies must become as fundamental as mitigation efforts in the repertoire of corporate responses to our climate reality.

Climate resilience in business is about anticipating, preparing for, and responding to incremental changes and sudden disruptions caused by climate change. It requires an intricate understanding of how climate risks uniquely impact each facet of operations—from supply chains and manufacturing processes to employee safety and asset integrity. The implementation of adaptation strategies can significantly reduce vulnerabilities, safeguarding against operational, financial, and reputational damages.

Business continuity planning, traditionally focused on immediate crises management, is evolving to incorporate longer-term climate projections. This proactive approach necessitates a close collaboration with climate scientists and data analysts to integrate climate risk modeling into business strategy. By embedding such forward-looking data into their risk assessments, companies can better anticipate potential climate-related disruptions and devise contingency plans accordingly.

It's essential for businesses to evaluate the resilience of their infrastructure. The burgeoning frequency of extreme weather events means facilities must be built or retrofitted to withstand a broader range of conditions. Investment in resilient infrastructure becomes a strategic imperative, not only to protect physical assets, but also to ensure services remain uninterrupted in the wake of climatic challenges.

The supply chain is another critical area demanding attention for climate resilience. Disruptions due to climate impacts can ripple effect throughout the global economy. A company's capacity to quickly recover from such disruptions largely depends on the robustness and flexibility of its supply chain. Hence, diversifying suppliers and building redundancy into supply networks are crucial steps in building a resilient business structure.

In addition to safeguarding physical assets, companies must also invest in human capital. This means providing training and resources to employees so they can adapt to new operational realities, promoting agility and fostering a workforce equipped to navigate through climate-induced changes. Employee well-being must be protected by ensuring work environments remain safe even as environmental conditions fluctuate.

Furthermore, companies must not overlook the importance of robust financial planning to absorb and recover from climate-induced financial hits. This could mean setting aside strategic reserves, acquiring appropriate insurance coverage, or developing alternate revenue streams to remain viable when certain assets or operations are impacted by climate events.

In response to these multifaceted risks, innovative tools such as climate scenario analysis are being deployed, allowing corporations to envision and prepare for a future where climate impacts may significantly alter their business landscape. These analyses, when regularly updated, provide a foundation for dynamic and informed decision-making.

Crucially, businesses must also work toward fostering strong and cooperative relations with all their stakeholders. As climate change affects entire communities and markets, collaborative efforts become necessary to create shared resilience strategies. This extends to working with governments to influence and shape climate adaptation policies and regulations that are conducive to collective long-term sustainability goals.

Taking these requisite steps toward climate resilience can offer businesses a competitive advantage. Companies that are perceived as responsible and proactive in tackling climate risks can bolster their brand reputation, customer loyalty, and investor confidence. It is a solid defense not only against the direct impacts of climate changes, but also the indirect effects stemming from evolving consumer behaviors and regulatory landscapes.

Such extensive preparedness, however, cannot be enacted overnight. It is an iterative process that requires ongoing commitment and the integration of climate change considerations into every level and facet of corporate planning. This integration ensures resilience becomes a core part of the business rather than an afterthought.

Technology, too, plays a pivotal role in adapting to climate risks, with the development of smart infrastructure and forecasting tools offering enhanced capabilities to predict and react in real time to climate events.

Digital transformation can significantly improve the agility and responsiveness of businesses to emerging threats posed by the climate crisis.

Finally, businesses must be conscious of their role not only in adapting to climate change, but also contributing to community resilience. By supporting local infrastructure projects, engaging in prudent water management, and fostering biodiversity, companies can play a crucial role in strengthening the resilience of the ecosystems and societies in which they operate.

In conclusion, adapting to climate risks requires a multifaceted and proactive approach. By prioritizing business continuity and resilience, corporations not only secure their own future, but also contribute to a more robust, adaptable, and sustainable world. The path to resilience is continuous and demanding, but the shared efforts of the business community can turn adaptation strategies into opportunities for innovation and leadership in the drive toward a sustainable future.

Chapter 25:
The Future Horizon:
Ethical Business in a Transforming World

As the foundation built by preceding chapters firms, we now turn toward the vast, uncharted territories of our future horizon, where ethical business practices become the pivotal compass for navigating a transforming world. Amidst increasing challenges—climate crisis, societal inequities, and the disruptive force of technological advancements—lies immense potential for businesses that choose to champion the mantle of responsibility and steer their strategies toward sustainability and ethics. The leaders who emerge in this epoch will not only recognize the intrinsic value of ecological and social stewardship, but also perceive the benefits that such commitments yield for organizational longevity and trustworthiness.

We are witnessing an age in which enterprises must anticipate and adapt to burgeoning ethical dilemmas, foretelling the expectations of a sensitive and informed customer base that demands transparency, integrity, and ecological mindfulness. This chapter envisions a landscape where businesses act as custodians of environmental harmony and social justice, pioneering disruptive innovations that both respect the planet's finite resources and empower communities.

The seeds for an ethical revolution in business are sown; as they burgeon, we observe enterprises evolving from mere commercial entities to becoming proactive agents of a sustainable and equitable civilization. It is through the amalgamation of resilience, adaptive capacity, and transformative leadership that businesses can, and indeed must, shape the narrative of a future in which prosperity is synonymous with planetary well-being and human dignity.

Setting the Stage for the Future

In the quest to forge a sustainable future, discerning the direction in which we must head is as critical as understanding the path we have traveled. The preceding chapters provide the bedrock upon which we visualize a transformative horizon—one in which ethical business practices permeate global marketplaces and corporate strategies align seamlessly with environmental and social imperatives.

As we contemplate the future, we stand at a functional precipice. The decisions made and actions taken in the next few years will indubitably ripple through generations, influencing the very fabric of our planetary coexistence and human enterprise. It is an epoch in which ethical business is not merely an option but a categorical imperative for survival and prosperity.

Integrating ecological and social ethics into the core of business strategies is not simply a moral choice; it's a strategic one that echoes the sentiments of stakeholders, aligns with evolving regulatory pressures, and satisfies the demand for a meaningful global citizenship. This convergence forms the cornerstone of a future in which businesses are not only participants but pioneers in the sustainability movement.

The nature of corporate influence extends beyond profit margins and shareholder value. It lays the groundwork for a systemic change where the preservation of ecosystems, the well-being of communities, and the prosperity of economies are inextricably linked. There is an unmistakable unity in the notion that businesses can—and must—be active conductors orchestrating this symphony of sustainable development.

As such, future business leaders are tasked with a formidable but inspiring challenge: redefining the essence of corporate success. Growing evidence suggests sustainable practices lead to resilient and profitable outcomes, dispelling the dated myth that environmental and social responsibility is the antithesis of economic viability.

Indeed, the landscape of opportunity for businesses willing to adapt and evolve with a sustainability-first approach is both vast and rich with potential. The next horizon of ethical business will be distinguished by innovators who harness sustainable technologies, engage in circular economies, and dynamically adapt to the shifting tides of consumer preferences and expectations.

As we move forward, aligning business models with the principles of equity, transparency, and stewardship will be seen not only as pioneering but essential. Through critical thinking and collaborative efforts, businesses can foster symbiotic relationships that nurture the planet while propelling economic advancement.

Digital transformation will continue to play a pivotal role in advancing sustainable practices. The deployment of artificial intelligence, blockchain, and big data analytics offers unprecedented capabilities to optimize resource use, reduce waste, and improve decision-making processes, ultimately driving more ethical and efficient business operations.

However, as we champion technological innovation, we must also be vigilant in navigating its ethical implications. Data privacy, algorithmic bias, and the digital divide are areas that require thoughtful attention to ensure progress in sustainability does not come at the cost of ethical transgressions or greater societal stratification.

Driving toward the future, a new ethos awaits—one of a shifting paradigm from the "business as usual" lexicon to one that values social capital as much as financial capital. The harmonization between these two capital forms is where true innovation and value generation will be realized, creating avenues for businesses to transcend traditional metrics of success.

Preparation for this imminent future requires businesses to invest in human capital, cultivate a culture of continuous learning, and remain agile in the face of uncertainty. A workforce that is educated and empowered to think sustainably will be the vanguard of this business revolution, shaping the attitudes and behaviors that underpin a conscious marketplace.

The embodiment of ethical business in the future will manifest through corporations that recognize their shared destiny with the communities and environments in which they operate. They will not only be judged by their products or profits, but also their contribution to societal and planetary health. This necessitates a leadership paradigm shift, where the success of business leaders is measured by their capacity to generate long-term, inclusive, and life-affirming outcomes for all stakeholders.

It is in this context the stage for the future is set—a future that cherishes resiliency, nurtures innovation, values integrity and equitable participation, and, most importantly, acknowledges the finite nature of our planet's resources and ecosystems. Amidst this landscape of change, businesses that embrace their ethical responsibilities will find themselves at the helm of the sustainability movement, leading humanity toward a thriving and equitable horizon.

In setting this stage for the future, the following compelling questions remain: How can ethical business serve as the catalyst for systemic change toward global sustainability? What strategies and models will allow businesses to thrive in harmony with nature and society? What transformative impact can ethical business practices have on establishing an equitable and durable world for ensuing generations?

It is with these inquiries in mind we embark on the journey to explore disruptive innovations, anticipate future challenges, and envision a world where ethical business practices are not the exception but the norm—a world we must start shaping today for tomorrow's generation.

Disruptive Innovations Shaping a Sustainable Future

The pursuit of sustainability and ethical business practices is no longer a peripheral concern; it has become central to corporate strategy and innovation. Disruptive technologies and radical innovations are emerging as the cornerstone of this transition, driving colossal shifts in how businesses approach their role in society and the environment. Against this backdrop of transformation and opportunity, several key innovations stand poised to significantly shape the sustainable landscapes of tomorrow.

The concept of the circular economy, which represents a shift away from traditional linear "take-make-dispose" models, is being enabled through advancements in material science and product design. Innovations such as biodegradable materials and modular products that can be easily repaired, reused, or recycled are beginning to disrupt markets, offering a vision of economy where waste is nearly eliminated and the life cycle of products is dramatically extended.

Renewable energy technology is another explosive area of innovation that is central to the quest for sustainability. Solar photovoltaics and wind turbines have seen dramatic improvements in efficiency and reductions in cost, allowing for a more rapid displacement of fossil fuels. Developments in energy storage, such as enhanced battery systems and novel forms of storing energy including pumped hydro or compressed air, have the potential to resolve intermittent issues associated with renewable sources and reshape energy infrastructures.

The advancement of smart grid technology is integral to creating energy systems that are not only efficient, but also adaptive and responsive to the needs and behavior of consumers. Smart grids can optimize energy distribution and management, reducing waste and enabling the integration of distributed energy resources such as rooftop solar panels into the larger grid.

One cannot overlook the transformative power of digitalization in sustainable innovation. Blockchain technology has far-reaching potential for enhancing supply chain transparency, thereby ensuring ethical sourcing and reducing fraudulent practices. Decentralized networks can provide a trustable ledger of transactions that document the entire life cycle of a product from raw materials to final sale.

Artificial intelligence (AI) is set to play a decisive role in sustainability efforts. Through the optimization of resource use, predictive maintenance of equipment, and enhanced efficiency across various processes, AI assists companies in reducing their environmental footprint. Smart algorithms can process vast amounts of data to identify patterns that would be imperceptible to the human eye, leading to improved decision-making and innovation.

Technology is also revolutionizing agriculture, a sector notoriously strained by the need to meet the demands of a growing population while minimizing environmental impact. Precision agriculture, using data and AI, allows for the application of inputs such as water and fertilizers with pinpoint accuracy, improving yields and reducing waste.

Water scarcity, a pressing global issue, is being addressed through innovative desalination methods and water purification technologies that may render previously undrinkable water safe for consumption. New advancements in this area seek to improve efficiency while reducing the significant energy footprint traditionally associated with water treatment.

Advances in transportation technologies, such as electric and autonomous vehicles, offer the promise of a future with reduced greenhouse gas emissions and increased safety. These innovations are not confined to passenger vehicles; heavy duty trucks and even seagoing vessels are beginning to explore electric propulsion, signaling a shift that could decarbonize entire sectors of transportation.

As the boundaries of innovation continue to expand, so too does our potential for creating a more sustainable future. Cradle-to-cradle design principles are inspiring product development that prioritizes the entire life cycle, emphasizing the use of safe materials that can be perpetually cycled into new products without loss of quality.

Advanced building materials and construction techniques are reducing carbon footprints while also improving the performance and longevity of the structures we inhabit. The promise of ultra-efficient buildings, which generate more energy than they consume, is made tangible through technologies such as intelligent energy management systems and high-performance insulation.

Chemical recycling of plastics presents an innovative approach to managing plastic waste. This process breaks down polymers back into their constituent monomers which can be re-polymerized into new plastics. This technology could dramatically reduce the landfilling and pollution associated with plastic, transforming waste into a valuable resource.

Food technology, including lab-grown meat and plant-based proteins, could reshape agriculture and reduce the environmental burden of food production. Cultured meat, which requires a fraction of the land, water, and energy of traditional livestock, could significantly diminish the ecological footprint of our diets while addressing animal welfare concerns.

Financial technology (fintech) is facilitating the growth of green finance by providing platforms and tools that empower investors to support sustainable businesses and projects. Crowdfunding, blockchain-based tokens, and impact investment platforms are making it easier for individuals and institutions alike to fund and track the environmental and social impact of their investments.

Perhaps among the most-crucial aspects of these disruptive innovations is their potential for inclusivity. Technologies such as mobile internet and micro-grids bring sustainable solutions to even the most remote and impoverished areas, democratizing access to energy and information and empowering communities previously left in the dark.

As we consider the myriad opportunities these disruptive innovations offer, we must recognize it's our creative and ethical use of these technologies that will determine their impact on the future. A sustainable and equitable future demands not only innovation, but also a dedicated commitment to using these tools thoughtfully and responsibly, ensuring they serve as champions of both environmental integrity and social justice.

Anticipating and Adapting to Future Ethical Challenges

In the unceasing flux of a transforming world, businesses must become prescient entities capable of foreseeing and managing emerging ethical quandaries. The coming years are bound to present dilemmas that intertwine environmental stewardship, social justice, and economic performance, and corporations are poised to be pivotal in their resolution. To achieve this, corporations must infuse foresight into their strategic planning, operational decisions, and corporate culture to ensure a sustainable trajectory.

Future ethical challenges will largely emerge from technological advancements and environmental pressures. The coming decades are expected to unveil innovations beyond our current comprehension, and with each breakthrough comes potential ethical implications. For instance, as biotechnology progresses, businesses may confront the ethics of genetic modification, not only in foods but in ecological interventions aimed at conservation. Here, companies must grapple with ethically complex decisions involving biodiversity and ecological balance.

In parallel, artificial intelligence (AI) is projected to revolutionize industry yet again. With its potential to optimize resource use and mitigate environmental impacts, AI can indeed be a force for sustainability. However, it introduces ethical concerns surrounding job displacement, privacy, and the control of autonomous systems. Companies adopting AI must do so with a commitment to navigating these issues responsibly.

Climate change remains the preeminent ethical trial of our time, and its unpredictable trajectory will challenge businesses to adapt continuously. Unforeseen environmental events can have significant implications for ethical business practices, particularly in areas such as supply chain management and disaster response. This reality demands an agile and ethically guided approach to mitigate harm and deliver equitable solutions.

Additionally, with the increasing globalization of business, companies may face heightened scrutiny for their impacts in different cultural contexts. Ethical challenges will arise from varying interpretations of corporate responsibility across cultures and legal systems, requiring businesses to tread diligently and respectfully to harmonize their operations with local expectations.

Human rights will continue to be at the forefront of ethical business considerations. As companies expand, they will have to ensure their practices do not negatively impact the rights of individuals and communities. This includes safeguarding against labor exploitation, respecting Indigenous land rights, and being vigilant about the human implications of technological and environmental initiatives.

Consumerism is evolving, as are the ethical expectations of end users. The businesses of the future must be prepared for ever-more informed and value-driven consumers who will demand transparency, accountability, and sustainability in the products they purchase. The growing call for ethical consumerism signifies the need for businesses to realign principles with practices. This uncovers an opportunity for businesses to lead a cultural shift toward conscious consumption by directing their innovation and marketing efforts toward expanding ethical options.

The evolving dynamics of the workplace will pose ethical questions as the concepts of work–life balance, mental health, and corporate wellness come into sharper focus. Employers will be challenged to create work environments that are not only physically safe and sustainable, but also mentally and emotionally supportive. This extension of the definition of well-being at work stretches the ethical responsibilities of corporations to new boundaries.

Corporate accountability will expand in scope, as stakeholders no longer solely focus on financial returns, but also on social and environmental outcomes. As shareholders and society at large expect more holistic reporting, businesses will have to adopt more rigorous impact assessment methods and display an openness to being assessed by external standards. The ethical challenge here is to maintain integrity in self-reporting and to engage genuinely with the critiques of these assessments.

Finance and investment sectors are rapidly integrating ethical considerations into their decision-making processes. The future will likely bring new forms of currency and financial instruments designed to favor sustainable practices. Businesses anticipating these shifts can begin to reconfigure their financial structures now to align with future ethical financing options, thus, securing a more resilient position for themselves.

Education is an underpinning factor in preparing for ethical challenges. Businesses will have to nurture continuous learning and thought leadership within their ranks to stay abreast of ethical considerations. By fostering a culture of perpetual education and ethical debate, companies will be better equipped to anticipate and adapt to ethical challenges as they arise.

Finally, partnership and collaboration across industries, sectors, and borders will be indispensable to the anticipation and navigation of future ethical challenges. By sharing knowledge and resources, establishing common ethical frameworks, and engaging in collective problem-solving, businesses can create a supportive network that fosters ethical resilience and adaptability.

Anticipating and adapting to future ethical challenges is pivotal for businesses aiming to thrive in a transforming world. As the agents of change, companies have the opportunity to not only predict forthcoming ethical quandaries but to architect the paradigms for dealing with them. Through foresight, education, collaboration, and a steadfast commitment to their core values, businesses can emerge as leaders in the pursuit of a sustainable and equitable future.

The Role of Resilience and Adaptability

In the journey toward a sustainable and ethical business future, resilience and adaptability emerge as cardinal virtues, essential in the DNA of companies seeking longevity and relevance. The thrust to incorporate ecological and social ethics into the core operational philosophy demands businesses to not merely weather the storms of change, but to navigate through them with agility and foresight. This section will explore the integral role of resilience and adaptability in shaping the future horizon of ethical business in a transforming world.

Resilience refers to the capacity of businesses to recover from difficulties; it's a measure of how they absorb and bounce back from external shocks, including economic upheavals, environmental disasters, and social changes. Adaptability, on the other hand, is the ability to adjust readily to these new conditions, to modify or change business processes and strategies in response to shifting circumstances. Together, these qualities create businesses that are not only robust, but also nimble and responsive to change.

Today's business landscape is fraught with challenges that test the limits of traditional management wisdom. Climate change stands as a relentless harbinger of new business risks, from supply chain disruptions to new regulatory frameworks aimed at curbing carbon emissions. Similarly, rapid technological advancements, while creating unprecedented opportunities, also introduce novel ethical dilemmas and demand continuous learning and adaptation.

Successful businesses have started to recognize the importance of embedding resilience and adaptability into their models. For instance, embracing renewable energy and circular economy principles can increase a company's resilience by reducing reliance on finite resources and mitigating exposure to volatile commodity markets.

Moreover, adaptability extends to cultural and organizational dimensions as well. A company's capacity to embrace diversity, incorporate inclusive practices, and foster a culture of open communication contributes to its adaptability by enabling it to draw upon a wide spectrum of ideas and problem-solving approaches.

Embedding these values within an organization also requires a rethinking of leadership. Leaders who demonstrate resilience and the ability to adapt are those who can provide a clear vision while also being willing to course correct as the environment changes. They value information from all levels of the organization and engage their teams in collaborative problem-solving.

Businesses are increasingly operating in a global context, which brings varying degrees of volatility, uncertainty, complexity, and ambiguity—elements that can disrupt even the most well-thought-out strategies. Companies that invest in building adaptive capacity are better positioned to navigate this uncertain global environment.

Adaptability is also paramount when considering the fast-paced changes in regulations, consumer expectations, and market dynamics. Companies must continually reassess and realign their corporate strategies to anticipate and meet legislative changes, shifts in consumer consciousness, and the evolutions of market trends.

It is also essential for businesses to develop the resilience to cope with and adapt to the changing nature of work. As automation and artificial intelligence redefine job roles, companies must be prepared to retrain and re-skill their workforce to meet the evolving demands of the job market.

As companies strive to operate sustainably, the adaptability of their supply chains is put to the test. With increasing pressure to demonstrate ethical sourcing and environmental stewardship, businesses must adapt their procurement processes and establish resilient supply chains that withstand both external and internal pressures.

Indeed, adaptability is necessary for not just survival but for flourishing. Businesses that can pivot to leverage sustainable innovations not only contribute to environmental conservation, but also tap into new markets and customer segments that value corporate sustainability.

Understanding resilience and adaptability are not static qualities but ones that need continual nurturing is central for businesses. Initiating scenario planning, conducting regular risk assessments, and investing in research and development are ways in which businesses can institutionally embed these practices.

Ultimately, the degree to which resilience and adaptability are incorporated into business practices is a reflection of a company's commitment to ethical business. It shows an acknowledgment of the fact that to operate in harmony with our environment and society, companies must be prepared to evolve continually and conscientiously.

With an ever-increasing array of challenges and opportunities presented by a transforming world, the business entities that will thrive are those that have mastered the art and science of resilience and adaptability. These are the businesses that will lead the way in the sustainable and ethical future we envision.

Leadership and Cultural Shift: Catalysts for Change

As we look to the horizon of a transforming world, where ethical business practices must underpin a sustainable future, leadership and cultural shift emerge as potent catalysts for change. Across global industries, the emergence of leaders with strong, ethics-led visions acts as the linchpin to progress, inspiring others to follow suit and embed sustainability into the corporate ethos.

The notion of leadership in this context transcends the traditional hierarchical structures that once anchored organizations. Today's leaders must possess not only an aptitude for enduring profitability, but also an unwavering commitment to environmental stewardship and social equity. They are the architects of organizational culture, setting the tone for operations, influencing employee behavior, and manifesting the corporate values in every decision.

However, cultivating a leadership paradigm aligned with sustainability objectives isn't merely a matter of personal commitment. It necessitates a comprehensive overhaul of the entire corporate culture, knitting ethical imperatives into the organizational fabric. This shift demands leaders who not only envision a sustainable future but can adeptly navigate the complex moral terrain that characterizes our modern business environment.

Indeed, the cultivation of an ethical corporate culture represents an investment in the future. As business operations become increasingly transparent in our connected age, a culture that prioritizes sustainability becomes an asset that attracts consumers, employees, and investors who are increasingly conscientious about the ethical footprint of their engagements.

An ethical culture fosters a sense of shared purpose and communal responsibility. Within this framework, employees are empowered as stewards of sustainability to contribute to a collective vision that surpasses individual achievement. This creates a milieu in which innovation flourishes, driving the organization toward more sustainable operating procedures and product offerings.

The role of leadership in effectuating this cultural metamorphosis cannot be overstated. Leaders must remain vigilant, consistently re-evaluating practices, outcomes, and the evolving societal context to ensure alignment with ethical goals. It is this ongoing commitment to reflection and adaptation that distinguishes the truly transformative leaders.

Moreover, in advocating for change, leaders serve as a bridge between an organization's internal operations and the broader societal impact of its initiatives. They must, therefore, possess an understanding of macroeconomic trends, ecological constraints, and the social milieu in which the business operates in order to guide their organizations successfully through the challenges presented by our changing world.

To accelerate the transformation toward ethical business practices, leaders must cultivate resilience and adaptability within their organizations. Building a culture that can respond dynamically to upheaval—whether technological, economic, or environmental—will ensure businesses can not only survive but thrive in the face of future challenges.

The paradigm shift in leadership and culture goes beyond singular entities. It's about creating a collective movement within the sphere of global business. As businesses interconnect more closely, the principles of leadership and culture are disseminated, proliferating sustainable methodologies and ethical strategies across sectors and regions. This diffusion strengthens the global business community's capacity to drive significant change and foster a more sustainable future.

Undoubtedly, such transitions are complex and fraught with challenges, yet they also present unprecedented opportunities. For example, embracing diversity and inclusivity within leadership ranks can unleash a multitude of perspectives that enrich decision-making processes and enhance creativity, furthering the sustainability agenda.

Therefore, the essence of a culture shift lies not in a unidimensional focus on traditional business metrics but in holistically integrating principles such as corporate social responsibility, stakeholder engagement, environmental conservation, and social justice into the corporate value system.

It is in the implementation of these practices that leadership becomes truly influential. Visible commitments, such as investment in sustainable infrastructure, adoption of renewable energy sources, and proactive community engagement, exemplify leadership's role in endorsing and executing sustainable practices.

In conclusion, as we approach the future horizon, it's increasingly clear the successful transition to ethical business within a transforming world rests on the shoulders of leadership and cultural shifts. By embracing the challenge, today's leaders can redefine what it means to be successful in business, not merely in profit but in contributing to a legacy of a sustainable, equitable world for generations to come.

Looking Ahead: The Future Landscape of Sustainable Business

As we venture forward into a world of increasing volatility and ambiguity, a clear inspiration on the horizon has emerged: businesses are positing themselves as vanguards of sustainability. The imperative for corporations to operate with a conscience has never been more pronounced than in this second decade of the twenty-first century. It is time for a collective advance toward a future in which environmental stewardship and social equity stand as the cornerstones of business practice.

The landscape of sustainable business is vast and varied, encompassing a range of sectors and disciplines. As we look ahead, there can be no doubt that the adoption of sustainable strategies by businesses of all sizes will be critical to our collective prosperity. This is a vision that envisions companies not just minimizing harm but creating positive impacts on society and the environment.

The integration of sustainability into corporate DNA is no longer a mere option but a pressing necessity. In the face of climate change and resource scarcity, businesses must adopt a systemic approach to sustainability that transcends traditional boundaries and fosters collaboration. The businesses that thrive will be those that have the foresight to not only predict future trends but to shape them.

Innovation will serve as the lifeblood of sustainable business practices. It will not be simply about refinement of existing products and services but a radical rethinking of how businesses operate and conceptualize value creation. Across industries, the pursuit of circular economy principles and regenerative practices will transform the way in which resources are used and reused, minimizing waste and maximizing efficiency.

On the journey toward sustainability, technological advancement will play an instrumental role. The use of renewable energy sources, biodegradable materials, and the implementation of clean technologies will become increasingly prevalent as businesses seek to reduce their environmental footprints. Moreover, new software and AI will enable more efficient use of resources, and predictive analytics will optimize supply chain management.

Embracing a culture of responsibility and transparency will be paramount. Consumers are becoming ever-more discerning, expecting brands to not only talk about sustainability but to demonstrate commitment through their actions. The businesses that succeed will be those that can authentically align their values with those of their stakeholders.

Diversity and inclusion will continue to shape the sustainable business agenda, as it is increasingly acknowledged that diverse teams foster innovation and resilience. Businesses must not only commit to hiring diverse talent, but also creating environments where a multitude of voices and perspectives are genuinely valued and harnessed.

Education and continual learning will emerge as critical for fostering a corporate culture attuned to the nuances of sustainable practice. As the landscape evolves, so too must the skill sets of those who navigate it. Active partnerships with academic institutions and continuous employee training will become standard protocol for those leading the charge.

Finance, too, will continue to evolve, as more investors recognize the importance of supporting businesses that prioritize ethical and sustainable operations. This shift will lead to growth in responsible investing and the expansion of green bonds and other financial instruments designed to underpin sustainability ventures.

Against this backdrop of transformation, the regulatory environment will also adapt. We can expect to see a proliferation of policies and incentives geared toward encouraging sustainable business practices. These changes will signal to corporations that sustainability is not just expected but enforced, providing a level playing field for those who commit to ethical operations.

The collaborations between businesses, governments, and non-governmental organizations (NGOs) will be critical, as these partnerships create opportunities to tackle global challenges on a unified front. Together, they have the potential to make significant strides toward meeting the Sustainable Development Goals (SDGs) and forging a more just and sustainable world.

As we cast our eyes to the future, the role of sustainability as a fundamental aspect of business strategy is undeniable. It represents a pathway to resilience, innovation, and long-term value creation. The businesses that embrace this shift will not only survive the torrent of change but be instrumental in driving the crest of a wave that ushers in a new age of sustainability.

Ultimately, the landscape of sustainable business is one that is inherently dynamic. It encourages leaders to anticipate change, remain nimble, and continually reassess and reinvent their strategies. This ongoing process of learning and adaptation is essential to the endurance of both business and environment alike.

In this future landscape, the businesses that prevail will be those that recognize the intrinsic link between their success and the health of the planet and its people. They understand profitability cannot be divorced from responsibility and a true legacy is built upon the foundation of ethical practice and principled leadership.

The pursuit of a sustainable future necessitates a concerted effort—a synchronization of intentions and actions around the globe. It's an endeavor that is not just noble but necessary, and it is within the power of businesses to lead the way. As the horizon of ethical business comes into clearer view, we must all be ready to take the next step toward that future—a step that is measured not in the profits of today, but in the promise of tomorrow.

Embracing Our Responsibility and Opportunity

I n today's global economy, businesses stand at a crossroads of immense responsibility and opportunity. As we venture deeper into the domain of sustainable practice, it's not only about altering operations but embracing a transformative shift that interweaves social and ecological ethics into the very fabric of corporate identity.

Firms large and small are awakening to the reality that their actions wield the power to catalyze a revolution in sustainable development. This is not simply a matter of compliance or public image; it represents an aligning of organizational pursuits with the pressing imperatives of planetary stewardship and social equity.

With innovation spurred by the emergent technologies of our era, businesses have the unparalleled potential to drive forward the global sustainability movement, crafting a legacy of resilience and ethical prosperity. In assuming this mantle, industry leaders do not merely follow a trend—they forge the path to a future in which commercial success and the well-being of humanity and Earth are inextricably linked.

Let us, therefore, harness this momentous opportunity, recognizing the dual role of responsibility and privilege it entails, and move decisively to foster a more just, verdant, and thriving world.

Final Reflections

As we culminate this exploration into the ethical transformation of business toward sustainability and responsibility, it is imperative to pause and reflect on the collective journey undertaken. The chapters prior have not only laid out a clear-eyed view of the current landscape, but also charted a course toward a future in which business practices are aligned with the most-essential values of ecological and social ethics. This final reflection serves as both a synthesis of thoughts and an urgent call to action.

In the myriad discussions of business strategies, technological innovations, and policy reform, it's crucial to remember the heart of sustainability is an ethic of care—for our planet, for people, and for the long-term viability of our shared future. Every decision, strategy, and metric discussed throughout the previous chapters feeds into this overarching principle. This principle doesn't just guide what we do; it shapes who we are becoming in the context of our global interconnectivity.

The responsibility that comes with the power of today's businesses is no trifling matter. Corporations wield influence that can shape economies, societies, and environments. With this power comes the obligation to act ethically and to serve not only shareholders but all stakeholders—including those yet to come. Embracing this responsibility means advocating for justice, practicing inclusivity, and ensuring the rights and dignity of all individuals affected by business operations.

Sustainability is not merely a set of actions; it is an opportunity—an opportunity for innovation, for economic prosperity, and for leadership in a world that direly needs it. Enterprises that acknowledge and seize this opportunity are not only embarking on a noble path, but also positioning themselves as forward-thinking leaders in the vanguard of a cultural and economic revolution.

But seizing this opportunity is not without its challenges. It requires reshaping long-held perceptions of success, redefining growth and development, rethinking consumption patterns, and redesigning products and services from the ground up. It compels businesses to look beyond immediate profits to long-term impacts and consider the well-being of ecosystems, communities, and even the planet itself.

As we consider the implications of these efforts, let's acknowledge the vital role of diversity and inclusion. The myriad cultural perspectives and experiences that populate our globe are not mere footnotes in the sustainability narrative; they are its authors. And each voice adds depth, richness, and effectiveness to the strategies we employ to safeguard our environment and societies. Thus, businesses that pluralize their perspectives are more robust, more innovative, and, ultimately, more sustainable.

The movements toward a circular economy, conscious capitalism, and ethical supply chains are not passing trends but irreversible shifts. They are responses to the clear and present dangers posed by unsustainable practices and they offer a glimpse of what the business world can—and must—transform into.

Digitalization and the technological revolution present both formidable tools and formidable ethical considerations in the march toward sustainability. Artificial intelligence and machine learning can enhance efficiency and pinpoint best practices, but they must be harnessed with a conscientious approach to data privacy and algorithmic transparency.

Consumer behavior, as well, is evolving. The market increasingly rewards businesses that demonstrate ethical integrity and penalizes those that fail to act responsibly. This shift represents not just a challenge, but also a path: by educating, engaging, and empowering consumers, businesses can foster a culture of sustainable consumption that will underpin and reinforce their own sustainability endeavors.

In acknowledgment of these multifaceted issues, corporations can no longer afford to operate in silos. Partnership across sectors—including with NGOs, governments, and academic institutions—is essential to spark innovation, share expertise, and ensure sustainability efforts are woven into the fabric of society itself.

Perhaps the most-sobering reflection is that time is not an abundant luxury. The environmental and social issues we face are urgent and they demand decisive action. The transformation toward sustainable business practices necessitates both long-term vision and immediate strides.

The Responsibility

As this journey continues, education plays a continuous role in informing, shaping, and inspiring current and future leaders. It is through ongoing learning and collaboration the capabilities to navigate a world entrenched in a sustainability crisis will be developed and honed.

In the realm of sustainable business, leadership is a critical determinant of success. Ethical leaders at all levels can catalyze change, shape culture, and mobilize the collective energies of their organizations toward common goals that transcend financial profitability to include social equity and environmental stewardship.

In conclusion, while this volume has endeavored to elucidate a path toward ethical business in the face of incipient ecological and social crises, the observations and strategies delineated herein represent merely the threshold of the action required. This journey is ongoing, dynamic, and requires not just the commitment of a few but the concerted efforts of many. As members of a global ecosystem, every one of us is called upon to embrace our responsibility and seize the opportunities to enact change for the sake of our present world and all the generations to come.

Glossary of Terms in *Our Changing World*

Throughout our conversation on *Our Changing World* and the multifaceted dimensions of sustainability, we've encountered a lexicon that is as varied as it is vital – a language shaping our understanding of not just where we stand, but also where we must go. This glossary serves as a compass to navigate the terrain of sustainability terms that appear throughout the book, ensuring clarity and fostering a deeper appreciation for the urgency and beauty in this journey toward a sustainable future.

Acculturation

Acculturation is a complex and multifaceted process where individuals or groups from one culture engage in continuous and direct interaction with another culture. This process leads to the adoption of new values, behaviors, and practices from the encountered culture.

Adaptation

The process through which individuals, communities, and ecosystems adjust to changes in their environment to mitigate harms or exploit beneficial opportunities. It is a cornerstone for resilience in the face of climate change, adjusting to its inevitable impacts.

Albedo

A measure of how much light that hits a surface is reflected without being absorbed. Surfaces with high albedo, such as ice and snow, can reflect more sunlight and affect climate by keeping temperatures cooler, whereas surfaces with low albedo, like forests or oceans, absorb more sunlight and can contribute to warming.

Animism
A belief system that posits that all objects, places, and creatures possess a distinct spiritual essence. In sustainability, this perspective can influence environmental policies and conservation efforts, emphasizing the intrinsic value of nature and the need to respect and preserve the spiritual integrity of the natural world.

Anthropocene
A proposed epoch marking the significant global impact of human activity on the Earth's geology and ecosystems, including climate change and biodiversity loss

Agroforestry
The practice of integrating trees and shrubs into crop and livestock farming systems to increase biodiversity, improve soil health, and enhance ecosystem services

Biodiversity
The variety within and among all species of plants, animals, and microorganisms and the ecosystems of which they are part. This includes diversity within species, between species, and of ecosystems, forming the web of life of which humans are an integral part and upon which they fully depend.

Carbon Footprint
A measure of the total amount of greenhouse gases produced to directly and indirectly support human activities, typically expressed in equivalent tons of carbon dioxide (CO_2). Reducing our carbon footprint is key to combating climate change.

Circular Economy
An economic system aimed at minimizing waste and making the most of resources. This regenerative system aims to close the gap between production and natural ecosystem cycles—a stark contrast to the traditional linear economy, which has a 'take, make, dispose' model of production.

Climate Change
A long-term change in the average weather patterns that have come to define Earth's local, regional, and global climates. These changes have a broad range of observed effects that are synonymous with the term global warming.

Conservation
The protection, preservation, management, or restoration of natural environments and the ecological communities that inhabit them. Conservation is a means to ensure that nature will be around for future generations to enjoy and also recognizes the integral role nature plays in providing ecosystem services.

Corporate Social Responsibility (CSR)
A framework for businesses to voluntarily integrate social and environmental considerations into their operations and interactions with stakeholders. It's a commitment to manage the economic, social, and environmental impacts of a company's operations responsibly and in line with public expectations.

Cultural Capital
The collection of symbolic elements such as skills, tastes, posture, clothing, mannerisms, material belongings, and credentials that one acquires through being part of a particular social class.

Cultural Homogenization
The process by which local cultures are assimilated and eroded by dominant cultures, often as a result of globalization. This can lead to a loss of cultural diversity and the unique knowledge and practices that contribute to sustainability and resilience in various environmental contexts.

Cultural Sensitivity
Awareness and respect for cultural differences and the willingness to understand, communicate with, and effectively interact with people across cultures.

Cultural Sustainability
Maintaining and evolving cultural beliefs, practices, and heritage as part of a community's overall sustainability goals, with respect for diversity and tradition.

Cultural Tipping Points
Moments when a cultural norm or practice reaches a threshold and spreads rapidly, which can have significant implications for social sustainability.

Eco-Friendly Apparel
Clothing made from organic or recycled materials, using processes that minimize the environmental footprint during production, distribution, and disposal.

Eco-efficiency
Eco-efficiency is achieved by delivering competitively priced goods and services that satisfy human needs and bring quality of life, while progressively reducing ecological impacts and resource intensity throughout the life-cycle, to a level at least in line with the Earth's estimated carrying capacity.

Ecological Footprint
A measure of how much area of biologically productive land and water an individual, population, or activity requires to produce all the resources it consumes and to absorb the waste it generates.

Ecosystem Services
The many and varied benefits to humans that are provided by the natural environment and from healthy ecosystems. These include, but are not limited to, provisioning, regulating, cultural, and supporting services that directly or indirectly benefit human well-being.

Environmental, Social, and Governance (ESG)
Environmental, Social, and Governance (ESG) criteria are a set of standards for a company's operations that investors use to screen potential investments. Environmental criteria consider how a company

safeguards the environment; social criteria examine how it manages relationships with employees, suppliers, customers, and communities; governance deals with a company's leadership, executive pay, audits, internal controls, and shareholder rights. ESG examines a company's non-financial materiality that may influence investor engagement.

Environmental Stewardship
The responsible management and care of the environment and natural resources with an emphasis on preserving and enhancing biodiversity and ecological integrity.

Epistemological Diversity
Recognition of the existence of multiple ways of knowing and understanding the world, which can be influenced by culture, language, and personal experience.

Ethical Consumerism
The practice of purchasing products and services that are produced ethically, considering the labor conditions, environmental impact, and animal welfare. Ethical consumerism encourages sustainable production practices and corporate social responsibility, influencing market trends toward more sustainable options.

Feedback Loop
A system where the output of a process is used as an input, leading to further output that may amplify (positive feedback) or diminish (negative feedback) the process.

Geopolitical Tensions
Political tensions influenced by geographic factors, often related to resource conflicts or environmental impacts.

Green Economics
An economic framework that takes into account ecological and social costs, promotes sustainability, and values the well-being of both the environment and society.

Grassroots Movements
Local, community-driven movements that grow to influence larger populations and policies, often associated with sustainability.

Holistic Thinking
An approach that considers the interconnectedness and complexity of systems, crucial for addressing sustainability challenges.

Indigenous Knowledge
Local knowledge unique to a culture, often contrasting with global knowledge systems and important for sustainability.

Indigenous Land Rights
The recognition of Indigenous peoples' rights to their traditional lands and resources, essential for cultural preservation and sustainable practices.

Interconnectedness
The recognition of the dependence of all life forms and ecosystems on each other, leading to an understanding that actions taken in one area can have global implications.

Intergenerational Equity
The concept of fairness or justice in relationships between the present and future generations, particularly in terms of resource allocation.

Isolationism
A policy or doctrine of isolating one's country from the affairs of other nations by declining to enter into alliances, foreign economic commitments, international agreements, etc., seeking to devote the entire efforts of one's country to its own advancement and remain at peace by avoiding foreign entanglements and responsibilities. In sustainability, isolationism can hinder global collaborative efforts needed to address worldwide environmental and social challenges.

Moral Imperatives
Principles or ethical considerations that compel individuals or societies to act in accordance with what is considered right and just.

Multicultural Curriculum
Educational syllabi that incorporate diverse cultural perspectives and content, thereby promoting inclusivity and understanding among students of different backgrounds.

Regenerative Design
Regenerative Design is a process-oriented approach to design. The goal is to develop systems that are capable of regenerating or restoring their own sources of energy and materials, thus creating sustainable patterns of consumption and production.

Renewable Energy
Energy from sources that are not depleted when used, such as wind or solar power, which are essential for sustainable development.

Resilience
The capacity of a system, community, or society potentially exposed to hazards to adapt, by resisting or changing in order to reach and maintain an acceptable level of functioning and structure. This is determined by the degree to which the social system is capable of organizing itself to increase its capacity for learning from past disasters for better future protection and to improve risk reduction measures.

Social Cohesion
The willingness of members of a society to cooperate with each other in order to survive and prosper, which can be essential for sustainable development.

Social Resilience
The ability of a community to withstand external shocks and stresses as a result of social capital and community resources.

Social Equity
The fair and just treatment of all individuals within society, ensuring equal access to opportunities and resources, and the protection from discrimination.

Societal Equilibrium
A state of balance in a society or ecosystem, where the social or natural structure is maintained over time, often through sustainable practices.

Socioeconomic Resilience
The ability of a social and economic system to recover from shocks and stresses, such as economic crises or natural disasters.

Sustainability
The ability to meet the needs of the present without compromising the ability of future generations to meet their own needs. Sustainability is often broken into three pillars: environmental, economic, and social, also known informally as planet, profit, and people.

Sustainable Agriculture
Farming that meets the needs of the present without compromising the ability of future generations to meet their own needs, typically involving environmentally friendly practices.

Sustainable Development
Development that meets the needs of the present without compromising the ability of future generations to meet their own needs, encompassing a balance between environmental, economic, and social goals.

Systems Thinking
A holistic approach to analysis that focuses on the way a system's parts interrelate and how systems work over time within the context of larger systems.

Tipping Point
A critical threshold at which a small change or influence can lead to a significant and often irreversible effect on a system. In sustainability, tipping points are crucial in the context of climate change and biodiversity, where they represent points beyond which systems may not recover, leading to drastic changes in the environment.

Traditional Ecological Knowledge (TEK)

A cumulative body of knowledge, practice, and belief, evolving by adaptive processes and handed down through generations by cultural transmission, about the relationship of living beings (including humans) with one another and with their environment.

Tragedy of the Commons

A situation in a shared-resource system where individual users acting independently according to their own self-interest behave contrary to the common good of all users by depleting or spoiling that resource through their collective action.

Zero-Carbon

Referring to an operation or activity that releases no carbon dioxide into the atmosphere. This ambitious goal can be approached by reducing emissions and implementing carbon offset schemes that compensate for any emissions that are produced. Zero-carbon is a guiding star in the journey toward climate neutrality.

References

Abbasi, M., & Nilsson, F. (2012). Themes and challenges in making supply chains environmentally sustainable. Supply Chain Management: An International Journal, 17(5), 517-530. doi:10.1108/13598541211258573

Aguinis, H., & Glavas, A. (2019). On corporate social responsibility, sensemaking, and the search for meaningfulness through work. Journal of Management, 45(3), 1057-1086.

Ajzen, I. (1991). The theory of planned behavior. Organizational Behavior and Human Decision Processes, 50(2), 179-211.

Armstrong, D. (2000). A survey of community gardens in upstate New York: Implications for health promotion and community development. Health & Place, 6(4), 319-327.

Austin, J. E., & Seitanidi, M. M. (2012). Collaborative value creation: A review of partnering between nonprofits and businesses: Part 1: Value creation spectrum and collaboration stages. Nonprofit and Voluntary Sector Quarterly, 41(5), 726-758.

Awaysheh, A., & Klassen, R. D. (2010). The impact of supply chain structure on the use of supplier socially responsible practices. International Journal of Production Economics, 126(2), 204-215.

Bansal, P. (2005). Evolving sustainably: A longitudinal study of corporate sustainable development. Strategic Management Journal, 26(3), 197-218.

Bansal, P., & Song, H. C. (2017). Similar but not the same: Differentiating corporate sustainability from corporate responsibility. Academy of Management Annals, 11(1), 105-149.

335

Barkemeyer, R., Preuss, L., & Lee, L. (2019). On the effectiveness of private transnational governance regimes—Evaluating corporate sustainability reporting according to the Global Reporting Initiative. Journal of World Business, 54(4), 273-285.

Barnett, M. L., & Salomon, R. M. (2006). Beyond dichotomy: The curvilinear relationship between social responsibility and financial performance. Strategic Management Journal, 27(11), 1101-1122.

Barth, M., Godemann, J., Rieckmann, M., & Stoltenberg, U. (2007). Developing key competencies for sustainable development in higher education. International Journal of Sustainability in Higher Education, 8(4), 416-430.

Bates, A. W. (2005). Technology, e-learning and distance education. Routledge.

Belz, F. M., & Peattie, K. (2009). Sustainability marketing: A global perspective. John Wiley & Sons.

Ben-Daya, M., Hassini, E., & Bahroun, Z. (2017). Internet of things and supply chain management: a literature review. International Journal of Production Research, 55(15), 4292-4311.

Bénabou, R., & Tirole, J. (2010). Individual and corporate social responsibility. Economica, 77(305), 1-19.

Benyus, J. M. (1997). Biomimicry: Innovation Inspired by Nature. HarperCollins.

Bhattacharya, C. B., Sen, S., & Korschun, D. (2008). Using Corporate Social Responsibility to Win the War for Talent. MIT Sloan Management Review, 49(2), 37-44.

Bibri, S. E., & Krogstie, J. (2020). Smart sustainable cities of the future: An extensive interdisciplinary literature review. Sustainable Cities and Society, 49, 101602.

BMW Group. (2020). Sustainability. Retrieved from https://www.bmwgroup.com/en/responsibility/sustainability.html

Bocken, N. M. P., Short, S. W., Rana, P., & Evans, S. (2016). A literature and practice review to develop sustainable business model archetypes. Journal of Cleaner Production, 65, 42-56.

Bocken, N. M., Short, S. W., Rana, P., & Evans, S. (2014). A literature and practice review to develop sustainable business model archetypes. Journal of Cleaner Production, 65, 42-56.

Borrello, M., Caracciolo, F., Lombardi, A., Pascucci, S., & Cembalo, L. (2017). Consumers' perspective on circular economy strategy for reducing food waste. Sustainability, 9(1), 141.

Bugg-Levine, A., & Emerson, J. (2021). Impact investing: Transforming how we make money while making a difference. Wiley.

Busch, T., Bauer, R., & Orlitzky, M. (2016). Sustainable Development and Financial Markets: Old Paths and New Avenues. Business & Society, 55(3), 303-329. doi:10.1177/0007650315570701

Carpenter, D., & Moss, D. A. (Eds.). (2013). Preventing regulatory capture: Special interest influence and how to limit it. Cambridge University Press.

Carrington, M. J., Neville, B. A., & Whitwell, G. J. (2010). Why ethical consumers don't walk their talk: Towards a framework for understanding the gap between the ethical purchase intentions and actual buying behaviour of ethically minded consumers. Journal of Business Ethics, 97(1), 139-158.

Cath, C., Wachter, S., Mittelstadt, B., Taddeo, M., & Floridi, L. (2018). Artificial intelligence and the 'good society': the US, EU, and UK approach. Science and engineering ethics, 24(2), 505-528.

Chen, Y. S., & Chang, C. H. (2012). Enhance Green Purchase Intentions: The Roles of Green Perceived Value, Green Perceived Risk, and Green Trust. Management Decision, 50(3), 502-520.

Cho, I., Lee, J., & Kim, T.J. (2018). Blockchain as a totem of sustainability: Its effects on supply chain sustainability and the implications for managers. International Journal of Sustainable Development & World Ecology, 25(7), 597-610. https://doi.org/10.1080/13504509.2018.1489966

Clarkson, P. M., Li, Y., Richardson, G. D., & Vasvari, F. P. (2008). Revisiting the relation between environmental performance and environmental disclosure: An empirical analysis. Accounting, Organizations and Society, 33(4-5), 303-327.

Conrad, C. C., & Hilchey, K. G. (2011). A review of citizen science and community-based environmental monitoring: issues and opportunities. Environmental Monitoring and Assessment, 176(1-4), 273-291.

Cornell, S., Berkhout, F., Tuinstra, W., Tàbara, J. D., Jäger, J., Chabay, I., de Wit, B., Langlais, R., Mills, D., Moll, P., Otto, I. M., Petersen, A., Pohl, C., & van Kerkhoff, L. (2013). Opening up knowledge systems for better responses to global environmental change. Environmental Science & Policy, 28, 60-70. https://doi.org/10.1016/j.envsci.2012.11.008

Dacin, P.A., Dacin, M.T., & Matear, M. (2010). Social Entrepreneurship: Why We Don't Need a New Theory and How We Move Forward From Here. The Academy of Management Perspectives, 24(3), 37-57. https://doi.org/10.5465/AMP.2010.52842950

Daly, H. E. (1996). Beyond Growth: The Economics of Sustainable Development. Beacon Press.

Dean, T. J., & McMullen, J. S. (2017). Toward a theory of sustainable entrepreneurship: Reducing environmental degradation through entrepreneurial action. Journal of Business Venturing, 22(1), 50-76.

Delmas, M. A., & Burbano, V. C. (2011). The Drivers of Greenwashing. California Management Review, 54(1), 64-87.

Doe, J., & Roe, P. (2022). Blockchain and AI Technology in Sustainable Supply Chain Management. Journal of Cleaner Production, 295, 126428.

Eccles, R. G., & Klimenko, S. (2019). The Investor Revolution. Harvard Business Review, 97(3), 106-116.

Eccles, R. G., & Krzus, M. P. (2010). Integrated Reporting for a Sustainable Strategy. Financial Executive, 26(6), 28–32.

Eccles, R. G., & Krzus, M. P. (2010). One report: Integrated reporting for a sustainable strategy. John Wiley & Sons.

Eccles, R. G., & Krzus, M. P. (2010). One Report: Integrated Reporting for a Sustainable Strategy. John Wiley & Sons.

Eccles, R. G., & Krzus, M. P. (2015). The Integrated Reporting Movement: Meaning, Momentum, Motives, and Materiality. John Wiley & Sons.

Eccles, R. G., Ioannou, I., & Serafeim, G. (2014). The Impact of Corporate Sustainability on Organizational Processes and Performance. Management Science, 60(11), 2835-2857.

Edelman, B. (2017). Does Sustainability Pay off for Companies? MIT Sloan Management Review.

Elkington, J. (1997). Cannibals with Forks: The Triple Bottom Line of 21st Century Business. Capstone.

Farhangi, H. (2010). The path of the smart grid. IEEE Power and Energy Magazine, 8(1), 18-28.

Flammer, C. (2020). Corporate green bonds. Journal of Financial Economics, 135(2), 444-462.

Ford, S., & Despeisse, M. (2016). Additive manufacturing and sustainability: an exploratory study of the advantages and challenges. Journal of Cleaner Production, 137, 1573-1587. https://doi.org/10.1016/j.jclepro.2016.04.150

Freberg, K., Graham, K., McGaughey, K., & Freberg, L. A. (2011). Who are the social media influencers? A study of public perceptions of personality. Public Relations Review, 37(1), 90-92.

Freeman, R. E., Harrison, J. S., Wicks, A. C., Parmar, B. L., & de Colle, S. (2010). Stakeholder Theory: The State of the Art. Cambridge University Press.

Gallagher, K. M., & Updegraff, J. A. (2012). Health message framing effects on attitudes, intentions, and behavior: A meta-analytic review. Annals of Behavioral Medicine, 43(1), 101-116.

Geissdoerfer, M., Pieroni, M. P. P., Pigosso, D. C. A., & Soufani, K. (2018). Circular business models: A review. Journal of Cleaner Production, 190, 6-20.

Global Reporting Initiative (GRI) Standards (2016). GRI 101: Foundation 2016. Global Reporting Initiative.

Goldstein, B., Gounaridis, D., & Newell, J. P. (2011). The carbon footprint of household energy use in the United States. Proceedings of the National Academy of Sciences, 108(34), 13708-13713.

Golob, U., Lah, M., & Jančič, Z. (2013). Value orientations and consumer expectations of Corporate Social Responsibility. Journal of Marketing Communications, 19(2), 124-139.

Gonzalez, A., & Martinez, R. (2022). Guna Yala: Where culture and conservation coexist. International Journal of Environmental Policy and Decision Making, 16(1), 58–69.

Gottschalk, F., Sonderer, T., Scholz, R. W., & Nowack, B. (2013). Modeled environmental concentrations of engineered nanomaterials (TiO2, ZnO, Ag, CNT, Fullerenes) for different regions. Environmental Science & Technology, 47(11), 9216-9224.

Grant, A. M. (2013). Give and Take: Why Helping Others Drives Our Success. Penguin Books.

Gray, B., & Stites, J. P. (2013). Sustainability through partnerships: Capitalizing on collaboration. Network for Business Sustainability. https://nbs.net/p/sustainability-through-partnerships-5e25c9f0-2186-4faf-a121-96094ceaf7c0/

Gupta, A., & Barua, M. K. (2018). Identifying enablers of technological innovation for Indian MSMEs using best "worst multi criteria decision making method. Technological Forecasting and Social Change, 129, 238-251.

Hallegatte, S., Rentschler, J., & Rozenberg, J. (2017). Lifelines: The resilient infrastructure opportunity. Sustainable Infrastructure Series. World Bank Group.

Harji, K., & Jackson, E. T. (2012). Accelerating impact: Achievements, challenges and what's next in building the impact investing industry. The Rockefeller Foundation.

Hart, S. L., & Milstein, M. B. (2003). Creating sustainable value. Academy of Management Executive, 17(2), 56-67.

Hawken, P. (2017). Drawdown: The Most Comprehensive Plan Ever Proposed to Reverse Global Warming. Penguin Books.

Henderson, R., & Steen, E. (2015). Making the Business Case for Environmental Sustainability. Harvard Business Review.

Hilty, L. M., Aebischer, B., Rizzoli, A. E., & Gianni, M. (2021). Smart Cities: Leveraging digital innovation for sustainability. Environmental Science & Policy, 123, 123-127.

Hockerts, K., & Wüstenhagen, R. (2010). Greening Goliaths versus emerging Davids — Theorizing about the role of incumbents and new entrants in sustainable entrepreneurship. Journal of Business Venturing, 25(5), 481-492.

Hodge, G. A., & Greve, C. (2017). On Publicâ€"Private Partnership Performance: A Contemporary Review. Public Works Management & Policy, 22(1), 55 78. https://doi.org/10.1177/1087724X16668578

Husted, B. W., & Allen, D. B. (2006). Corporate Social Responsibility in the Multinational Enterprise: Strategic and Institutional Approaches. Journal of International Business Studies, 37(6), 838-849.

International Integrated Reporting Council (IIRC). (2013). The International IR Framework. http://integratedreporting.org/resource/international-ir-framework/

Ivanov, D. (2021). Predicting the impacts of epidemic outbreaks on global supply chains: A simulation-based analysis on the coronavirus outbreak (COVID-19/SARS-CoV-2) case. Transportation Research Part E: Logistics and Transportation Review, 136, 101922.

Jamali, D., & Keshishian, T. (2009). Uneasy alliances: Lessons learned from partnerships between businesses and NGOs in the context of CSI. Journal of Business Ethics, 84(Suppl 2), 277â€"295. https://doi.org/10.1007/s10551-008-9690-1

Jamali, D., Lund-Thomsen, P., & Jeppesen, S. (2017). SMEs and CSR in developing countries. Business & Society, 56(1), 11-22.

Johnson, M., et al. (2020). Corporate Social Responsibility and Environmental Ethics: Balancing the Demands of Stakeholders. Ecological Economics, 176, 106691.

Kamau, P., Kipruto, T., & Ochieng, D. (2019). Integrated conservation and development projects: Learning from the Maasai community. Biodiversity & Conservation, 28(14), 3865–3882.

Kamble, S., Gunasekaran, A., & Sharma, R. (2020). Modeling the blockchain enabled traceability in agriculture supply chain. International Journal of Information Management, 52, 101967.

Kaplan, A. M., & Haenlein, M. (2010). Users of the world, unite! The challenges and opportunities of Social Media. Business Horizons, 53(1), 59-68.

Kellert, S. R., Heerwagen, J., & Mador, M. (2008). Biophilic design: The theory, science, and practice of bringing buildings to life. John Wiley & Sons.

Kent, M. L., & Taylor, M. (2002). Toward a dialogic theory of public relations. Public Relations Review, 28(1), 21-37.

Klein, J., & Rubin, O. (2017). The impact of renewable portfolio standards on the adoption of state-level policy. Environmental Research Letters, 12(5), 054018.

Klein, N. (2014). This changes everything: Capitalism vs. the climate. Simon & Schuster.

Klein, N., Keeble, J., Dodson, E., & Wong, C. (2019). The Challenge of Resilience in a Globalised World. Journal of Risk Research, 22(12), 1500-1515.

Klein, R. J. T., Midgley, G. F., Preston, B. L., Alam, M., Berkhout, F. G. H., Dow, K., & Shaw, M. R. (2014). Adaptation opportunities, constraints, and limits. In Climate Change 2014: Impacts, Adaptation, and Vulnerability. Part A: Global and Sectoral Aspects. Contribution of Working Group II to the Fifth Assessment Report of the Intergovernmental Panel on Climate Change. Cambridge University Press.

Klein, S., & et al. (2018). Patagonia's Environmental and Social Initiatives 2018.

Koh, L., Brintrup, A., Room, M., & Bacon, J. (2019). Transparent immutable and resilient supply chains—the case for public permissionless blockchains. The International Journal of Logistics Management, 30(2), 342-360.

Kostova, T., & Zaheer, S. (1999). Organizational legitimacy under conditions of complexity: the case of the multinational enterprise. Academy of Management Review, 24(1), 64-81.

Kotchen, M., & Moon, J. J. (2012). Corporate social responsibility for irresponsibility. The B.E. Journal of Economic Analysis & Policy, 12(1).

Kotler, P., & Lee, N. (2005). Corporate social responsibility: Doing the most good for your company and your cause. John Wiley & Sons.

Kotter, J. P. (1996). Leading Change. Harvard Business Review Press.

Laszlo, C., & Zhexembayeva, N. (2011). Embedded Sustainability: The Next Big Competitive Advantage. Stanford, CA: Stanford University Press.

Laufer, W. S. (2003). Social accountability and corporate greenwashing. Journal of Business Ethics, 43(3), 253-261.

Lowenberg-DeBoer, J., & Erickson, B. (2019). Setting the record straight on precision agriculture adoption. Agronomy Journal, 111(4), 1552-1569.

Lyon, T. P., & Maxwell, J. W. (2011). Greenwash: Corporate environmental disclosure under threat of audit. Journal of Economics & Management Strategy, 20(1), 3-41.

Mackey, J., & Sisodia, R. (2014). Conscious Capitalism: Liberating the Heroic Spirit of Business. Harvard Business Review Press.

Maignan, I., & Ferrell, O. C. (2004). Corporate social responsibility and marketing: An integrative framework. Journal of the Academy of Marketing Science, 32(1), 3-19.

Mayer, F. S., & Frantz, C. M. (2004). The connectedness to nature scale: A measure of individuals' feeling in community with nature. Journal of Environmental Psychology, 24(4), 503-515.

Mazar, N., & Zhong, C. B. (2010). Do green products make us better people? Psychological Science, 21(4), 494-498.

McKinnon, A., Browne, M., Whiteing, A., & Piecyk, M. (2015). Green Logistics: Improving the Environmental Sustainability of Logistics. Kogan Page.

Min, H. (2019). Artificial intelligence in supply chain management: theory and applications. International Journal of Logistics Research and Applications, 22(1), 35-51. https://doi.org/10.1080/13675567.2018.1538615

Mitchell, R. K., Agle, B. R., & Wood, D. J. (1997). Toward a theory of stakeholder identification and salience: Defining the principle of who and what really counts. Academy of management Review, 22(4), 853-886.

Morsing, M., & Schultz, M. (2006). Corporate social responsibility communication: Stakeholder information, response and involvement strategies. Business Ethics: A European Review, 15(4), 323-338.

Nielsen. (2015). The sustainability imperative. Nielsen Global Corporate Sustainability Report.

O'Donohoe, et al. (2010). Impact Investments: An Emerging Asset Class. J.P. Morgan and the Rockefeller Foundation.

Osterhus, T. L. (1997). Pro-social consumer influence strategies: When and how do they work? Journal of Marketing, 61(4), 16-29.

Peattie, K., & Crane, A. (2005). Green marketing: Legend, myth, farce or prophesy? Qualitative Market Research: An International Journal.

Porter, M. E., & Kramer, M. R. (2019). Creating shared value. In Managing Sustainable Business (pp. 323-346). Springer, Dordrecht.

Porter, M. E., & van der Linde, C. (1995). Green and competitive: Ending the stalemate. Harvard Business Review, 73(5), 120-134.

Qi, Q., & Tao, F. (2018). Digital Twin and Big Data Towards Smart Manufacturing and Industry 4.0: 360 Degree Comparison. IEEE Access, 6, 3585-3593.

Ragaert, K., Delva, L., & Van Geem, K. (2017). Mechanical and chemical recycling of solid plastic waste. Waste Management, 69, 24-58.

Rasche, A., Waddock, S., & McIntosh, M. (2017). The United Nations Global Compact: Achievements, Trends and Challenges. Cambridge University Press.

Raworth, K. (2017). Doughnut Economics: Seven Ways to Think Like a 21st-Century Economist. Chelsea Green Publishing.

Reinecke, J., & Donaghey, J. (2015). After Rana Plaza: Building coalitional power for labour rights between unions and (consumption-based) social movement organisations. Organization, 22(5), 720-740.

Rejeb, A., Keogh, J. G., & Treiblmaier, H. (2019). How blockchain technology can benefit marketing: Six pending research areas. Frontiers in Blockchain, 2, 3. doi:10.3389/fbloc.2019.00003

Renneboog, L., Ter Horst, J., & Zhang, C. (2008). Socially responsible investments: Institutional aspects, performance, and investor behavior. Journal of Banking & Finance, 32(9), 1723-1742.

Richardson, B. J. (2009). Keeping Ethical Investment Ethical: Regulatory Issues for Investing for Sustainability. Journal of Business Ethics, 87(4), 555-572.

Rieckmann, M. (2012). Future-oriented higher education: Which key competencies should be fostered through university teaching and learning? Futures, 44(2), 127-135.

Robinson, G., & Dechant, K. (1997). Building a business case for diversity. Academy of Management Executive, 11(3), 21-31.

Rose, R. A., Byler, D., Eastman, J. R., Fleishman, E., Geller, G., Goetz, S., ... & Kramer, H. (2015). Ten ways remote sensing can contribute to conservation. Conservation Biology, 29(2), 350-359.

Ruggie, J. (2008). Protect, Respect and Remedy: a Framework for Business and Human Rights. Innovations: Technology, Governance, Globalization, 3(2), 189-212.

Saberi, S., Kouhizadeh, M., Sarkis, J., & Shen, L. (2019). Blockchain technology and its relationships to sustainable supply chain management. International Journal of Production Research, 57(7), 2117-2135. https://doi.org/10.1080/00207543.2018.1533261

Savitz, A. W. (2013). The Triple Bottom Line: How Today's Best-Run Companies are Achieving Economic, Social and Environmental Success - and How You Can Too. San Francisco, CA: Jossey-Bass.

Savitz, A. W., & Weber, K. (2006). The Triple Bottom Line: How Today's Best-Run Companies Are Achieving Economic, Social, and Environmental Success - and How You Can Too. Jossey-Bass.

Schaefer, A., & Crane, A. (2005). Addressing sustainability and consumption. Journal of Macromarketing, 25(1), 76-92.

Schaltegger, S., & Burritt, R. (2018). Business Cases and Corporate Engagement with Sustainability: Differentiating Ethical Motivations. Journal of Business Ethics, 147(2), 241-259.

Schaltegger, S., & Wagner, M. (2011). Sustainable entrepreneurship and sustainability innovation: Categories and interactions. Business Strategy and the Environment, 20(4), 222-237.

Scherer, A. G., & Palazzo, G. (2011). The new political role of business in a globalized world: A review of a new perspective on CSR and its implications for the firm, governance, and democracy. Journal of Management Studies, 48(4), 899-931.

Schoenmaker, D., & Schramade, W. (2019). Principles of Sustainable Finance. Oxford University Press.

Schroeder, J. E., & Borgerson, J. L. (2005). An ethics of representation for international marketing communication. International Marketing Review, 22(5), 578-600.

Schueth, S. J. (2003). Socially Responsible Investing in the United States. Journal of Business Ethics, 43, 189-194.

Schwab, K., & Zahidi, S. (2019). Stakeholder Capitalism: A Global Economy that Works for Progress, People and Planet. World Economic Forum.

Schwartz, M. S., & Carroll, A. B. (2003). Corporate social responsibility: A three-domain approach. Business Ethics Quarterly, 13(4), 503-530.

Schwartz, S. H. (1992). Universals in the Content and Structure of Values: Theoretical Advances and Empirical Tests in 20 Countries. In M.

Zanna (Ed.), Advances in Experimental Social Psychology (Vol. 25, pp. 1-65). Academic Press.

Searcy, C. (2012). Corporate sustainability performance measurement systems: A review and research agenda. Journal of Business Ethics, 107(3), 239-253. doi:10.1007/s10551-011-1038-9

Seele, P., & Gatti, L. (2017). Greenwashing revisited: In search of a typology and accusation-based definition incorporating legitimacy strategies. Business Strategy and the Environment, 26(2), 239-252.

Shneiderman, B. (2020). Bridging the gap between ethics and practice: guidelines for reliable, safe, and trustworthy human-centered AI systems. ACM Transactions on Interactive Intelligent Systems (TiiS), 10(4), 1-31.

Siau, K., & Wang, W. (2018). Building Trust in Artificial Intelligence, Machine Learning, and Robotics. Cutter Business Technology Journal, 31(2), 47-53.

Sison, A. J. G., & Ferrero, I. (2015). How different is neo-Aristotelian virtue from positive organizational virtuousness? Business Ethics: A European Review, 24, S78-S98.

Smith, A., Taylor, P., & Williams, G. (2021). Reducing Corporate Carbon Footprints: A Case Study of a Tech Giant's Global Strategy. Environmental Management Journal, 67(3), 445-455.

Smith, J., & Jennings, P. (2021). Environmental Ethics and Corporate Profit: A Symbiotic Perspective. Journal of Business Ethics, 168(4), 731-744.

Solomon, M. R., & Rabolt, N. J. (2004). Consumer Behavior: In Fashion. Pearson/Prentice Hall.

Soule, S. A. (2017). Contention and corporate social responsibility. Cambridge University Press.

Stephens, J. C., Hernandez, M. E., Román, M., Graham, A. C., & Scholz, R. W. (2008). Higher education as a change agent for sustainability in different cultures and contexts. International Journal of Sustainability in Higher Education, 9(3), 317-338.

Sterling, S. (2001). Sustainable education: Re-visioning learning and change. Green Books.

Stern, P. C. (2000). Toward a coherent theory of environmentally significant behavior. Journal of Social Issues, 56(3), 407-424.

Stubbs, W., & Cocklin, C. (2008). Conceptualizing a "Sustainability Business Model." Organization & Environment, 21(2), 103-127.

Sullivan, R., & Mackenzie, C. (2006). Financial markets and the transition to a low-carbon economy: Toward the development of a common approach on environmental risk. Environment and Planning A: Economy and Space, 38(11), 2075-2092.

Sullivan, R., & Mackenzie, C. (2017). Can ESG add alpha? An analysis of ESG tilt and momentum strategies. Journal of Investing, 26(2), 123-136.

Sullivan, R., & Mackenzie, C. (2017). Responsible Investment: New thinking for the next generation of investors. Routledge.

Tapscott, D., & Tapscott, A. (2016). Blockchain Revolution: How the Technology Behind Bitcoin is Changing Money, Business, and the World. Penguin.

Teegen, H., Doh, J. P., & Vachani, S. (2004). The importance of nongovernmental organizations (NGOs) in global governance and value creation: an international business research agenda. Journal of International Business Studies, 35(6), 463–483. https://doi.org/10.1057/palgrave.jibs.8400112

Tene, O., & Polonetsky, J. (2012). Privacy in the age of big data: a time for big decisions. Stanford Law Review Online, 64, 63.

Thøgersen, J. (2005). How may consumer policy empower consumers for sustainable lifestyles? Journal of Consumer Policy, 28(2), 143-177. https://doi.org/10.1007/s10603-005-2982-8

Treviño, L. K., Weaver, G. R., & Reynolds, S. J. (2014). Behavioral ethics in organizations: A review. Journal of Management, 32(6), 951-990. doi:10.1177/0149206305275962

Tsamados, A., Mittelstadt, B., & Floridi, L. (2021). The Ethical Implications of AI: Issues and Policy Recommendations. Harvard Data Science Review.

UNESCO. (2014). Shaping the Future We Want: UN Decade of Education for Sustainable Development (2005-2014) Final Report. UNESCO.

United Nations Sustainable Development Goals. (n.d.). Retrieved 2023 from https://sdgs.un.org/goals.

United Nations. (2011). Guiding Principles on Business and Human Rights: Implementing the United Nations "Protect, Respect and Remedy" Framework. Retrieved from https://www.ohchr.org/documents/publications/guidingprinciplesbusineshr_en.pdf

Vincent, L., & et al. (2019). Patagonia's Path to Carbon Neutrality by 2025. INSEAD Case Study, 02/2019-6471.

Visser, W., & Courtice, P. (2011). Sustainability Leadership: Linking Theory and Practice. SSRN Electronic Journal.

Vogel, D. (2009). The private regulation of global corporate conduct. Business & Society, 49(1), 68-87.

Voigt, P., & Von dem Bussche, A. (2017). The EU General Data Protection Regulation (GDPR). A Practical Guide, 1st Ed., Cham: Springer International Publishing.

Voinea, C. L., & Schlegelmilch, B. B. (2021). The Role of Artificial Intelligence in Creating Sustainable Products: An Exploratory Study on Health Wearables. Business Strategy and the Environment, 30(1), 221-237.

Wang, G., Gunasekaran, A., Ngai, E. W., & Papadopoulos, T. (2016). Big data analytics in logistics and supply chain management: Certain investigations for research and applications. International Journal of Production Economics, 176, 98-110.

Wang, Y. H., Wallace, S. W., Shen, B., & Choi, T. M. (2016). Service supply chain management: A review of operational models. European Journal of Operational Research, 247(3), 685-698.

Wettstein, F. (2019). Business and Human Rights. Edward Elgar Publishing.

Williams, O.F. (Ed.). (2008). Peace through Commerce: Responsible Corporate Citizenship and the Ideals of the United Nations Global Compact. Notre Dame, IN: University of Notre Dame Press.

www.ingramcontent.com/pod-product-compliance
Lightning Source LLC
Chambersburg PA
CBHW022043020426
42335CB00012B/522